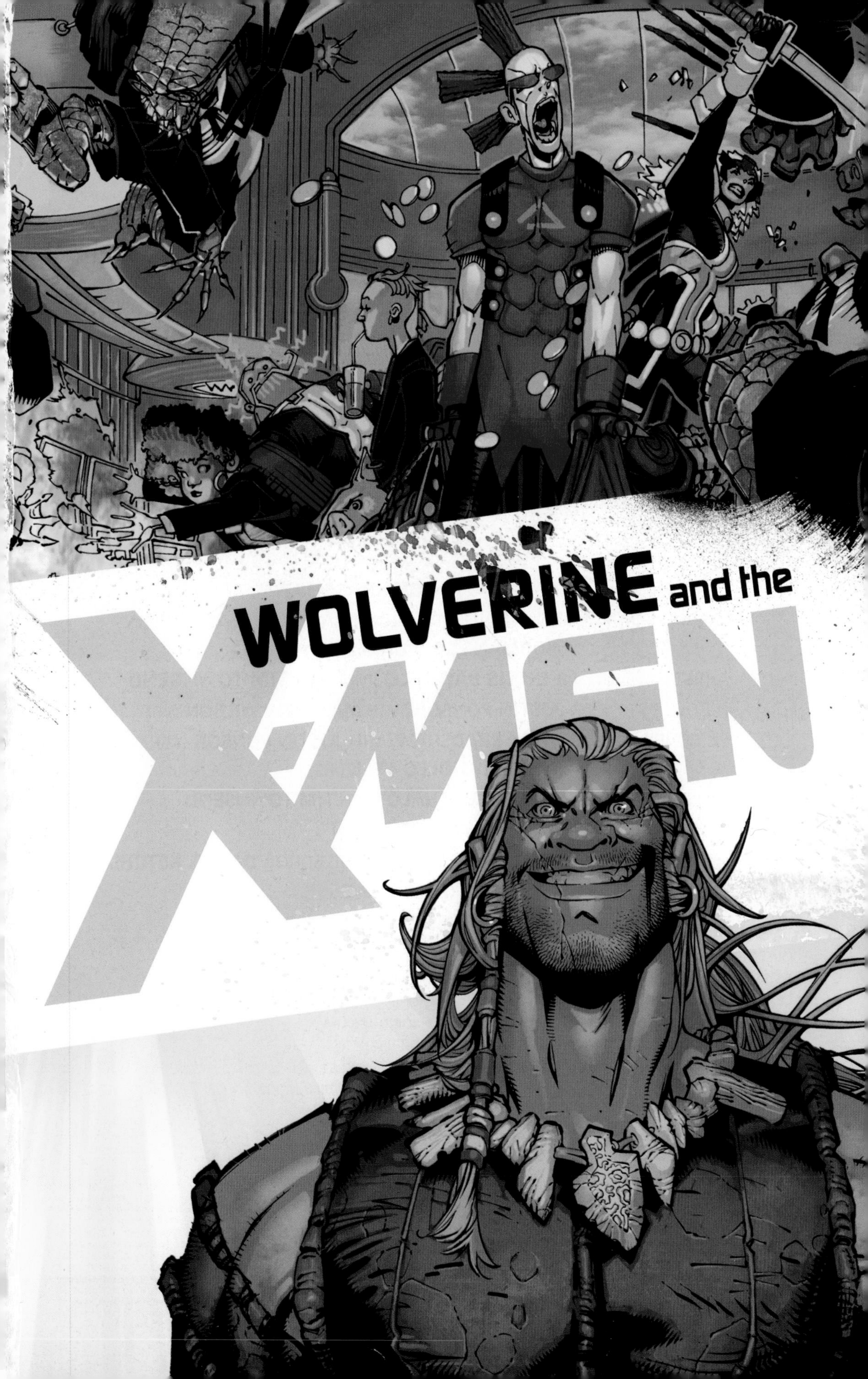
WOLVERINE and the
X-MEN

WOLVERINE and the X-MEN

WRITER: **JASON AARON**

PENCILER, #5-7: **NICK BRADSHAW**

INKERS, #5-7: **WALDEN WONG** WITH **NICK BRADSHAW, JAY LEISTEN, NORMAN LEE** & **CAM SMITH**

ARTIST/COLORIST, #8: **CHRIS BACHALO** INKER, #8: **TIM TOWNSEND**

COLORISTS, #5-7: **JUSTIN PONSOR** WITH **MATTHEW WILSON** (#6)

COVER ART, #5-7: **NICK BRADSHAW** WITH **JUSTIN PONSOR** (#5) & **MORRY HOLLOWELL** (#6-7)

COVER ART, #8: **CHRIS BACHALO** WITH **TIM TOWNSEND**

LETTERER: **ROB STEEN**

ASSISTANT EDITOR: **JORDAN D. WHITE** • ASSOCIATE EDITOR: **DANIEL KETCHUM**

EDITOR: **NICK LOWE**

COLLECTION EDITOR: **JENNIFER GRÜNWALD**
ASSISTANT EDITORS:
ALEX STARBUCK & **NELSON RIBEIRO**
EDITOR, SPECIAL PROJECTS: **MARK D. BEAZLEY**
SENIOR EDITOR, SPECIAL PROJECTS:
JEFF YOUNGQUIST
SENIOR VICE PRESIDENT OF SALES: **DAVID GABRIEL**
SVP OF BRAND PLANNING & COMMUNICATIONS:
MICHAEL PASCIULLO
BOOK DESIGNER: **RODOLFO MURAGUCHI**

EDITOR IN CHIEF:
AXEL ALONSO
CHIEF CREATIVE OFFICER:
JOE QUESADA
PUBLISHER:
DAN BUCKLEY
EXECUTIVE PRODUCER:
ALAN FINE

WOLVERINE & THE X-MEN BY JASON AARON VOL. 2. Contains material originally published in magazine form as WOLVERINE & THE X-MEN #5-8. First printing 2012. Hardcover ISBN# 978-0-7851-5681-9. Softcover ISBN# 978-0-7851-5682-6. Published by MARVEL WORLDWIDE, INC., a subsidiary of MARVEL ENTERTAINMENT, LLC. OFFICE OF PUBLICATION: 135 West 50th Street, New York, NY 10020. Copyright © 2012 and 2013 Marvel Characters, Inc. All rights reserved. Hardcover: $19.99 per copy in the U.S. and $21.99 in Canada (GST #R127032852). Softcover: $16.99 per copy in the U.S. and $18.99 in Canada (GST #R127032852). Canadian Agreement #40668537. All characters featured in this issue and the distinctive names and likenesses thereof, and all related indicia are trademarks of Marvel Characters, Inc. No similarity between any of the names, characters, persons, and/or institutions in this magazine with those of any living or dead person or institution is intended, and any such similarity which may exist is purely coincidental. **Printed in the U.S.A.** ALAN FINE, EVP - Office of the President, Marvel Worldwide, Inc. and EVP & CMO Marvel Characters B.V.; DAN BUCKLEY, Publisher & President - Print, Animation & Digital Divisions; JOE QUESADA, Chief Creative Officer; TOM BREVOORT, SVP of Publishing; DAVID BOGART, SVP of Operations & Procurement, Publishing; RUWAN JAYATILLEKE, SVP & Associate Publisher, Publishing; C.B. CEBULSKI, SVP of Creator & Content Development; DAVID GABRIEL, SVP of Publishing Sales & Circulation; MICHAEL PASCIULLO, SVP of Brand Planning & Communications; JIM O'KEEFE, VP of Operations & Logistics; DAN CARR, Executive Director of Publishing Technology; SUSAN CRESPI, Editorial Operations Manager; ALEX MORALES, Publishing Operations Manager; STAN LEE, Chairman Emeritus. For information regarding advertising in Marvel Comics or on Marvel.com, please contact Niza Disla, Director of Marvel Partnerships, at ndisla@marvel.com. For Marvel subscription inquiries, please call 800-217-9158. **Manufactured between 6/25/2012 and 8/6/2012 (hardcover), and 6/25/2012 and 2/4/2013 (softcover), by R.R. DONNELLEY, INC., SALEM, VA, USA.**

10 9 8 7 6 5 4 3 2 1

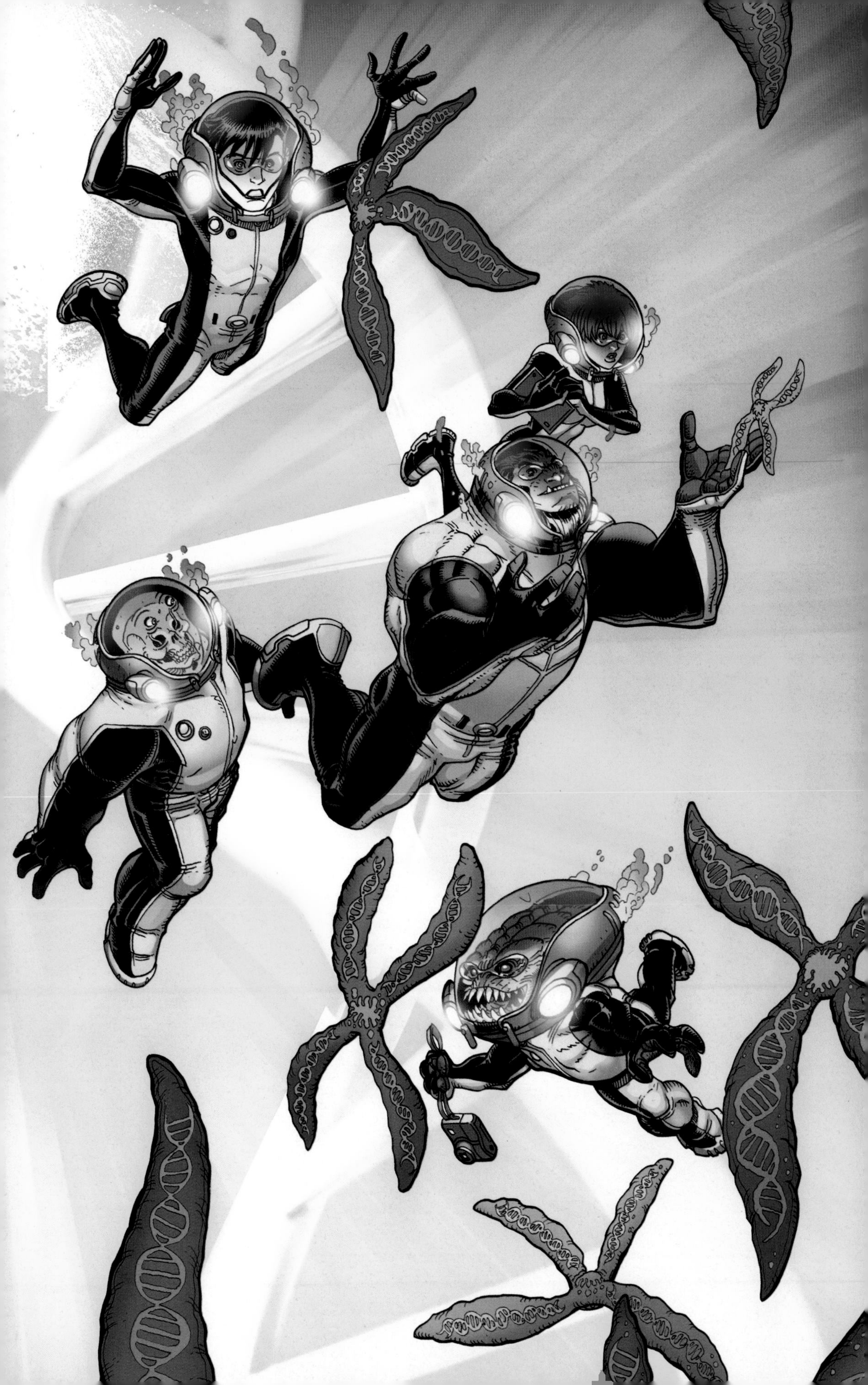

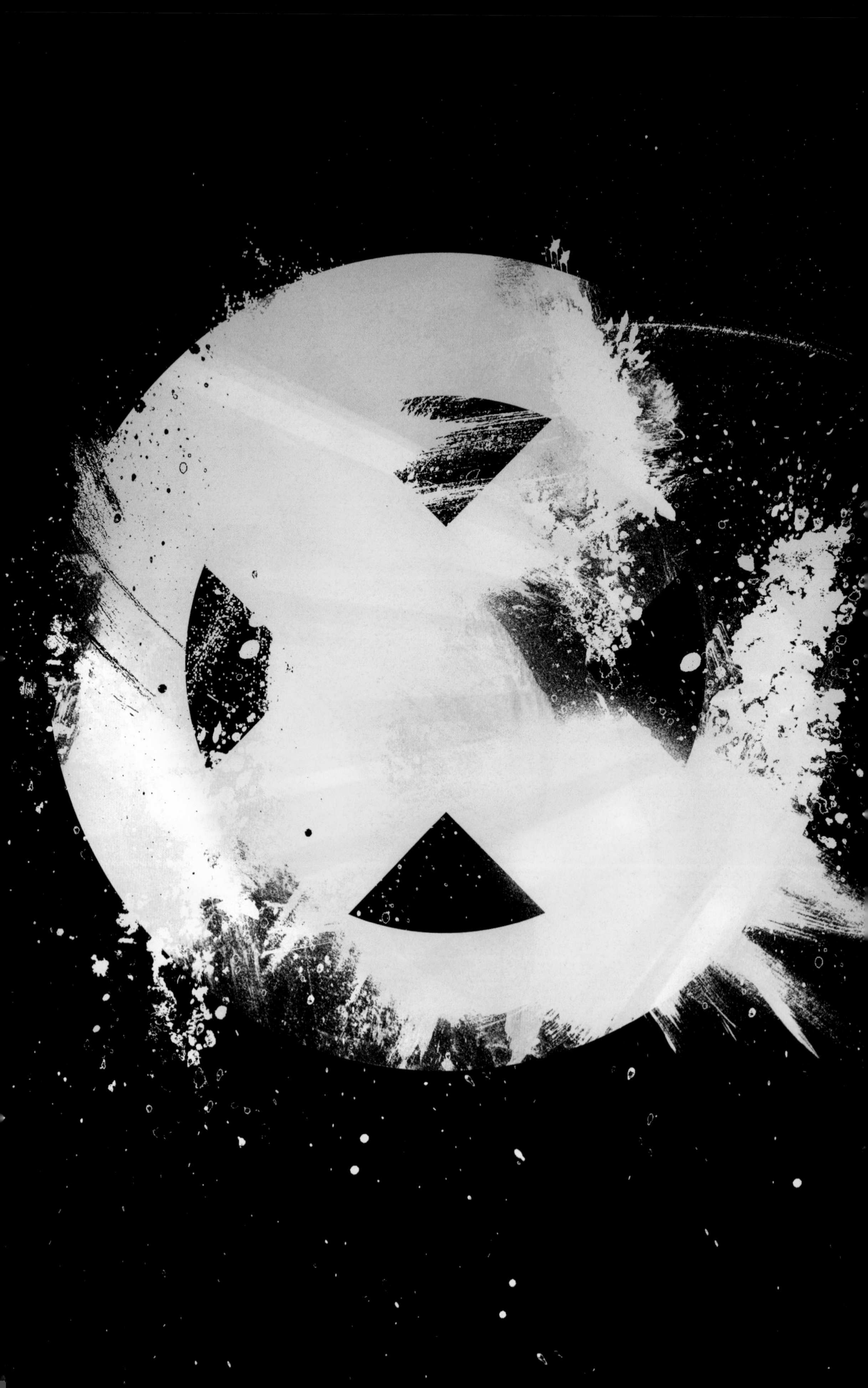

"MUTATIS MUTANDIS" 5
PART ONE: CONGRATULATIONS! IT'S A BROOD!

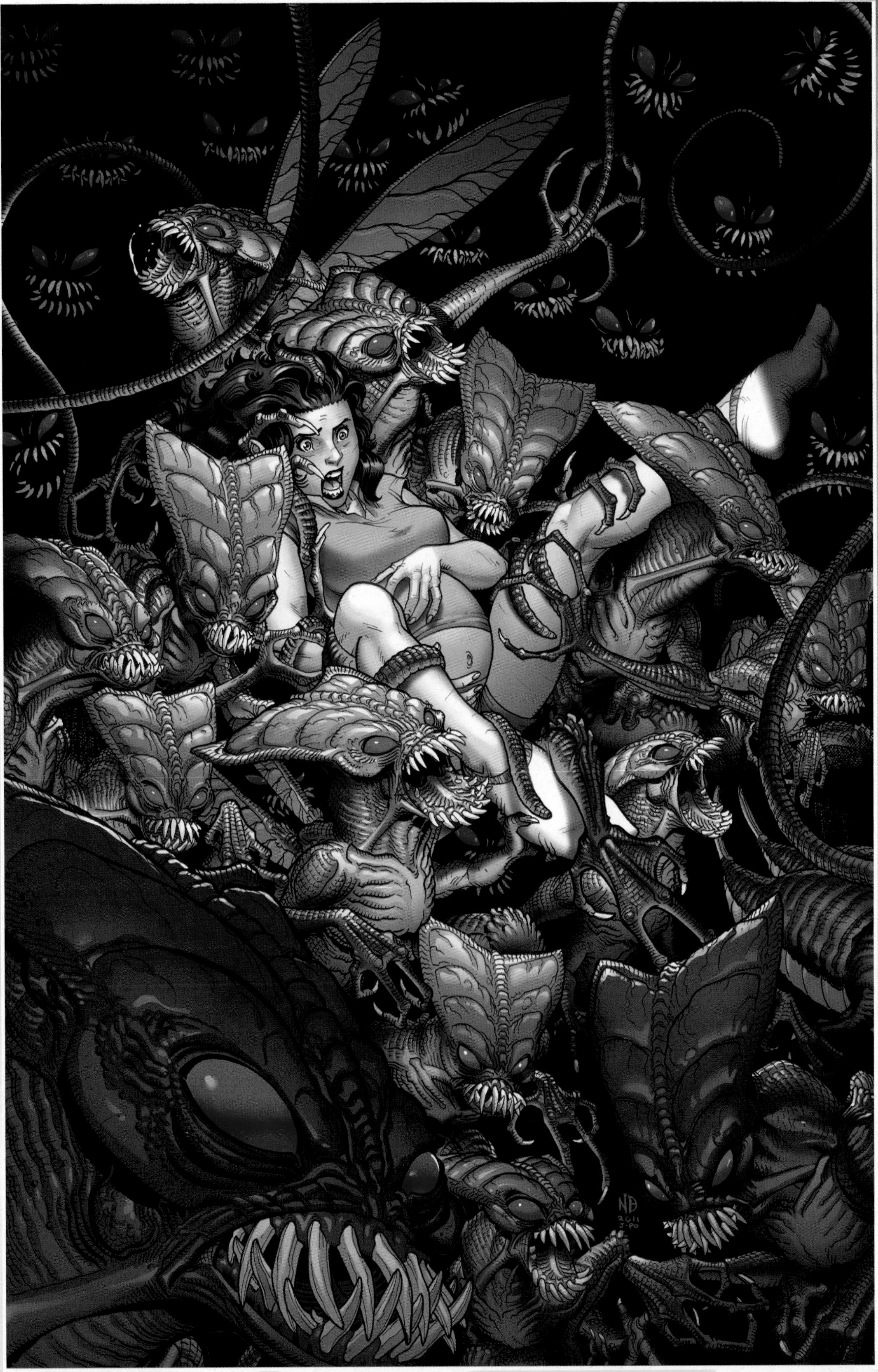

WOLVERINE and the X-MEN

If you were born different with mutant super-powers, the Jean Grey School for Higher Learning is the school for you. Founded by Wolverine and staffed by experienced X-Men, you will learn everything you need to know to survive in a world that hates and fears you.

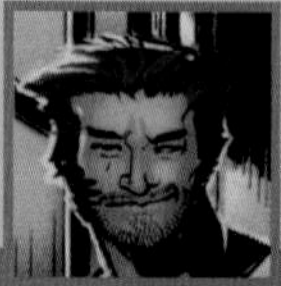

WOLVERINE
Clawed Headmaster

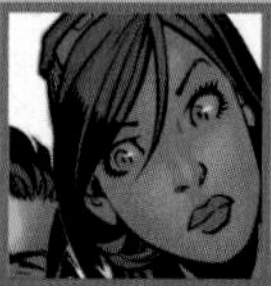

KITTY PRYDE
Phasing Headmistress

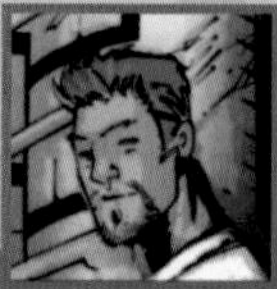

ICEMAN
Ice-Controlling Teacher

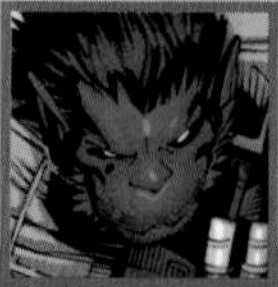

BEAST
Animalistic Intellectual Vice-Principal

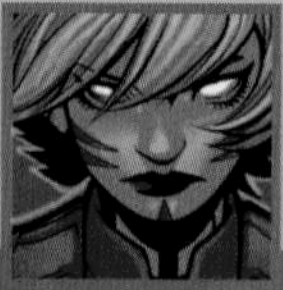

RACHEL GREY
Telekinetic Telepathic Teacher

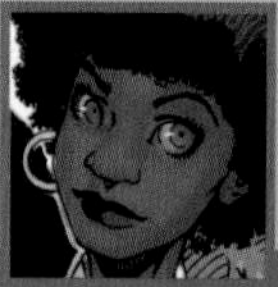

IDIE OKONKWO
Temperature-Controlling Student

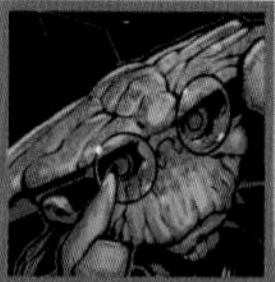

BROO
Alien Student

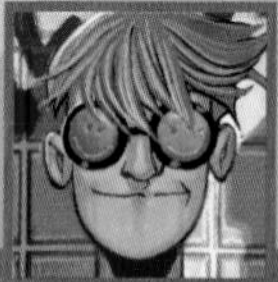

QUENTIN QUIRE
Telepathic Student

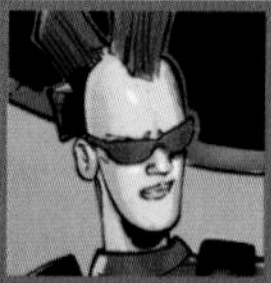

KID GLADIATOR
Superstrong Alien Student

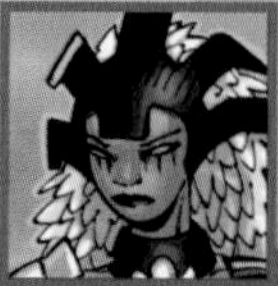

WARBIRD
Shi'ar Bodyguard

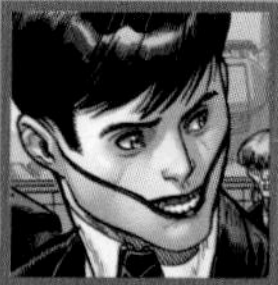

GENESIS
Flight & Eyebeams

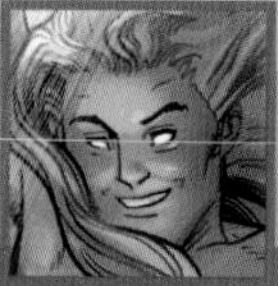

ANGEL
Metal Wings

PREVIOUSLY

It's been a rough time for Wolverine, starting a school for young mutants. He may have managed to fend off an attack from the new pubescent Hellfire Club, but he burned through all his operating costs to do so. At the same time, Wolverine's OTHER team, X-Force, adds two new students to the school: Genesis, who is a young clone of X-Men villain Apocalypse, and Angel, a founding member of the X-Men whose memory has been erased. Fortunately for the school, Angel also happens to be the incredibly wealthy CEO of a Fortune 500 corporation.

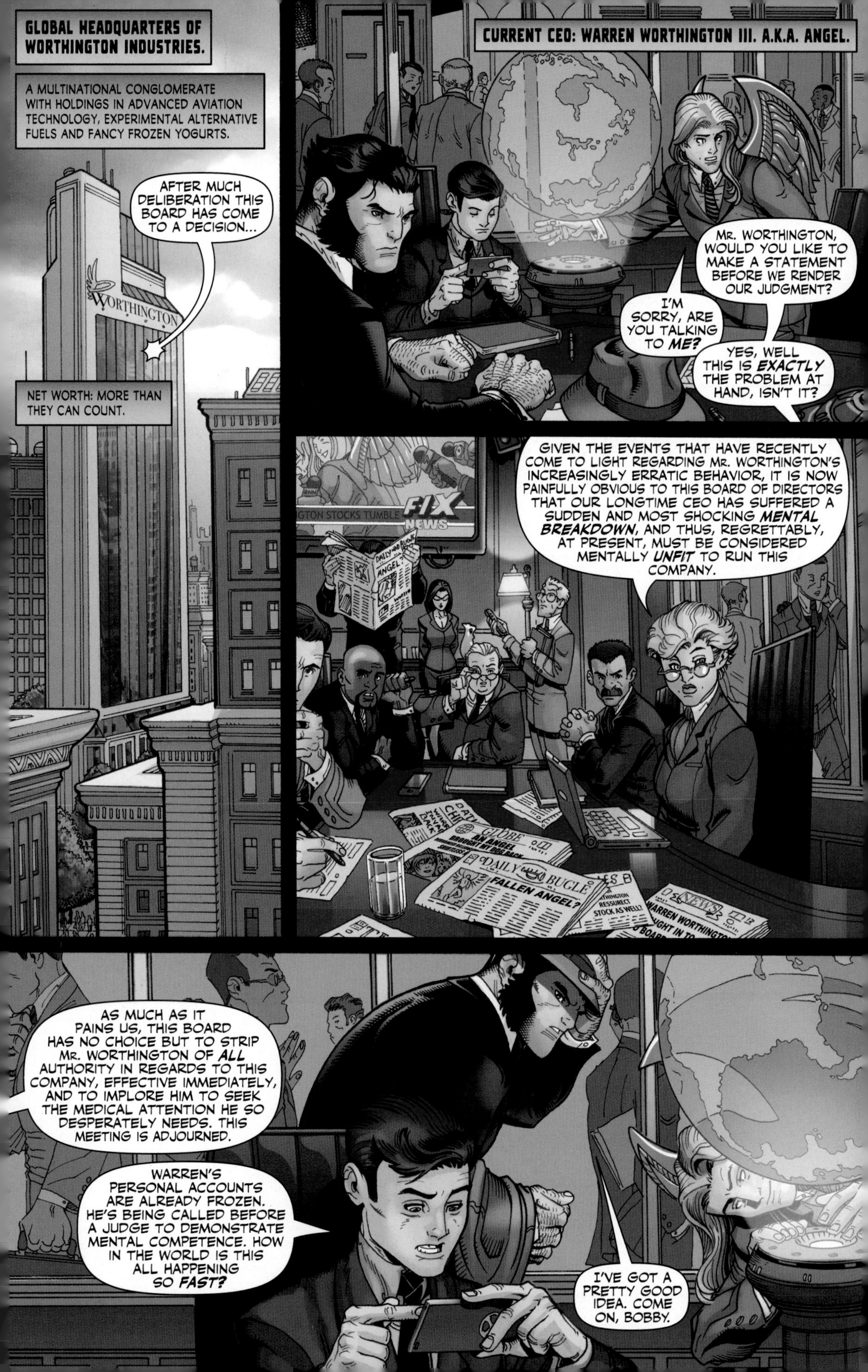
GLOBAL HEADQUARTERS OF WORTHINGTON INDUSTRIES.
A MULTINATIONAL CONGLOMERATE WITH HOLDINGS IN ADVANCED AVIATION TECHNOLOGY, EXPERIMENTAL ALTERNATIVE FUELS AND FANCY FROZEN YOGURTS.
AFTER MUCH DELIBERATION THIS BOARD HAS COME TO A DECISION...
WORTHINGTON
NET WORTH: MORE THAN THEY CAN COUNT.
CURRENT CEO: WARREN WORTHINGTON III. A.K.A. ANGEL.
MR. WORTHINGTON, WOULD YOU LIKE TO MAKE A STATEMENT BEFORE WE RENDER OUR JUDGMENT?
I'M SORRY, ARE YOU TALKING TO *ME?*
YES, WELL THIS IS *EXACTLY* THE PROBLEM AT HAND, ISN'T IT?
GIVEN THE EVENTS THAT HAVE RECENTLY COME TO LIGHT REGARDING MR. WORTHINGTON'S INCREASINGLY ERRATIC BEHAVIOR, IT IS NOW PAINFULLY OBVIOUS TO THIS BOARD OF DIRECTORS THAT OUR LONGTIME CEO HAS SUFFERED A SUDDEN AND MOST SHOCKING *MENTAL BREAKDOWN*, AND THUS, REGRETTABLY, AT PRESENT, MUST BE CONSIDERED MENTALLY *UNFIT* TO RUN THIS COMPANY.
GTON STOCKS TUMBLE
FIX NEWS
DAILY BUGLE
FALLEN ANGEL?
GLOBE
WARREN WORTHINGTON
AS MUCH AS IT PAINS US, THIS BOARD HAS NO CHOICE BUT TO STRIP MR. WORTHINGTON OF *ALL* AUTHORITY IN REGARDS TO THIS COMPANY, EFFECTIVE IMMEDIATELY, AND TO IMPLORE HIM TO SEEK THE MEDICAL ATTENTION HE SO DESPERATELY NEEDS. THIS MEETING IS ADJOURNED.
WARREN'S PERSONAL ACCOUNTS ARE ALREADY FROZEN. HE'S BEING CALLED BEFORE A JUDGE TO DEMONSTRATE MENTAL COMPETENCE. HOW IN THE WORLD IS THIS ALL HAPPENING SO *FAST?*
I'VE GOT A PRETTY GOOD IDEA. COME ON, BOBBY.

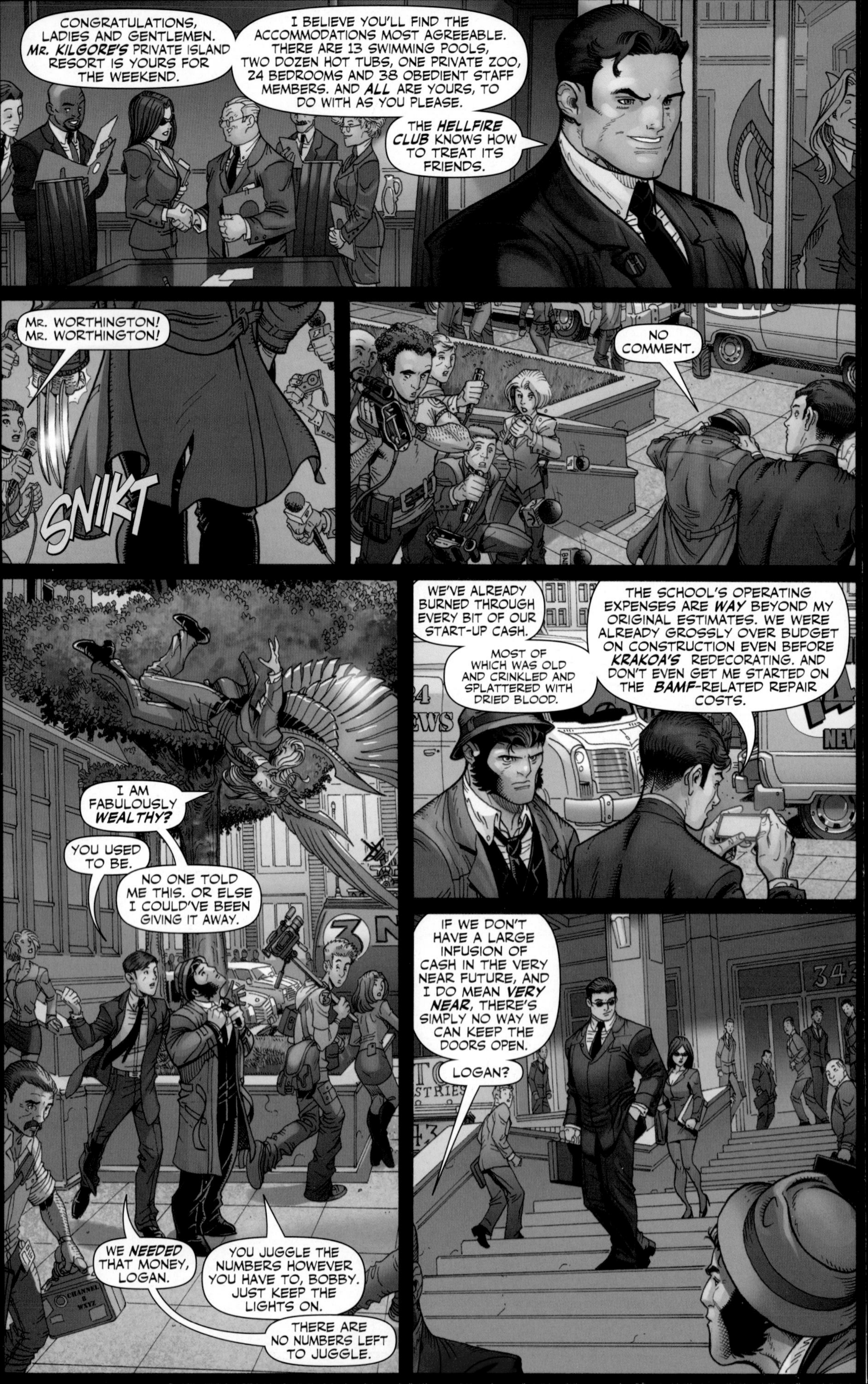
CONGRATULATIONS, LADIES AND GENTLEMEN. MR. KILGORE'S PRIVATE ISLAND RESORT IS YOURS FOR THE WEEKEND.
I BELIEVE YOU'LL FIND THE ACCOMMODATIONS MOST AGREEABLE. THERE ARE 13 SWIMMING POOLS, TWO DOZEN HOT TUBS, ONE PRIVATE ZOO, 24 BEDROOMS AND 38 OBEDIENT STAFF MEMBERS. AND ALL ARE YOURS, TO DO WITH AS YOU PLEASE.
THE HELLFIRE CLUB KNOWS HOW TO TREAT ITS FRIENDS.
MR. WORTHINGTON! MR. WORTHINGTON!
SNIKT
NO COMMENT.
I AM FABULOUSLY WEALTHY?
YOU USED TO BE.
NO ONE TOLD ME THIS. OR ELSE I COULD'VE BEEN GIVING IT AWAY.
WE NEEDED THAT MONEY, LOGAN.
YOU JUGGLE THE NUMBERS HOWEVER YOU HAVE TO, BOBBY. JUST KEEP THE LIGHTS ON.
THERE ARE NO NUMBERS LEFT TO JUGGLE.
WE'VE ALREADY BURNED THROUGH EVERY BIT OF OUR START-UP CASH.
MOST OF WHICH WAS OLD AND CRINKLED AND SPLATTERED WITH DRIED BLOOD.
THE SCHOOL'S OPERATING EXPENSES ARE WAY BEYOND MY ORIGINAL ESTIMATES. WE WERE ALREADY GROSSLY OVER BUDGET ON CONSTRUCTION EVEN BEFORE KRAKOA'S REDECORATING. AND DON'T EVEN GET ME STARTED ON THE BAMF-RELATED REPAIR COSTS.
IF WE DON'T HAVE A LARGE INFUSION OF CASH IN THE VERY NEAR FUTURE, AND I DO MEAN VERY NEAR, THERE'S SIMPLY NO WAY WE CAN KEEP THE DOORS OPEN.
LOGAN?

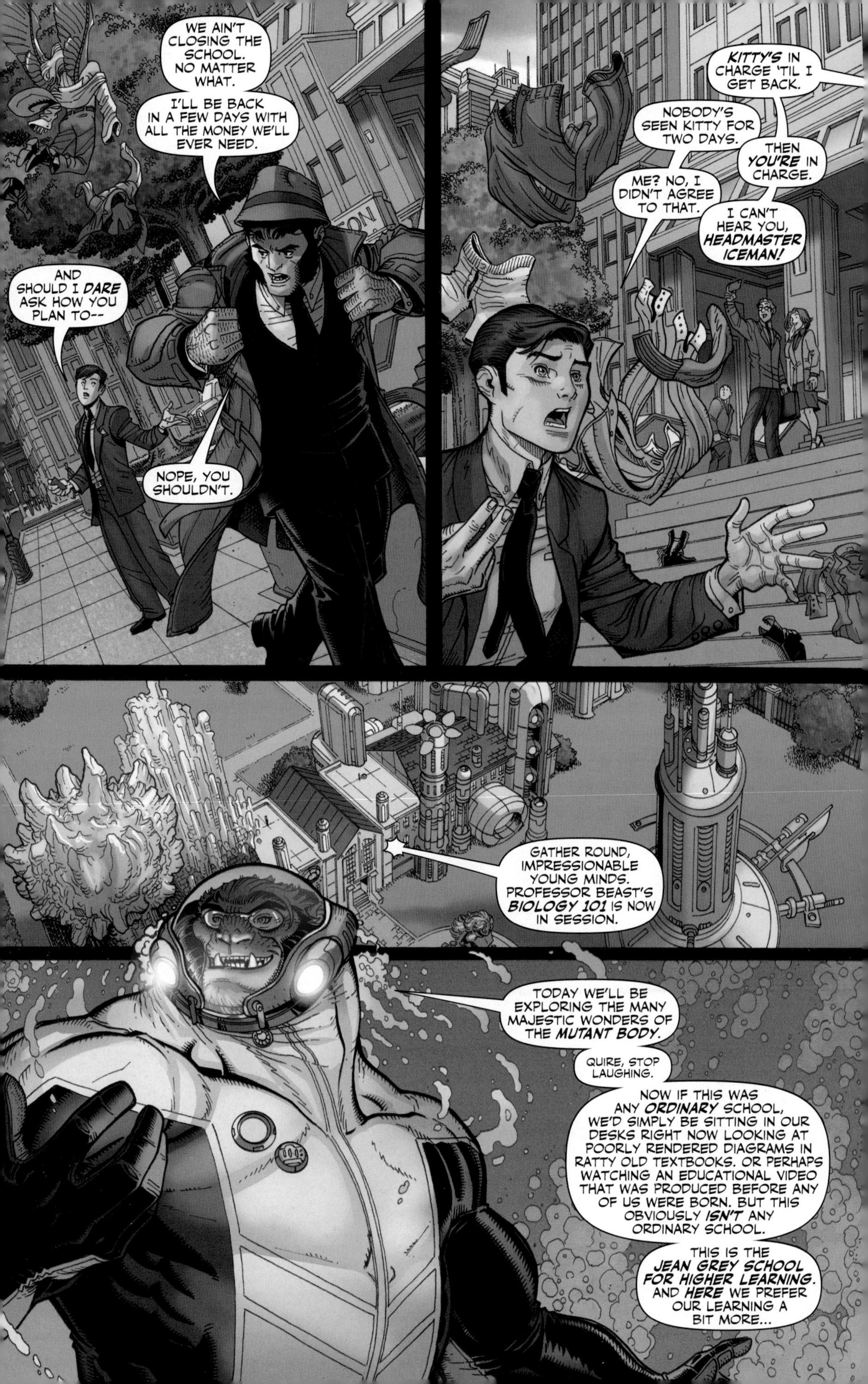
WE AIN'T CLOSING THE SCHOOL. NO MATTER WHAT.
I'LL BE BACK IN A FEW DAYS WITH ALL THE MONEY WE'LL EVER NEED.
AND SHOULD I *DARE* ASK HOW YOU PLAN TO--
NOPE, YOU SHOULDN'T.
KITTY'S IN CHARGE 'TIL I GET BACK.
NOBODY'S SEEN KITTY FOR TWO DAYS.
THEN *YOU'RE* IN CHARGE.
ME? NO, I DIDN'T AGREE TO THAT.
I CAN'T HEAR YOU, *HEADMASTER ICEMAN!*
GATHER ROUND, IMPRESSIONABLE YOUNG MINDS. PROFESSOR BEAST'S *BIOLOGY 101* IS NOW IN SESSION.
TODAY WE'LL BE EXPLORING THE MANY MAJESTIC WONDERS OF THE *MUTANT BODY*.
QUIRE, STOP LAUGHING.
NOW IF THIS WAS ANY *ORDINARY* SCHOOL, WE'D SIMPLY BE SITTING IN OUR DESKS RIGHT NOW LOOKING AT POORLY RENDERED DIAGRAMS IN RATTY OLD TEXTBOOKS. OR PERHAPS WATCHING AN EDUCATIONAL VIDEO THAT WAS PRODUCED BEFORE ANY OF US WERE BORN. BUT THIS OBVIOUSLY *ISN'T* ANY ORDINARY SCHOOL.
THIS IS THE *JEAN GREY SCHOOL FOR HIGHER LEARNING*. AND *HERE* WE PREFER OUR LEARNING A BIT MORE...

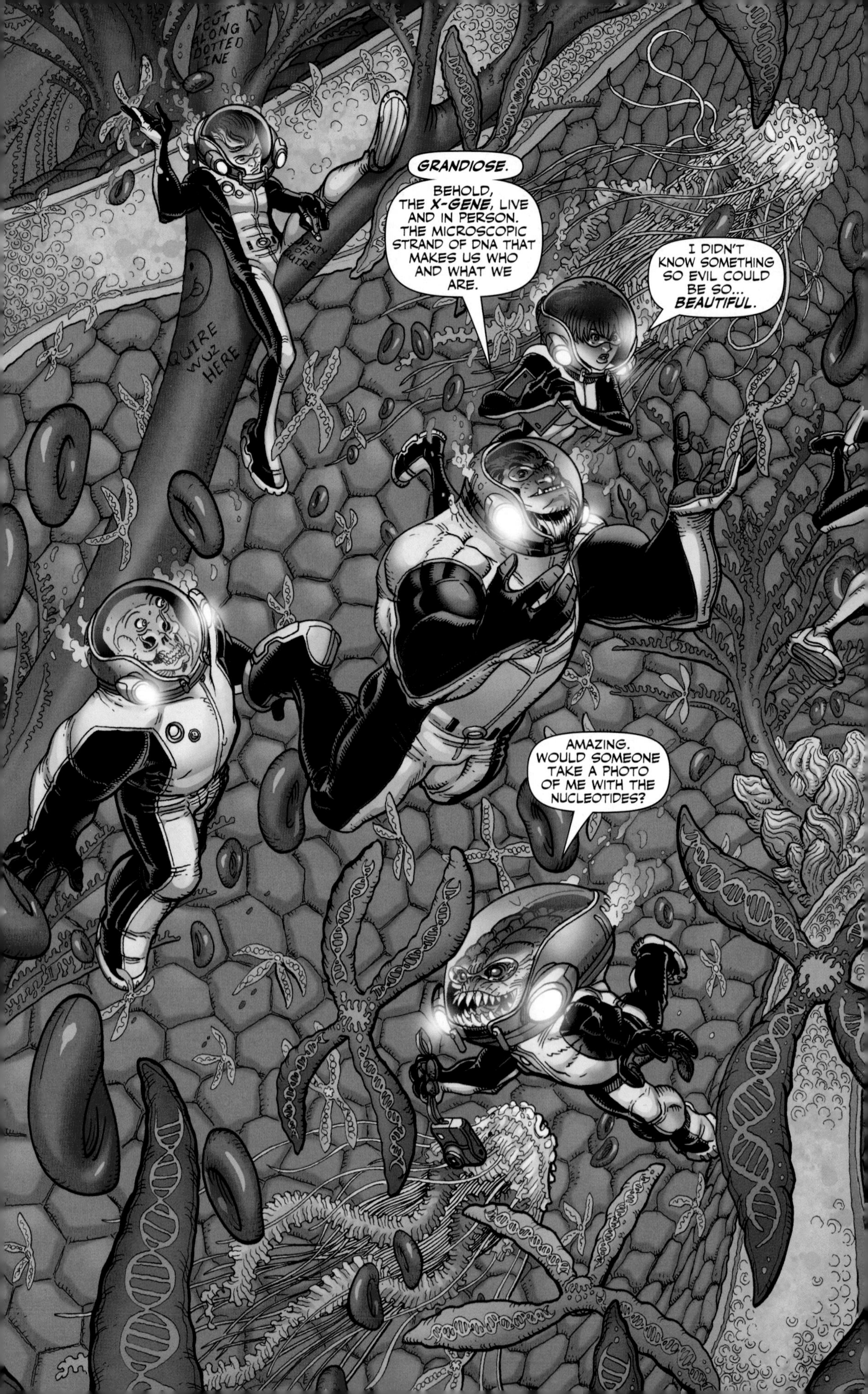
CUT ALONG DOTTED
GRANDIOSE.
BEHOLD, THE X-GENE, LIVE AND IN PERSON. THE MICROSCOPIC STRAND OF DNA THAT MAKES US WHO AND WHAT WE ARE.
I DIDN'T KNOW SOMETHING SO EVIL COULD BE SO... BEAUTIFUL.
QUIRE WUZ HERE
AMAZING. WOULD SOMEONE TAKE A PHOTO OF ME WITH THE NUCLEOTIDES?

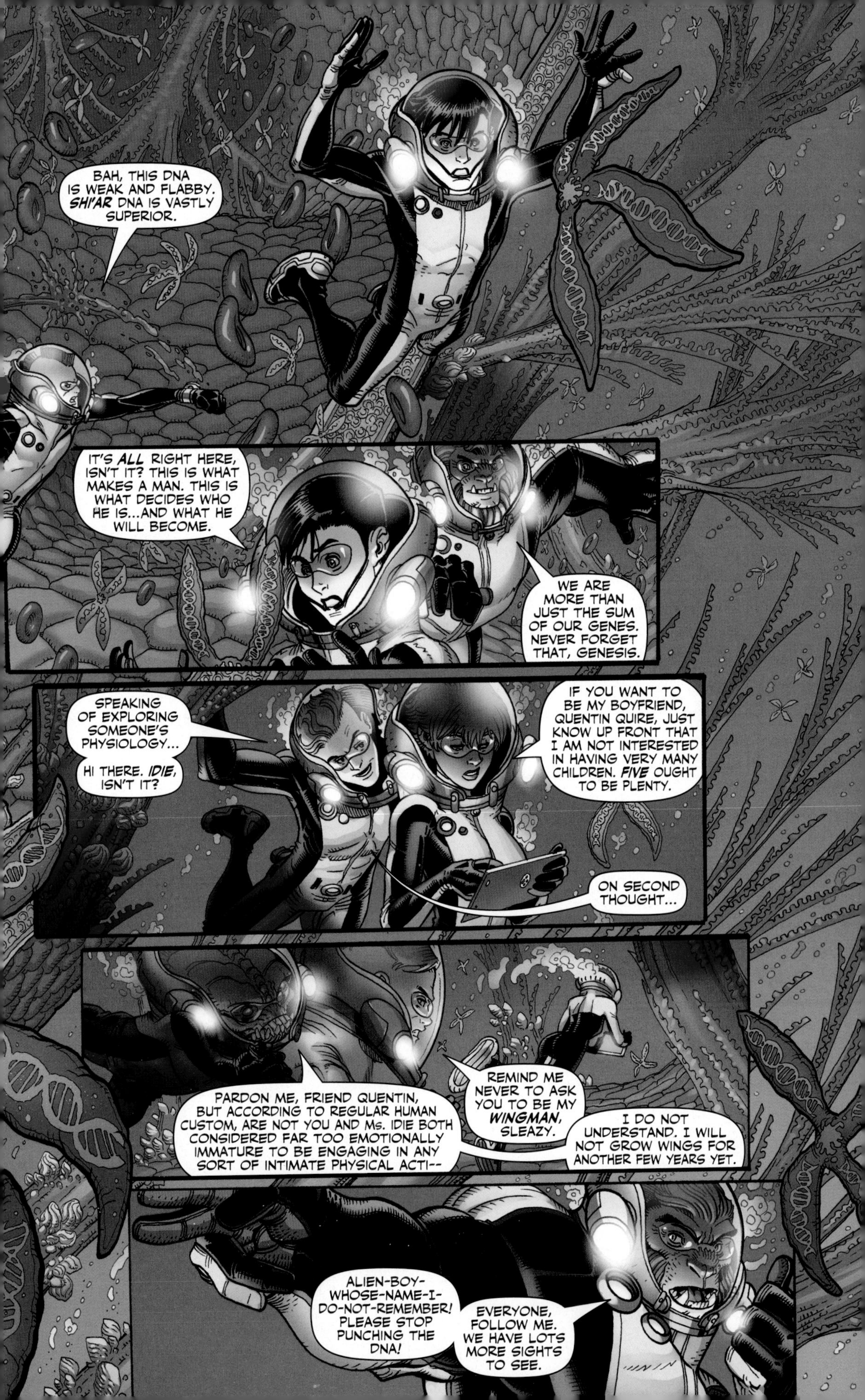
BAH, THIS DNA IS WEAK AND FLABBY. SHI'AR DNA IS VASTLY SUPERIOR.
IT'S ALL RIGHT HERE, ISN'T IT? THIS IS WHAT MAKES A MAN. THIS IS WHAT DECIDES WHO HE IS...AND WHAT HE WILL BECOME.
WE ARE MORE THAN JUST THE SUM OF OUR GENES. NEVER FORGET THAT, GENESIS.
SPEAKING OF EXPLORING SOMEONE'S PHYSIOLOGY...
HI THERE. IDIE, ISN'T IT?
IF YOU WANT TO BE MY BOYFRIEND, QUENTIN QUIRE, JUST KNOW UP FRONT THAT I AM NOT INTERESTED IN HAVING VERY MANY CHILDREN. FIVE OUGHT TO BE PLENTY.
ON SECOND THOUGHT...
PARDON ME, FRIEND QUENTIN, BUT ACCORDING TO REGULAR HUMAN CUSTOM, ARE NOT YOU AND Ms. IDIE BOTH CONSIDERED FAR TOO EMOTIONALLY IMMATURE TO BE ENGAGING IN ANY SORT OF INTIMATE PHYSICAL ACTI--
REMIND ME NEVER TO ASK YOU TO BE MY WINGMAN, SLEAZY.
I DO NOT UNDERSTAND. I WILL NOT GROW WINGS FOR ANOTHER FEW YEARS YET.
ALIEN-BOY-WHOSE-NAME-I-DO-NOT-REMEMBER! PLEASE STOP PUNCHING THE DNA!
EVERYONE, FOLLOW ME. WE HAVE LOTS MORE SIGHTS TO SEE.

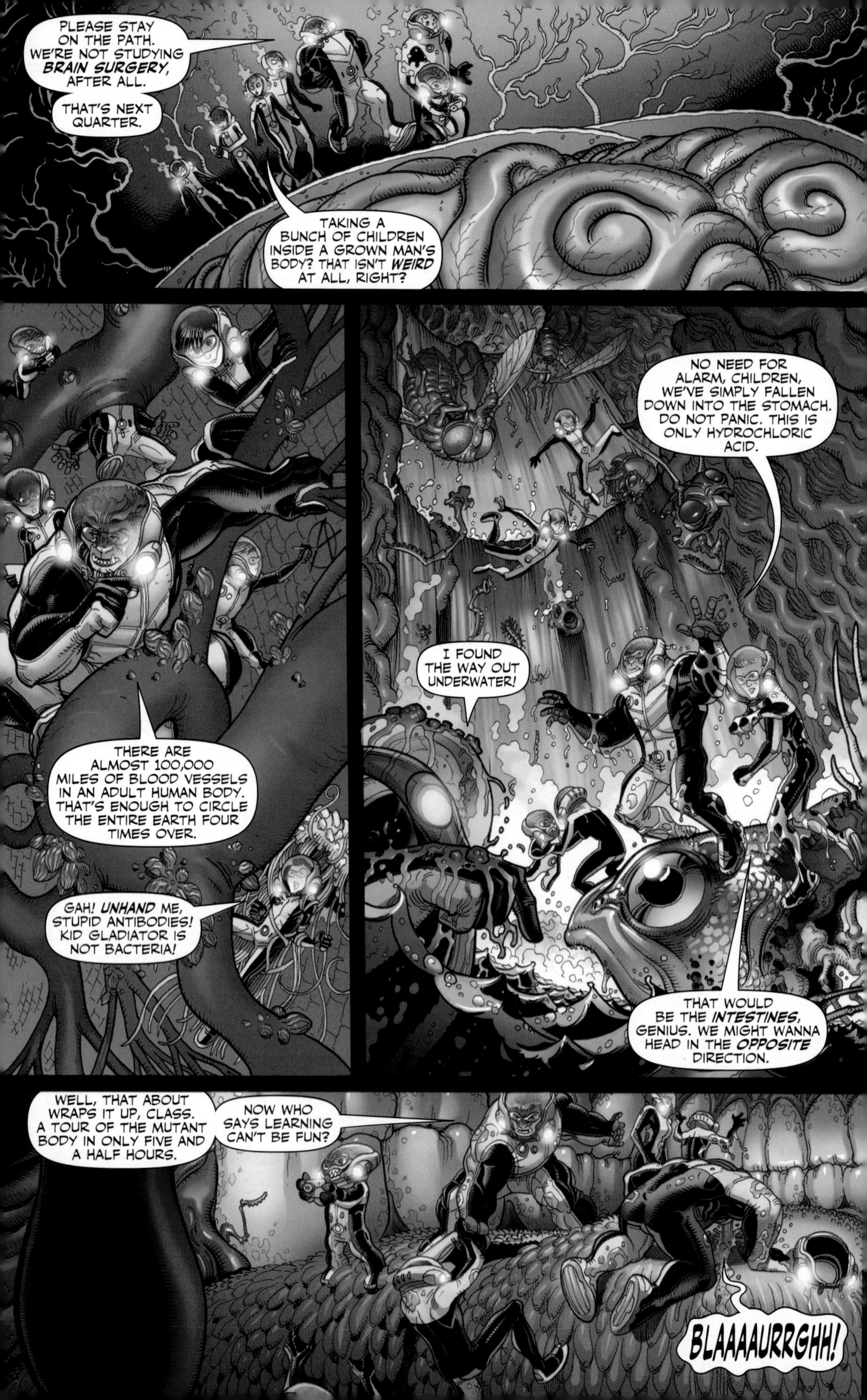
PLEASE STAY ON THE PATH. WE'RE NOT STUDYING BRAIN SURGERY, AFTER ALL.
THAT'S NEXT QUARTER.
TAKING A BUNCH OF CHILDREN INSIDE A GROWN MAN'S BODY? THAT ISN'T WEIRD AT ALL, RIGHT?
THERE ARE ALMOST 100,000 MILES OF BLOOD VESSELS IN AN ADULT HUMAN BODY. THAT'S ENOUGH TO CIRCLE THE ENTIRE EARTH FOUR TIMES OVER.
GAH! UNHAND ME, STUPID ANTIBODIES! KID GLADIATOR IS NOT BACTERIA!
NO NEED FOR ALARM, CHILDREN, WE'VE SIMPLY FALLEN DOWN INTO THE STOMACH. DO NOT PANIC. THIS IS ONLY HYDROCHLORIC ACID.
I FOUND THE WAY OUT UNDERWATER!
THAT WOULD BE THE INTESTINES, GENIUS. WE MIGHT WANNA HEAD IN THE OPPOSITE DIRECTION.
WELL, THAT ABOUT WRAPS IT UP, CLASS. A TOUR OF THE MUTANT BODY IN ONLY FIVE AND A HALF HOURS.
NOW WHO SAYS LEARNING CAN'T BE FUN?
BLAAAAURRGHH!

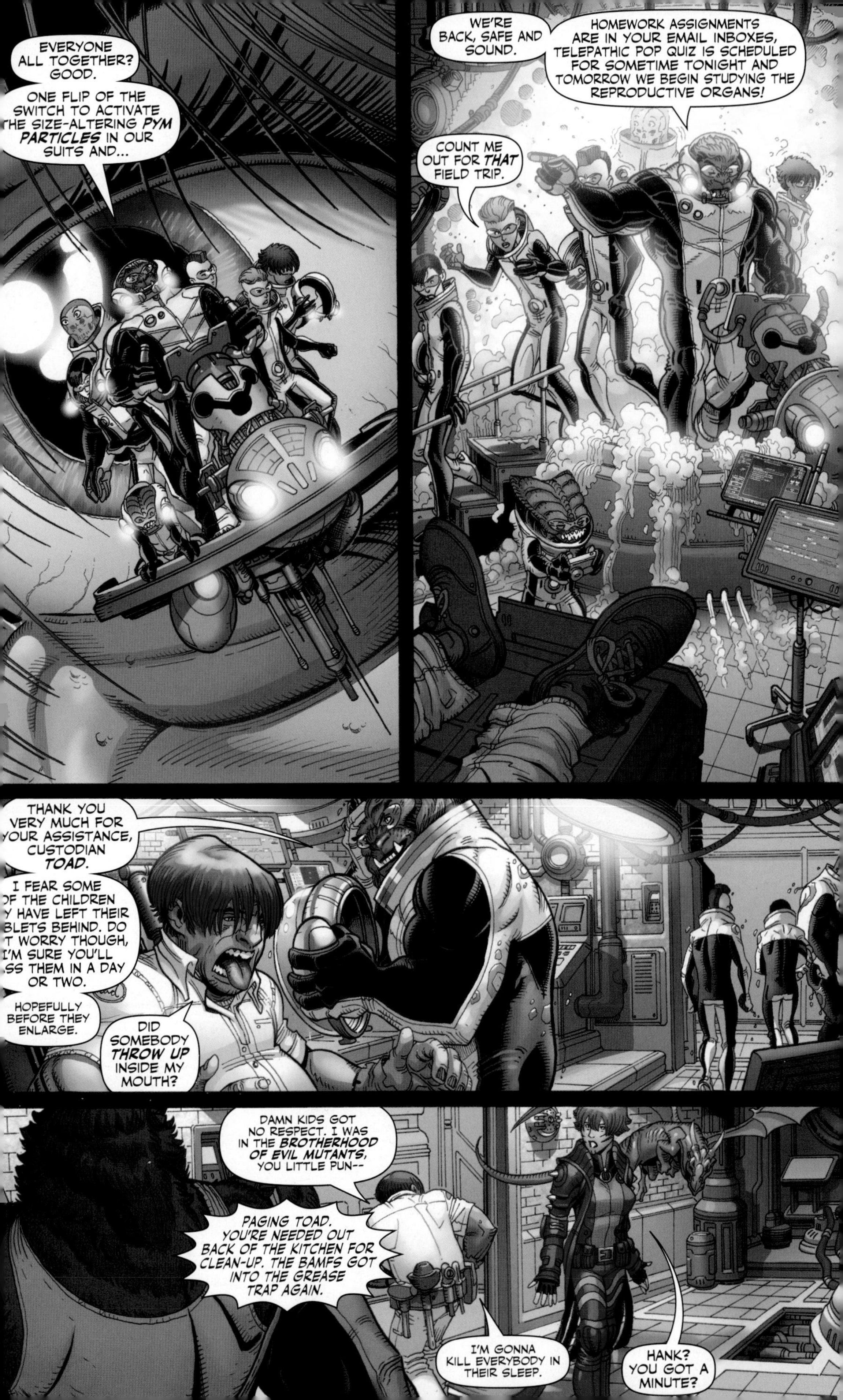

EVERYONE ALL TOGETHER? GOOD.
ONE FLIP OF THE SWITCH TO ACTIVATE THE SIZE-ALTERING PYM PARTICLES IN OUR SUITS AND...
WE'RE BACK, SAFE AND SOUND.
HOMEWORK ASSIGNMENTS ARE IN YOUR EMAIL INBOXES, TELEPATHIC POP QUIZ IS SCHEDULED FOR SOMETIME TONIGHT AND TOMORROW WE BEGIN STUDYING THE REPRODUCTIVE ORGANS!
COUNT ME OUT FOR THAT FIELD TRIP.
THANK YOU VERY MUCH FOR YOUR ASSISTANCE, CUSTODIAN TOAD.
I FEAR SOME OF THE CHILDREN Y HAVE LEFT THEIR BLETS BEHIND. DO T WORRY THOUGH, I'M SURE YOU'LL SS THEM IN A DAY OR TWO.
HOPEFULLY BEFORE THEY ENLARGE.
DID SOMEBODY THROW UP INSIDE MY MOUTH?
DAMN KIDS GOT NO RESPECT. I WAS IN THE BROTHERHOOD OF EVIL MUTANTS, YOU LITTLE PUN--
PAGING TOAD. YOU'RE NEEDED OUT BACK OF THE KITCHEN FOR CLEAN-UP. THE BAMFS GOT INTO THE GREASE TRAP AGAIN.
I'M GONNA KILL EVERYBODY IN THEIR SLEEP.
HANK? YOU GOT A MINUTE?

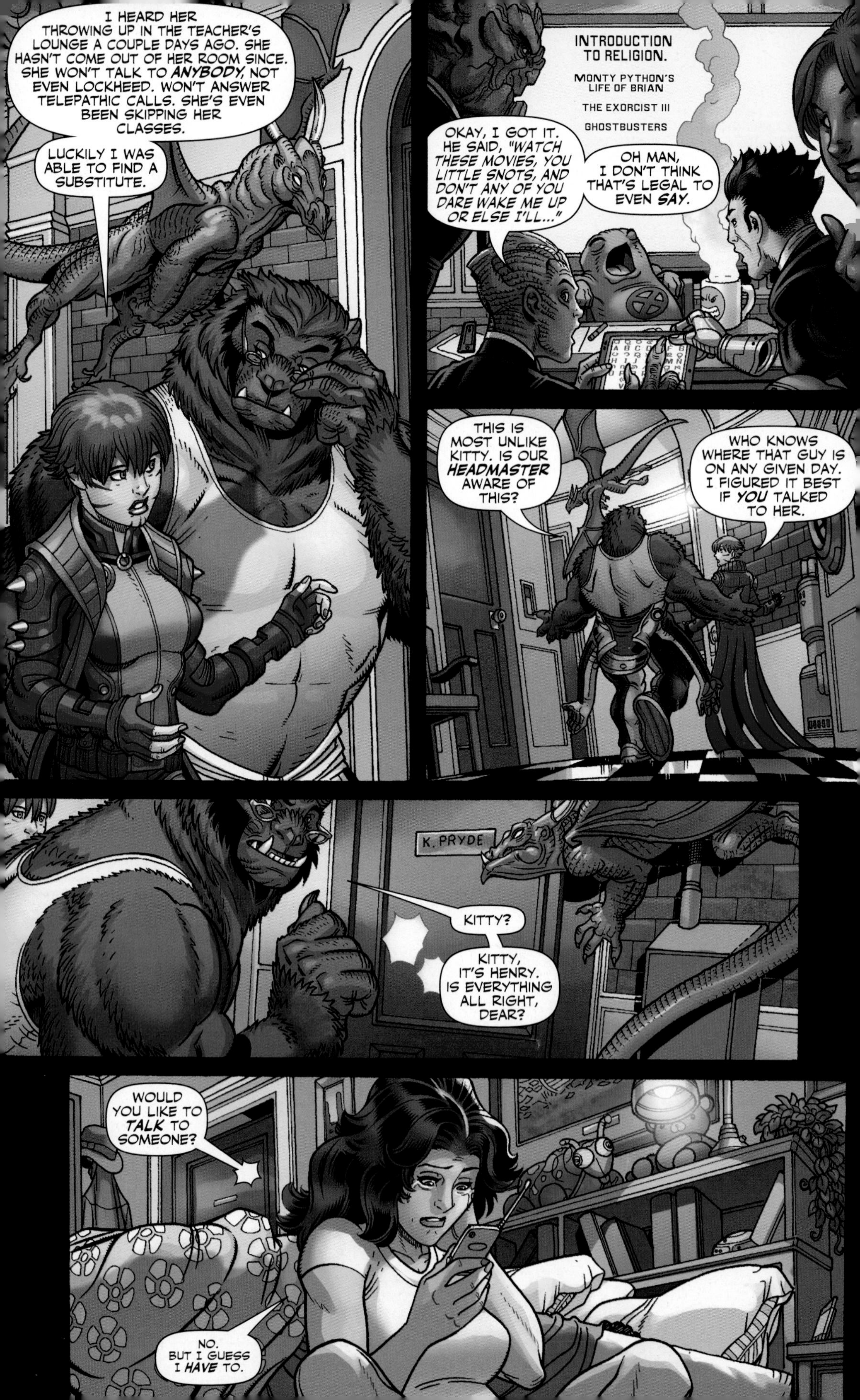
I HEARD HER THROWING UP IN THE TEACHER'S LOUNGE A COUPLE DAYS AGO. SHE HASN'T COME OUT OF HER ROOM SINCE. SHE WON'T TALK TO ANYBODY, NOT EVEN LOCKHEED. WON'T ANSWER TELEPATHIC CALLS. SHE'S EVEN BEEN SKIPPING HER CLASSES.
LUCKILY I WAS ABLE TO FIND A SUBSTITUTE.
INTRODUCTION TO RELIGION.
MONTY PYTHON'S LIFE OF BRIAN
THE EXORCIST III
GHOSTBUSTERS
OKAY, I GOT IT. HE SAID, "WATCH THESE MOVIES, YOU LITTLE SNOTS, AND DON'T ANY OF YOU DARE WAKE ME UP OR ELSE I'LL..."
OH MAN, I DON'T THINK THAT'S LEGAL TO EVEN SAY.
THIS IS MOST UNLIKE KITTY. IS OUR HEADMASTER AWARE OF THIS?
WHO KNOWS WHERE THAT GUY IS ON ANY GIVEN DAY. I FIGURED IT BEST IF YOU TALKED TO HER.
K. PRYDE
KITTY?
KITTY, IT'S HENRY. IS EVERYTHING ALL RIGHT, DEAR?
WOULD YOU LIKE TO TALK TO SOMEONE?
NO. BUT I GUESS I HAVE TO.

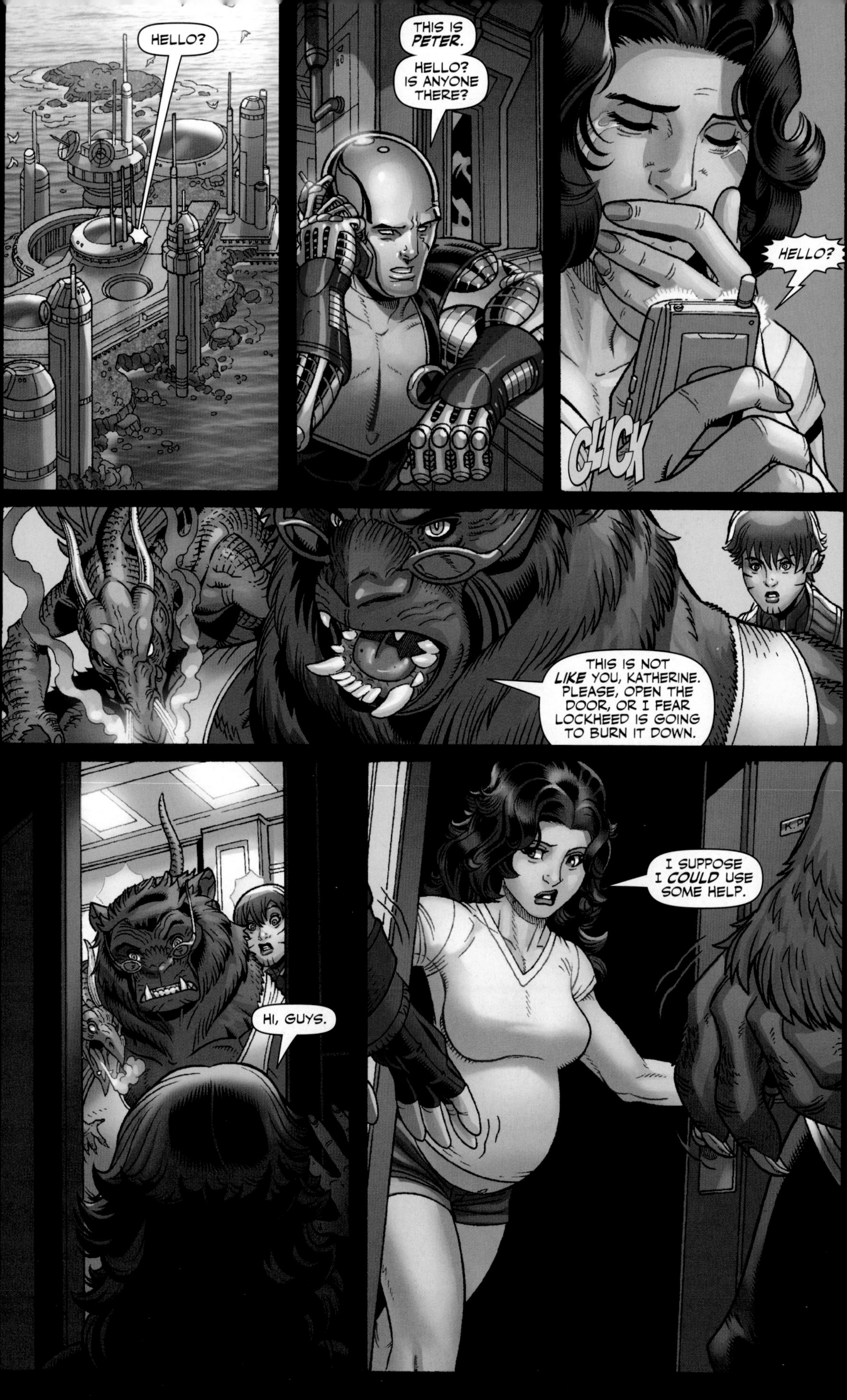
HELLO?
THIS IS PETER.
HELLO? IS ANYONE THERE?
HELLO?
CLICK
THIS IS NOT LIKE YOU, KATHERINE. PLEASE, OPEN THE DOOR, OR I FEAR LOCKHEED IS GOING TO BURN IT DOWN.
HI, GUYS.
I SUPPOSE I COULD USE SOME HELP.

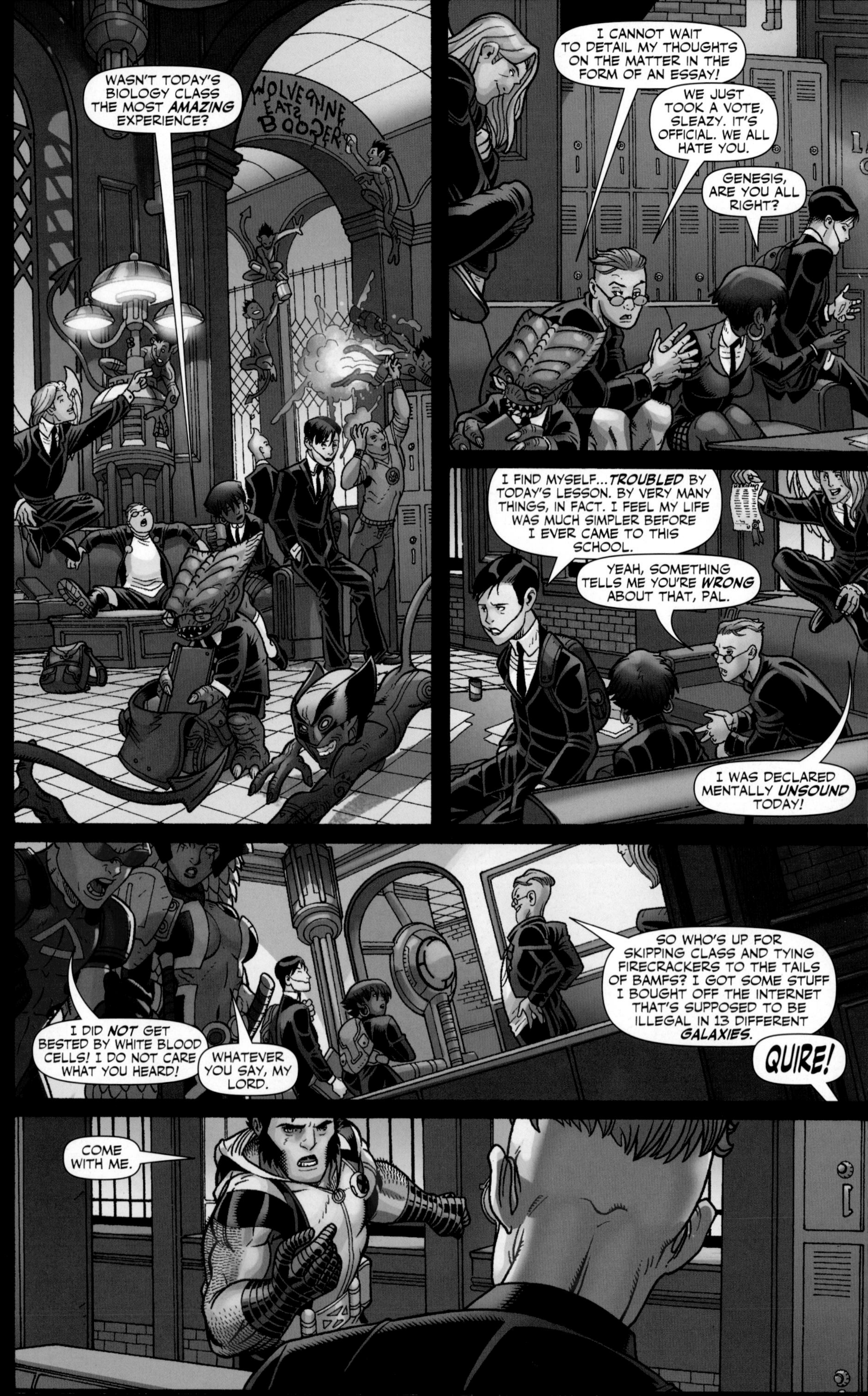
WASN'T TODAY'S BIOLOGY CLASS THE MOST AMAZING EXPERIENCE?
WOLVERINE EATS BOOGERS
I CANNOT WAIT TO DETAIL MY THOUGHTS ON THE MATTER IN THE FORM OF AN ESSAY!
WE JUST TOOK A VOTE, SLEAZY. IT'S OFFICIAL. WE ALL HATE YOU.
GENESIS, ARE YOU ALL RIGHT?
I FIND MYSELF...TROUBLED BY TODAY'S LESSON. BY VERY MANY THINGS, IN FACT. I FEEL MY LIFE WAS MUCH SIMPLER BEFORE I EVER CAME TO THIS SCHOOL.
YEAH, SOMETHING TELLS ME YOU'RE WRONG ABOUT THAT, PAL.
I WAS DECLARED MENTALLY UNSOUND TODAY!
I DID NOT GET BESTED BY WHITE BLOOD CELLS! I DO NOT CARE WHAT YOU HEARD!
WHATEVER YOU SAY, MY LORD.
SO WHO'S UP FOR SKIPPING CLASS AND TYING FIRECRACKERS TO THE TAILS OF BAMFS? I GOT SOME STUFF I BOUGHT OFF THE INTERNET THAT'S SUPPOSED TO BE ILLEGAL IN 13 DIFFERENT GALAXIES.
QUIRE!
COME WITH ME.

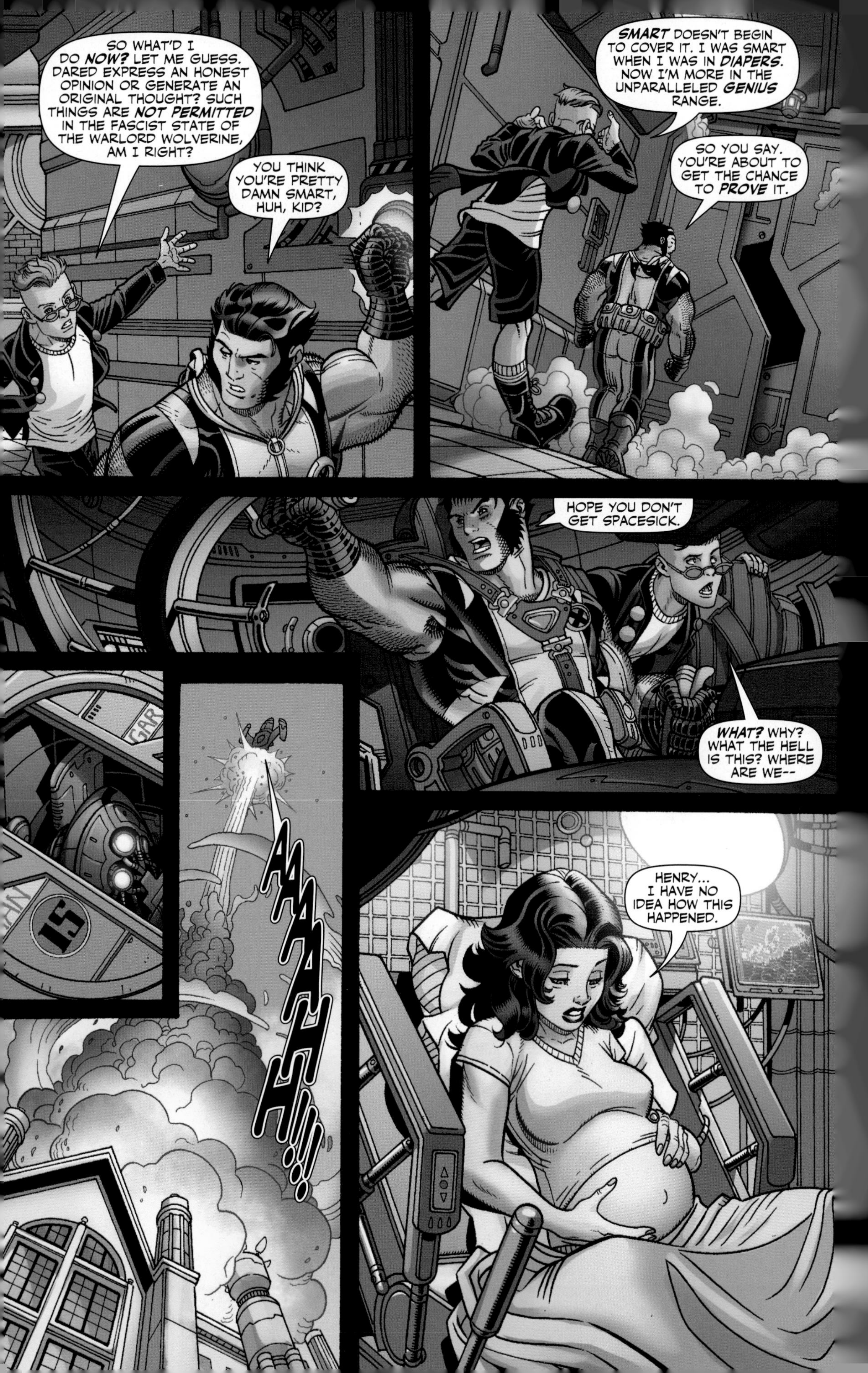
SO WHAT'D I DO NOW? LET ME GUESS. DARED EXPRESS AN HONEST OPINION OR GENERATE AN ORIGINAL THOUGHT? SUCH THINGS ARE NOT PERMITTED IN THE FASCIST STATE OF THE WARLORD WOLVERINE, AM I RIGHT?
YOU THINK YOU'RE PRETTY DAMN SMART, HUH, KID?
SMART DOESN'T BEGIN TO COVER IT. I WAS SMART WHEN I WAS IN DIAPERS. NOW I'M MORE IN THE UNPARALLELED GENIUS RANGE.
SO YOU SAY. YOU'RE ABOUT TO GET THE CHANCE TO PROVE IT.
HOPE YOU DON'T GET SPACESICK.
WHAT? WHY? WHAT THE HELL IS THIS? WHERE ARE WE--
AAAAHHH!!!
HENRY... I HAVE NO IDEA HOW THIS HAPPENED.

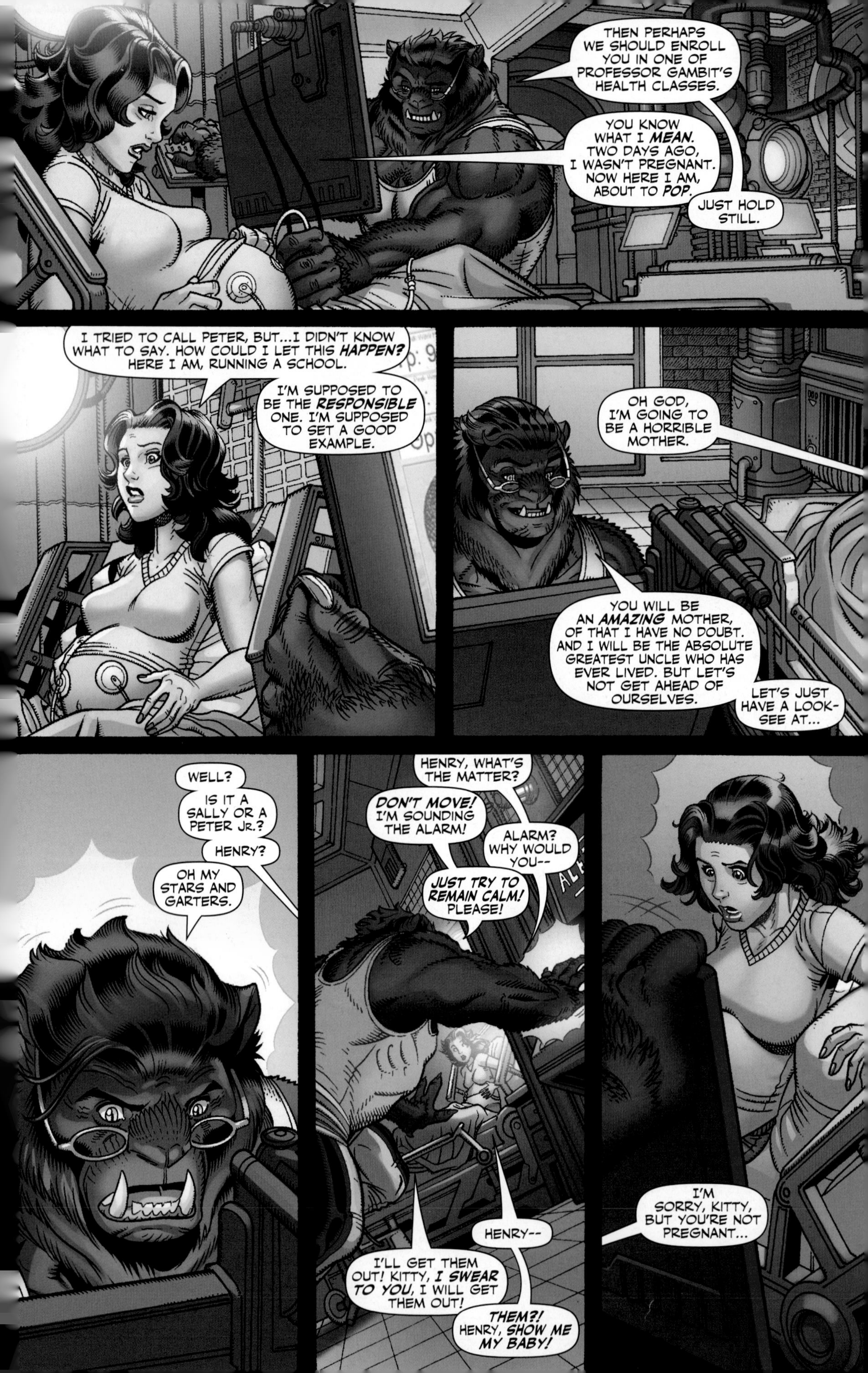
THEN PERHAPS WE SHOULD ENROLL YOU IN ONE OF PROFESSOR GAMBIT'S HEALTH CLASSES.
YOU KNOW WHAT I MEAN. TWO DAYS AGO, I WASN'T PREGNANT. NOW HERE I AM, ABOUT TO POP.
JUST HOLD STILL.
I TRIED TO CALL PETER, BUT...I DIDN'T KNOW WHAT TO SAY. HOW COULD I LET THIS HAPPEN? HERE I AM, RUNNING A SCHOOL.
I'M SUPPOSED TO BE THE RESPONSIBLE ONE. I'M SUPPOSED TO SET A GOOD EXAMPLE.
OH GOD, I'M GOING TO BE A HORRIBLE MOTHER.
YOU WILL BE AN AMAZING MOTHER, OF THAT I HAVE NO DOUBT. AND I WILL BE THE ABSOLUTE GREATEST UNCLE WHO HAS EVER LIVED. BUT LET'S NOT GET AHEAD OF OURSELVES.
LET'S JUST HAVE A LOOK-SEE AT...
WELL?
IS IT A SALLY OR A PETER JR.?
HENRY?
OH MY STARS AND GARTERS.
HENRY, WHAT'S THE MATTER?
DON'T MOVE! I'M SOUNDING THE ALARM!
ALARM? WHY WOULD YOU--
JUST TRY TO REMAIN CALM! PLEASE!
HENRY--
I'LL GET THEM OUT! KITTY, I SWEAR TO YOU, I WILL GET THEM OUT!
THEM?! HENRY, SHOW ME MY BABY!
I'M SORRY, KITTY, BUT YOU'RE NOT PREGNANT...

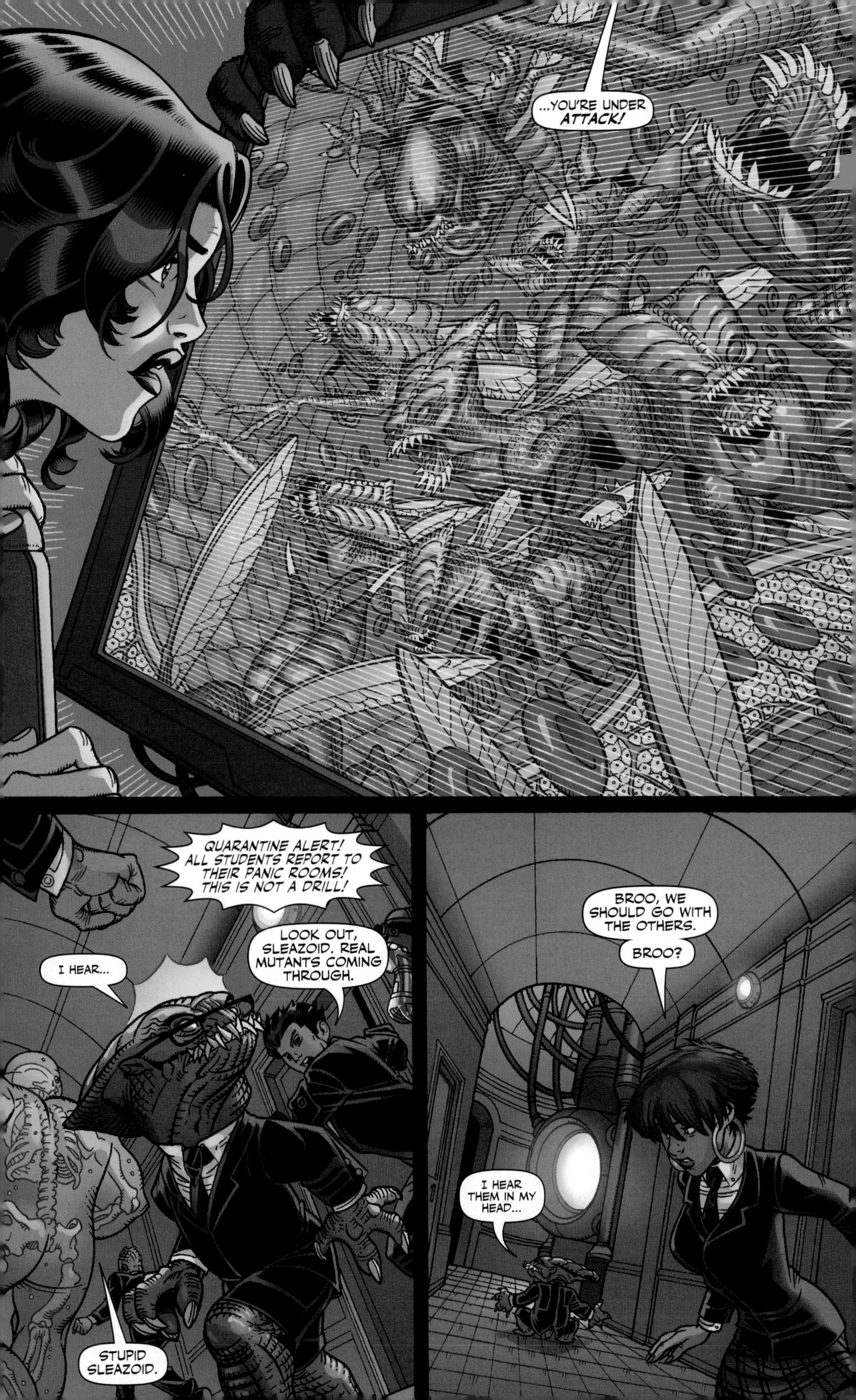
...YOU'RE UNDER ATTACK!
QUARANTINE ALERT! ALL STUDENTS REPORT TO THEIR PANIC ROOMS! THIS IS NOT A DRILL!
I HEAR...
LOOK OUT, SLEAZOID. REAL MUTANTS COMING THROUGH.
STUPID SLEAZOID.
BROO, WE SHOULD GO WITH THE OTHERS.
BROO?
I HEAR THEM IN MY HEAD...

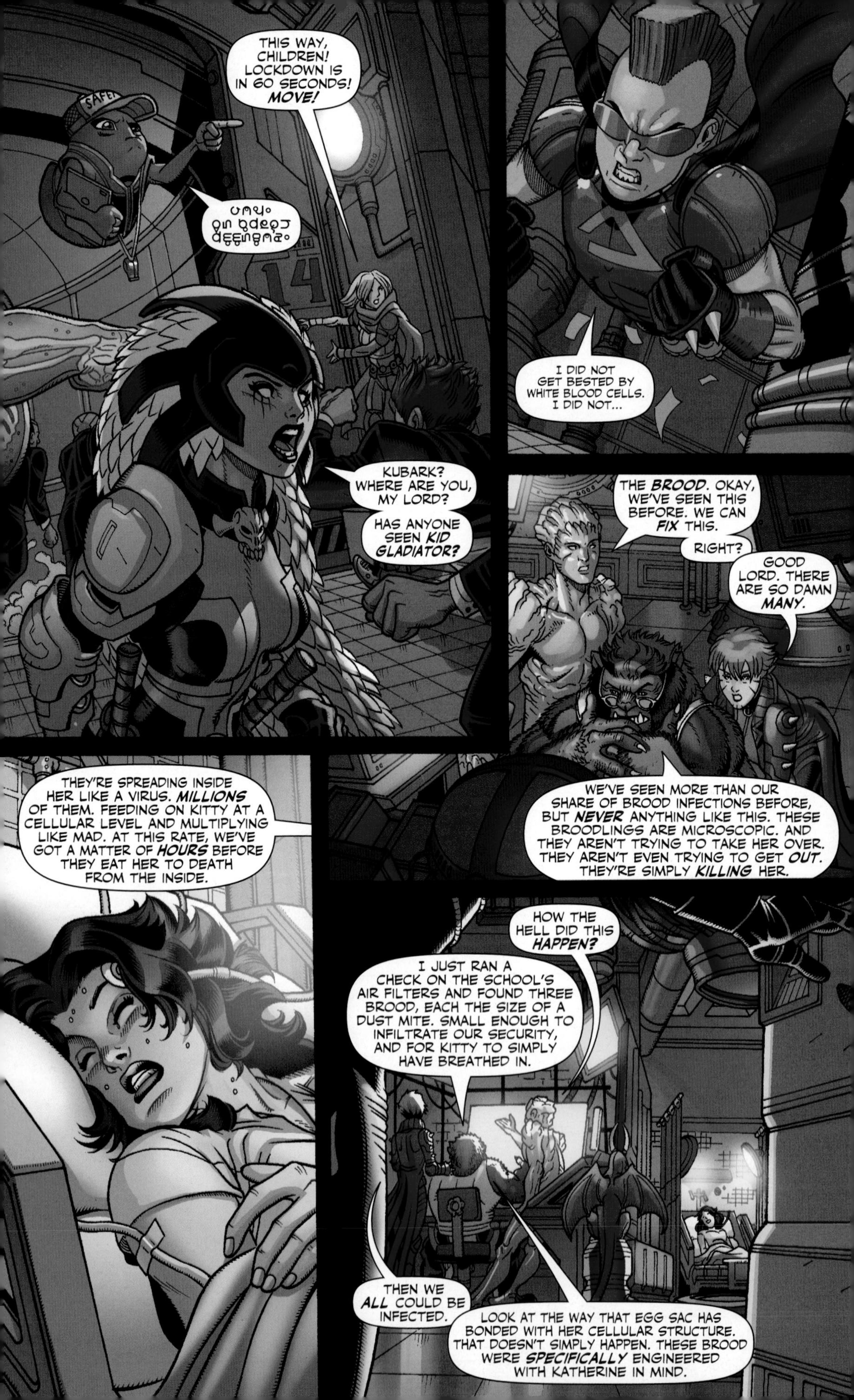
THIS WAY, CHILDREN! LOCKDOWN IS IN 60 SECONDS! MOVE!
KUBARK? WHERE ARE YOU, MY LORD?
HAS ANYONE SEEN KID GLADIATOR?
I DID NOT GET BESTED BY WHITE BLOOD CELLS. I DID NOT...
THE BROOD. OKAY, WE'VE SEEN THIS BEFORE. WE CAN FIX THIS.
RIGHT?
GOOD LORD. THERE ARE SO DAMN MANY.
THEY'RE SPREADING INSIDE HER LIKE A VIRUS. MILLIONS OF THEM. FEEDING ON KITTY AT A CELLULAR LEVEL AND MULTIPLYING LIKE MAD. AT THIS RATE, WE'VE GOT A MATTER OF HOURS BEFORE THEY EAT HER TO DEATH FROM THE INSIDE.
WE'VE SEEN MORE THAN OUR SHARE OF BROOD INFECTIONS BEFORE, BUT NEVER ANYTHING LIKE THIS. THESE BROODLINGS ARE MICROSCOPIC. AND THEY AREN'T TRYING TO TAKE HER OVER. THEY AREN'T EVEN TRYING TO GET OUT. THEY'RE SIMPLY KILLING HER.
HOW THE HELL DID THIS HAPPEN?
I JUST RAN A CHECK ON THE SCHOOL'S AIR FILTERS AND FOUND THREE BROOD, EACH THE SIZE OF A DUST MITE. SMALL ENOUGH TO INFILTRATE OUR SECURITY, AND FOR KITTY TO SIMPLY HAVE BREATHED IN.
THEN WE ALL COULD BE INFECTED.
LOOK AT THE WAY THAT EGG SAC HAS BONDED WITH HER CELLULAR STRUCTURE. THAT DOESN'T SIMPLY HAPPEN. THESE BROOD WERE SPECIFICALLY ENGINEERED WITH KATHERINE IN MIND.

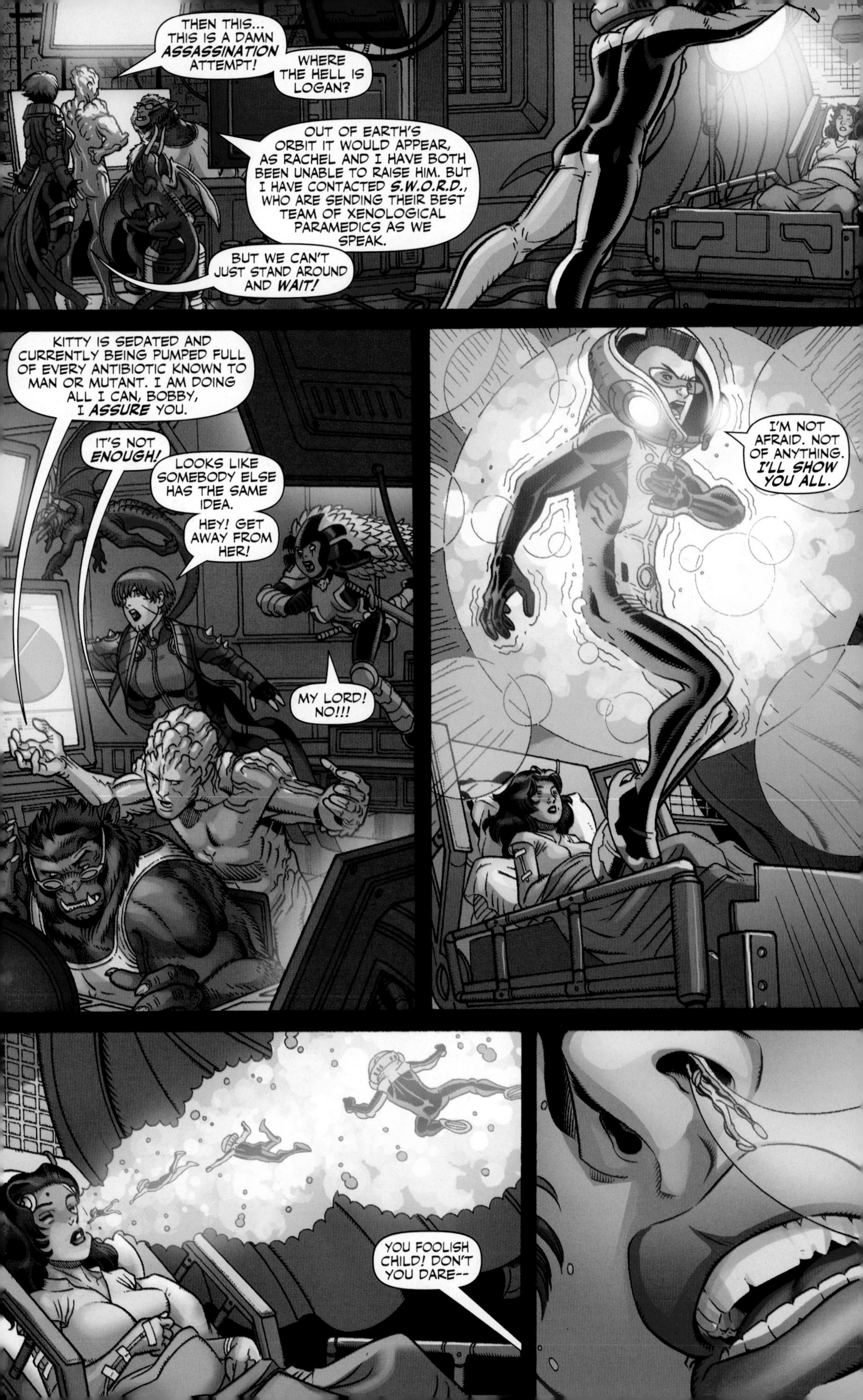

THEN THIS... THIS IS A DAMN ASSASSINATION ATTEMPT!
WHERE THE HELL IS LOGAN?
OUT OF EARTH'S ORBIT IT WOULD APPEAR, AS RACHEL AND I HAVE BOTH BEEN UNABLE TO RAISE HIM. BUT I HAVE CONTACTED S.W.O.R.D., WHO ARE SENDING THEIR BEST TEAM OF XENOLOGICAL PARAMEDICS AS WE SPEAK.
BUT WE CAN'T JUST STAND AROUND AND WAIT!
KITTY IS SEDATED AND CURRENTLY BEING PUMPED FULL OF EVERY ANTIBIOTIC KNOWN TO MAN OR MUTANT. I AM DOING ALL I CAN, BOBBY, I ASSURE YOU.
IT'S NOT ENOUGH!
LOOKS LIKE SOMEBODY ELSE HAS THE SAME IDEA.
HEY! GET AWAY FROM HER!
MY LORD! NO!!!
I'M NOT AFRAID. NOT OF ANYTHING. I'LL SHOW YOU ALL.
YOU FOOLISH CHILD! DON'T YOU DARE--

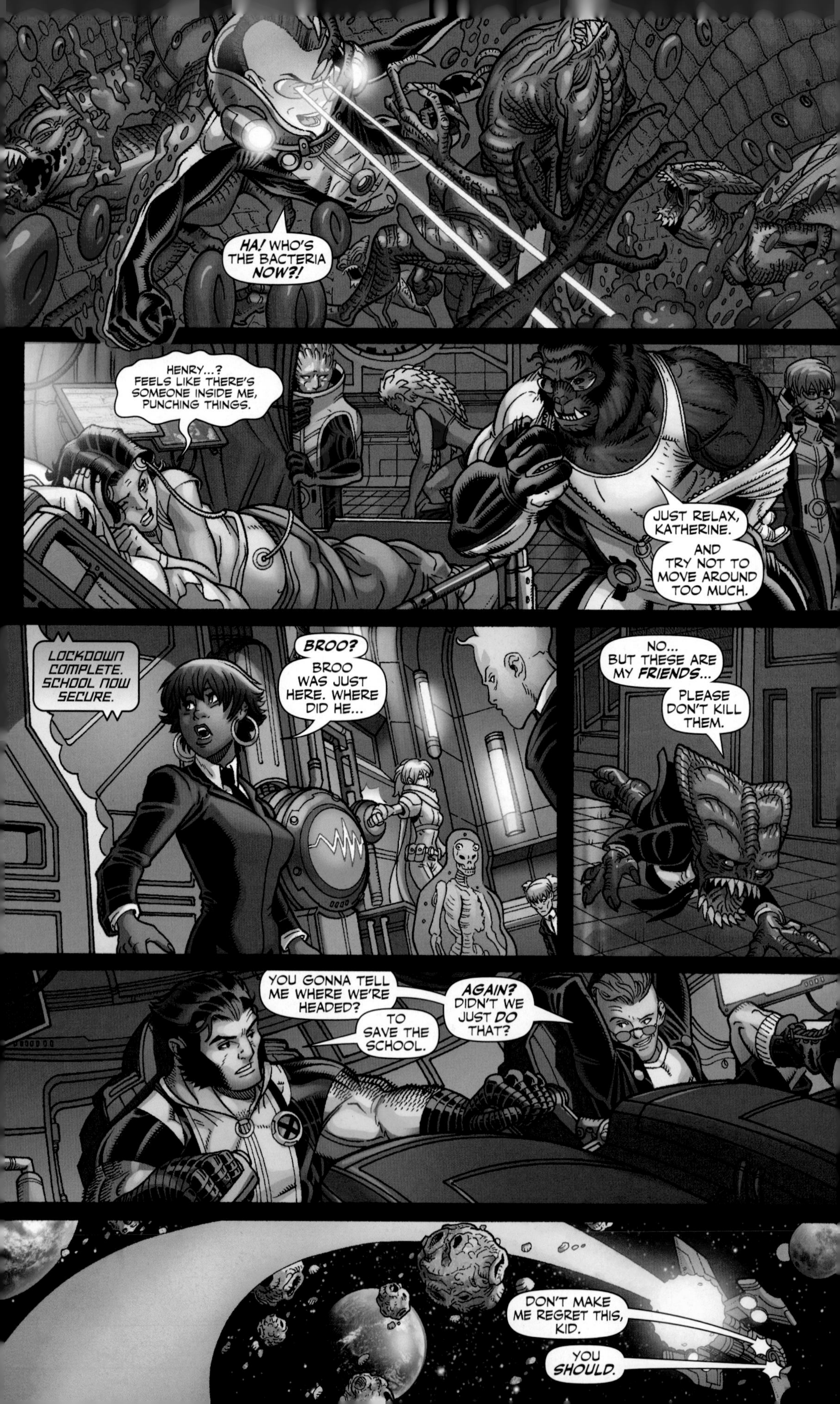
HA! WHO'S THE BACTERIA NOW?!
HENRY...? FEELS LIKE THERE'S SOMEONE INSIDE ME, PUNCHING THINGS.
JUST RELAX, KATHERINE.
AND TRY NOT TO MOVE AROUND TOO MUCH.
LOCKDOWN COMPLETE. SCHOOL NOW SECURE.
BROO?
BROO WAS JUST HERE. WHERE DID HE...
NO... BUT THESE ARE MY FRIENDS...
PLEASE DON'T KILL THEM.
YOU GONNA TELL ME WHERE WE'RE HEADED?
TO SAVE THE SCHOOL.
AGAIN? DIDN'T WE JUST DO THAT?
DON'T MAKE ME REGRET THIS, KID.
YOU SHOULD.

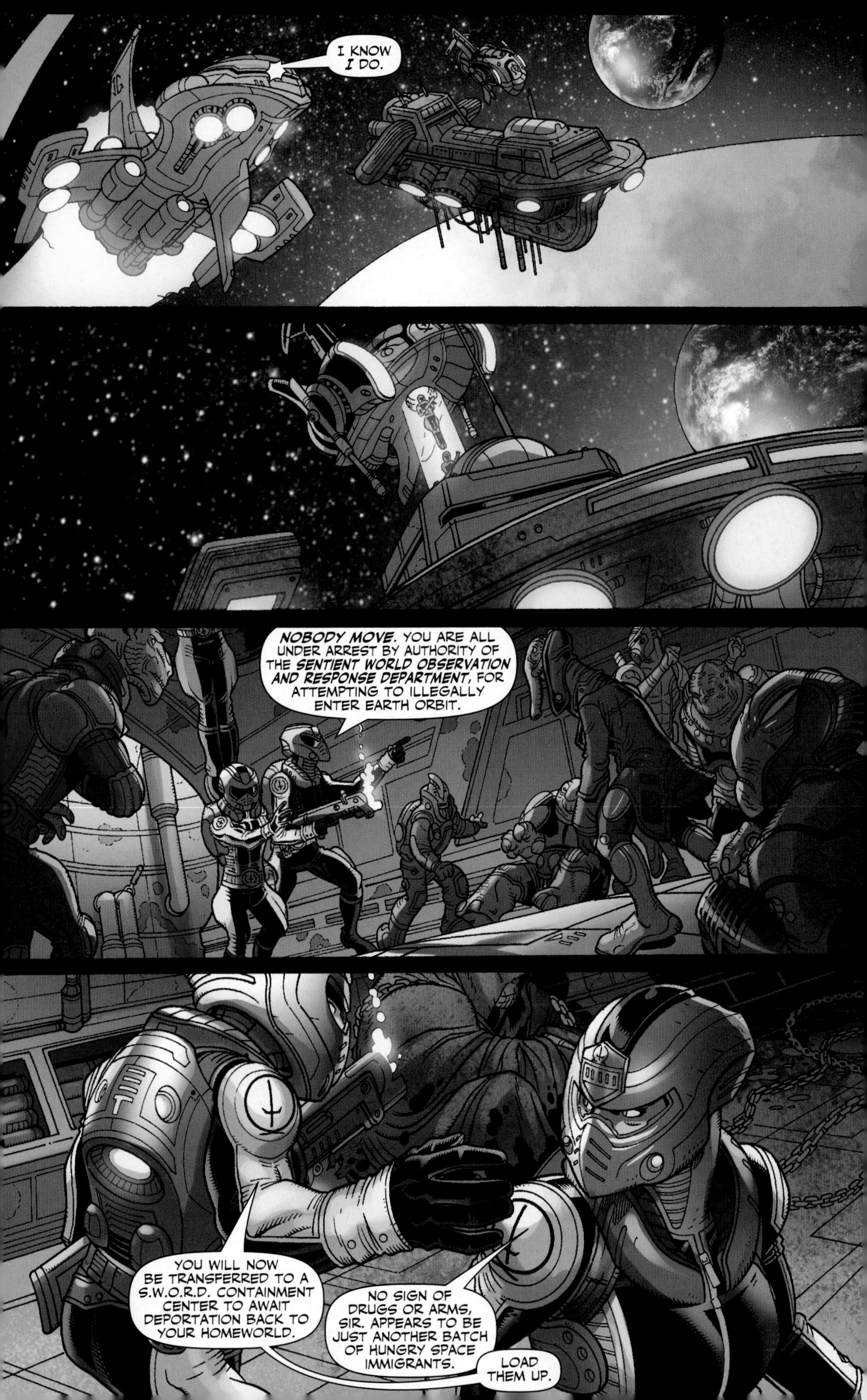
I KNOW I DO.
NOBODY MOVE. YOU ARE ALL UNDER ARREST BY AUTHORITY OF THE SENTIENT WORLD OBSERVATION AND RESPONSE DEPARTMENT, FOR ATTEMPTING TO ILLEGALLY ENTER EARTH ORBIT.
YOU WILL NOW BE TRANSFERRED TO A S.W.O.R.D. CONTAINMENT CENTER TO AWAIT DEPORTATION BACK TO YOUR HOMEWORLD.
NO SIGN OF DRUGS OR ARMS, SIR. APPEARS TO BE JUST ANOTHER BATCH OF HUNGRY SPACE IMMIGRANTS.
LOAD THEM UP.

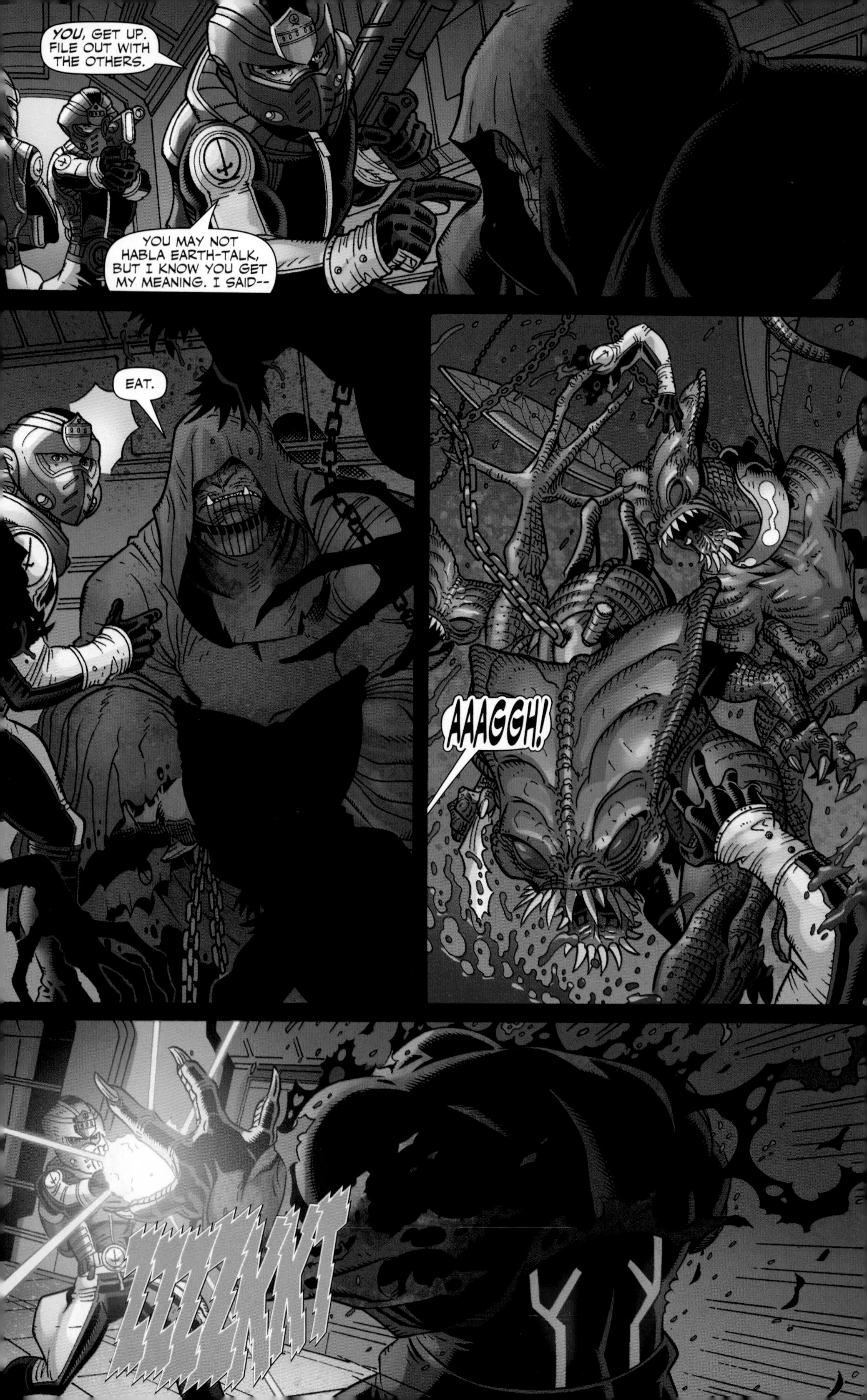
YOU, GET UP. FILE OUT WITH THE OTHERS.
YOU MAY NOT HABLA EARTH-TALK, BUT I KNOW YOU GET MY MEANING. I SAID--
EAT.
AAAGGH!
ZZZZKKT

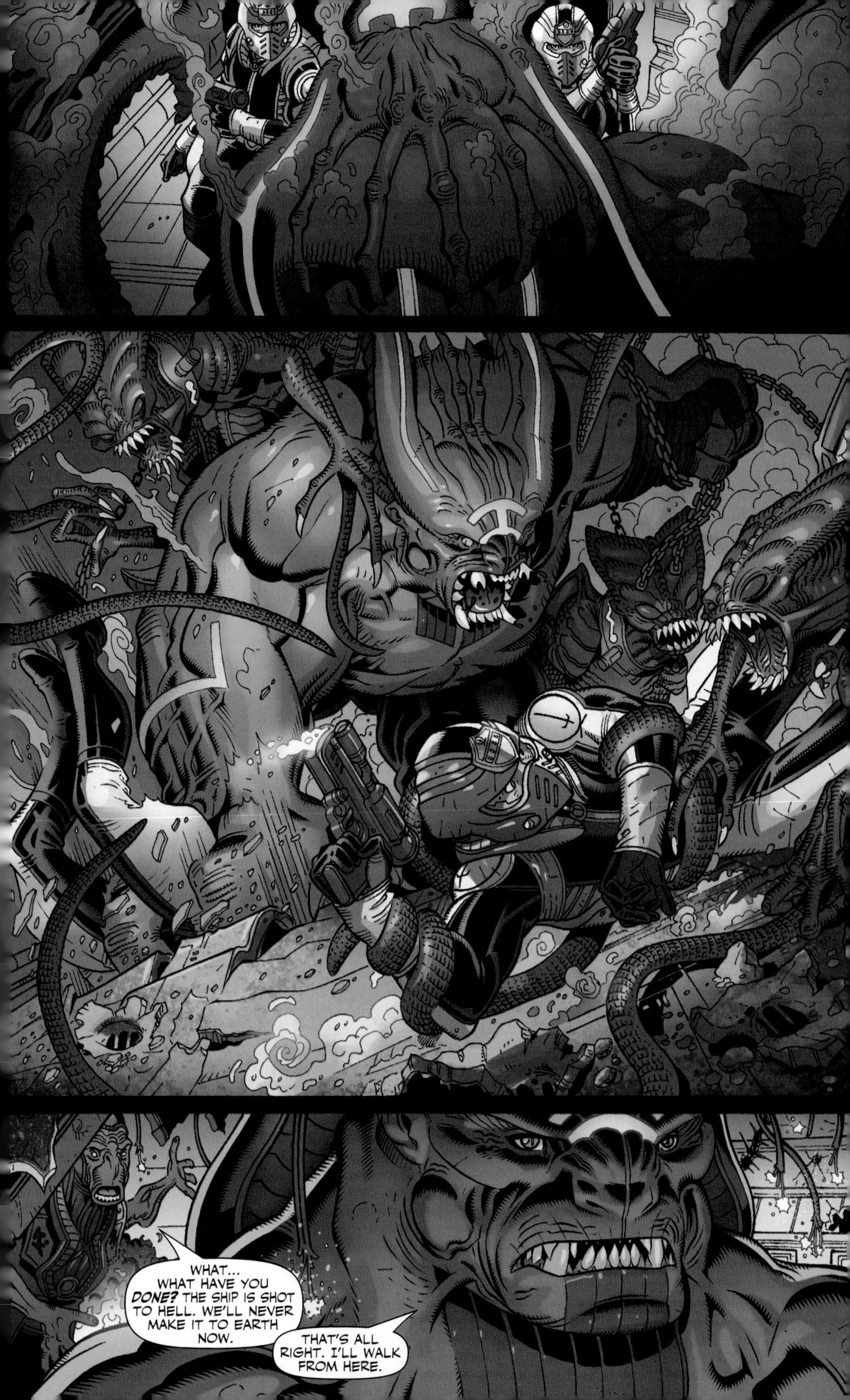
WHAT... WHAT HAVE YOU *DONE?* THE SHIP IS SHOT TO HELL. WE'LL NEVER MAKE IT TO EARTH NOW.
THAT'S ALL RIGHT. I'LL WALK FROM HERE.

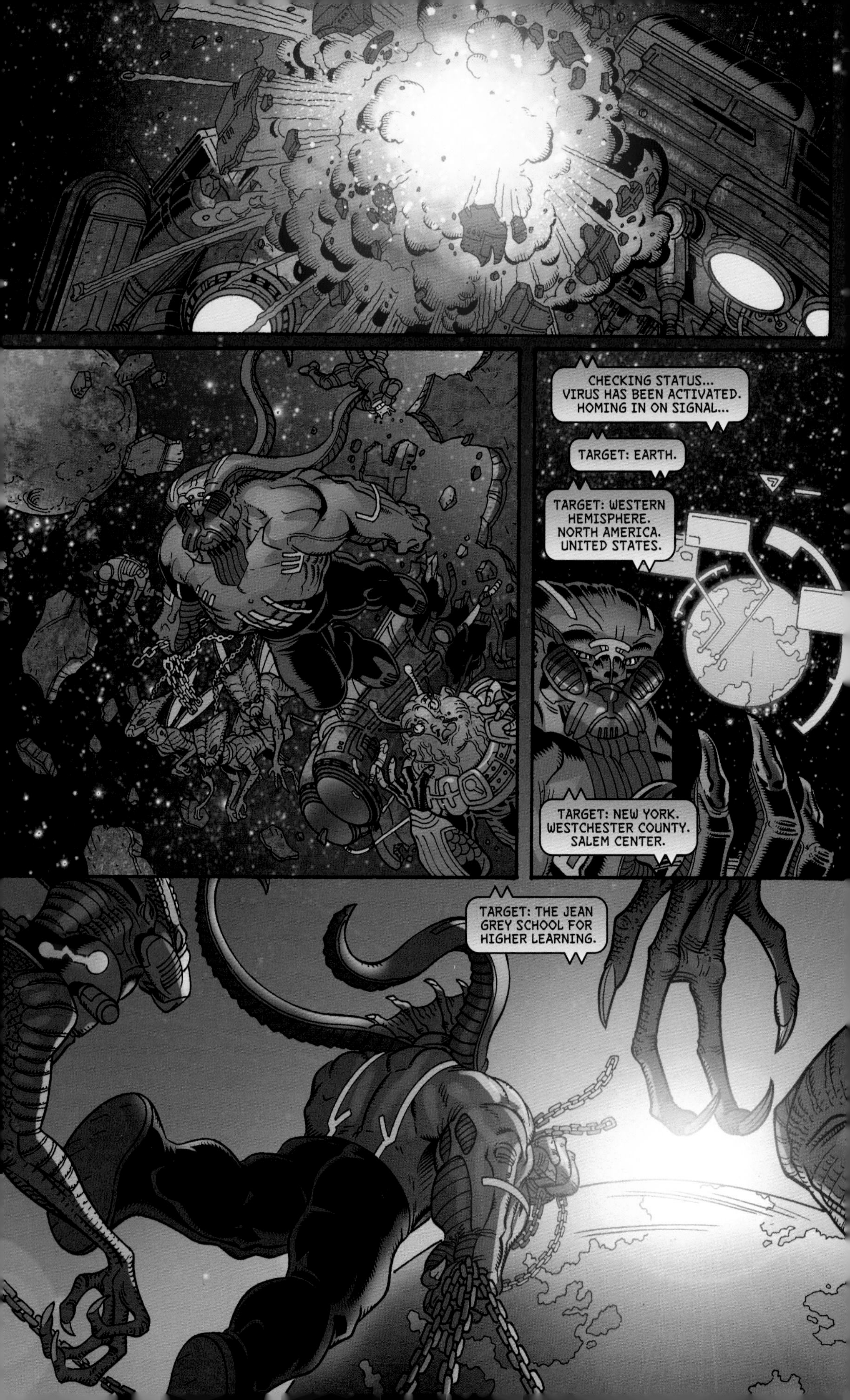
CHECKING STATUS...
VIRUS HAS BEEN ACTIVATED.
HOMING IN ON SIGNAL...
TARGET: EARTH.
TARGET: WESTERN HEMISPHERE. NORTH AMERICA. UNITED STATES.
TARGET: NEW YORK. WESTCHESTER COUNTY. SALEM CENTER.
TARGET: THE JEAN GREY SCHOOL FOR HIGHER LEARNING.

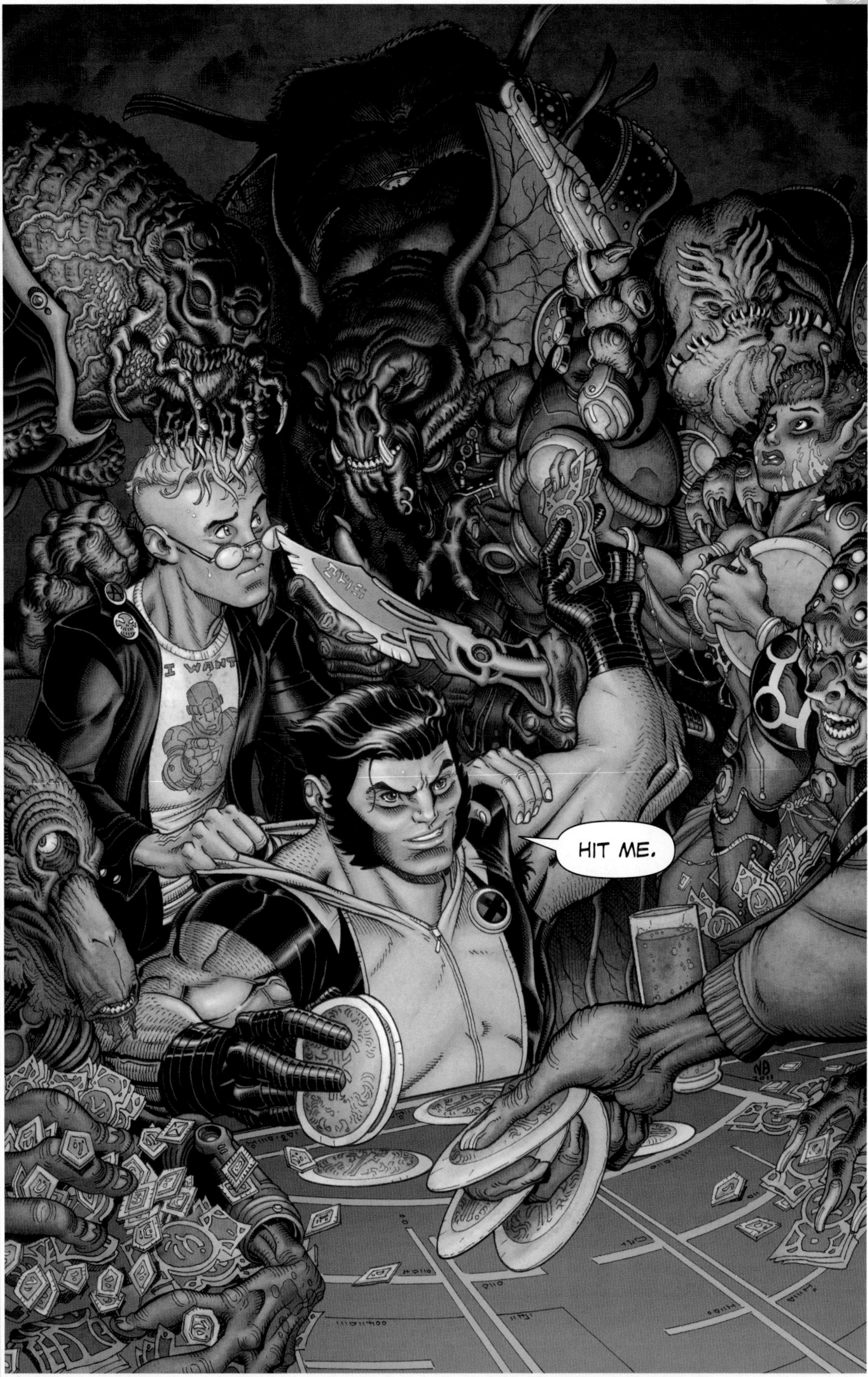
HIT ME.

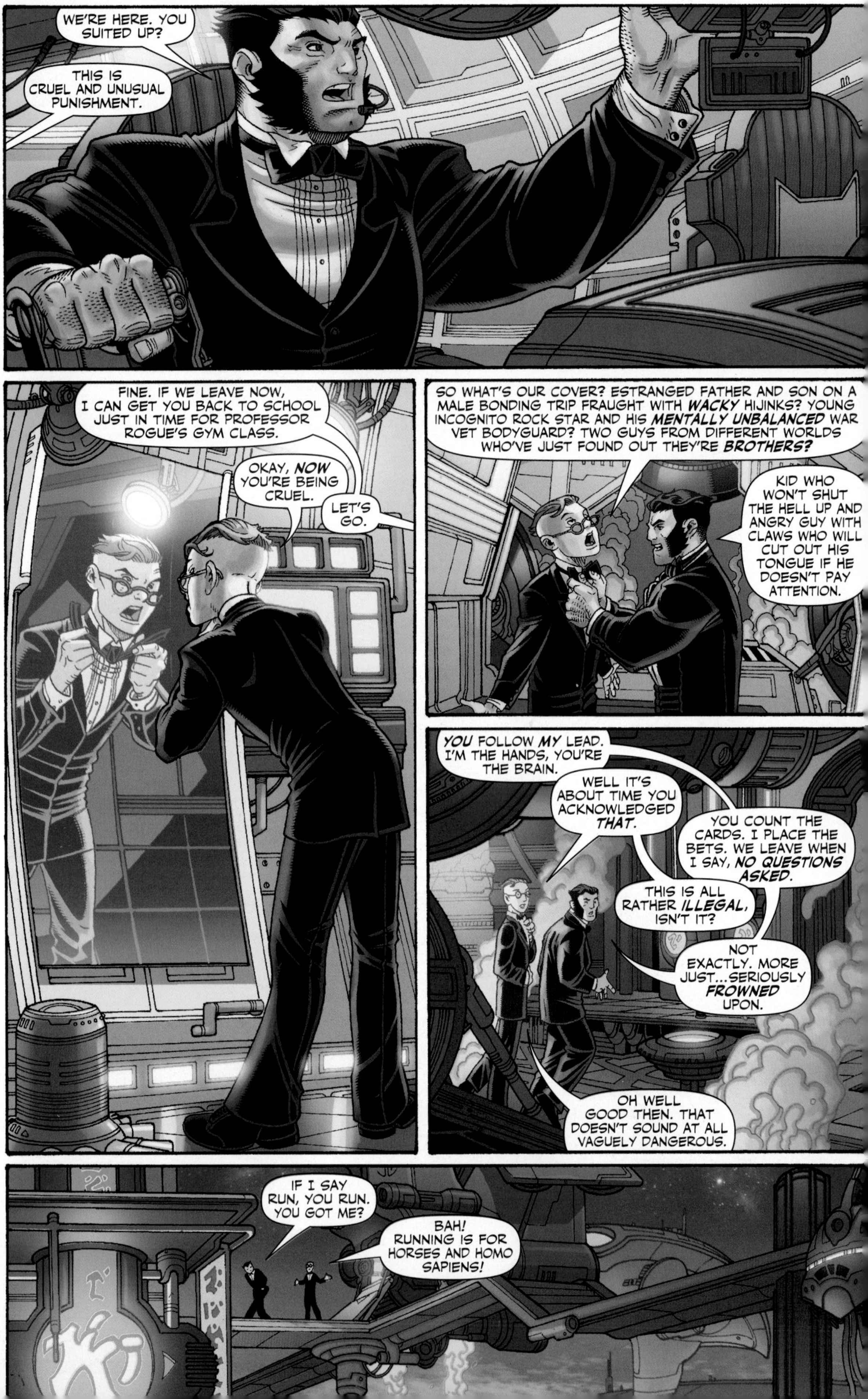
WE'RE HERE. YOU SUITED UP?
THIS IS CRUEL AND UNUSUAL PUNISHMENT.
FINE. IF WE LEAVE NOW, I CAN GET YOU BACK TO SCHOOL JUST IN TIME FOR PROFESSOR ROGUE'S GYM CLASS.
OKAY, NOW YOU'RE BEING CRUEL.
LET'S GO.
SO WHAT'S OUR COVER? ESTRANGED FATHER AND SON ON A MALE BONDING TRIP FRAUGHT WITH WACKY HIJINKS? YOUNG INCOGNITO ROCK STAR AND HIS MENTALLY UNBALANCED WAR VET BODYGUARD? TWO GUYS FROM DIFFERENT WORLDS WHO'VE JUST FOUND OUT THEY'RE BROTHERS?
KID WHO WON'T SHUT THE HELL UP AND ANGRY GUY WITH CLAWS WHO WILL CUT OUT HIS TONGUE IF HE DOESN'T PAY ATTENTION.
YOU FOLLOW MY LEAD. I'M THE HANDS, YOU'RE THE BRAIN.
WELL IT'S ABOUT TIME YOU ACKNOWLEDGED THAT.
YOU COUNT THE CARDS. I PLACE THE BETS. WE LEAVE WHEN I SAY, NO QUESTIONS ASKED.
THIS IS ALL RATHER ILLEGAL, ISN'T IT?
NOT EXACTLY. MORE JUST...SERIOUSLY FROWNED UPON.
OH WELL GOOD THEN. THAT DOESN'T SOUND AT ALL VAGUELY DANGEROUS.
IF I SAY RUN, YOU RUN. YOU GOT ME?
BAH! RUNNING IS FOR HORSES AND HOMO SAPIENS!

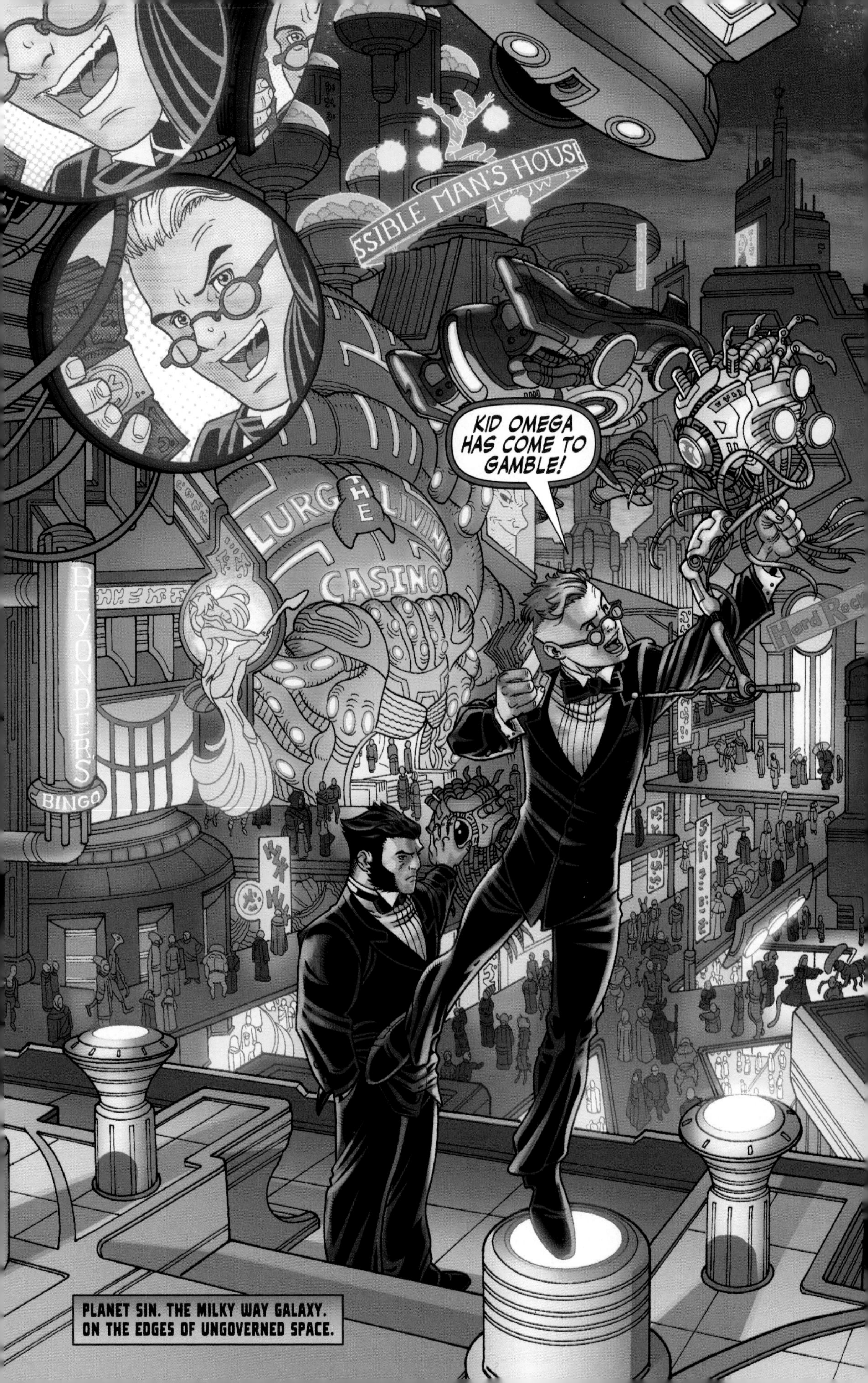

SSIBLE MAN'S HOUSE
LURG THE LIVING CASINO
BEYONDER'S BINGO
Hard Rock
KID OMEGA HAS COME TO GAMBLE!
PLANET SIN. THE MILKY WAY GALAXY. ON THE EDGES OF UNGOVERNED SPACE.

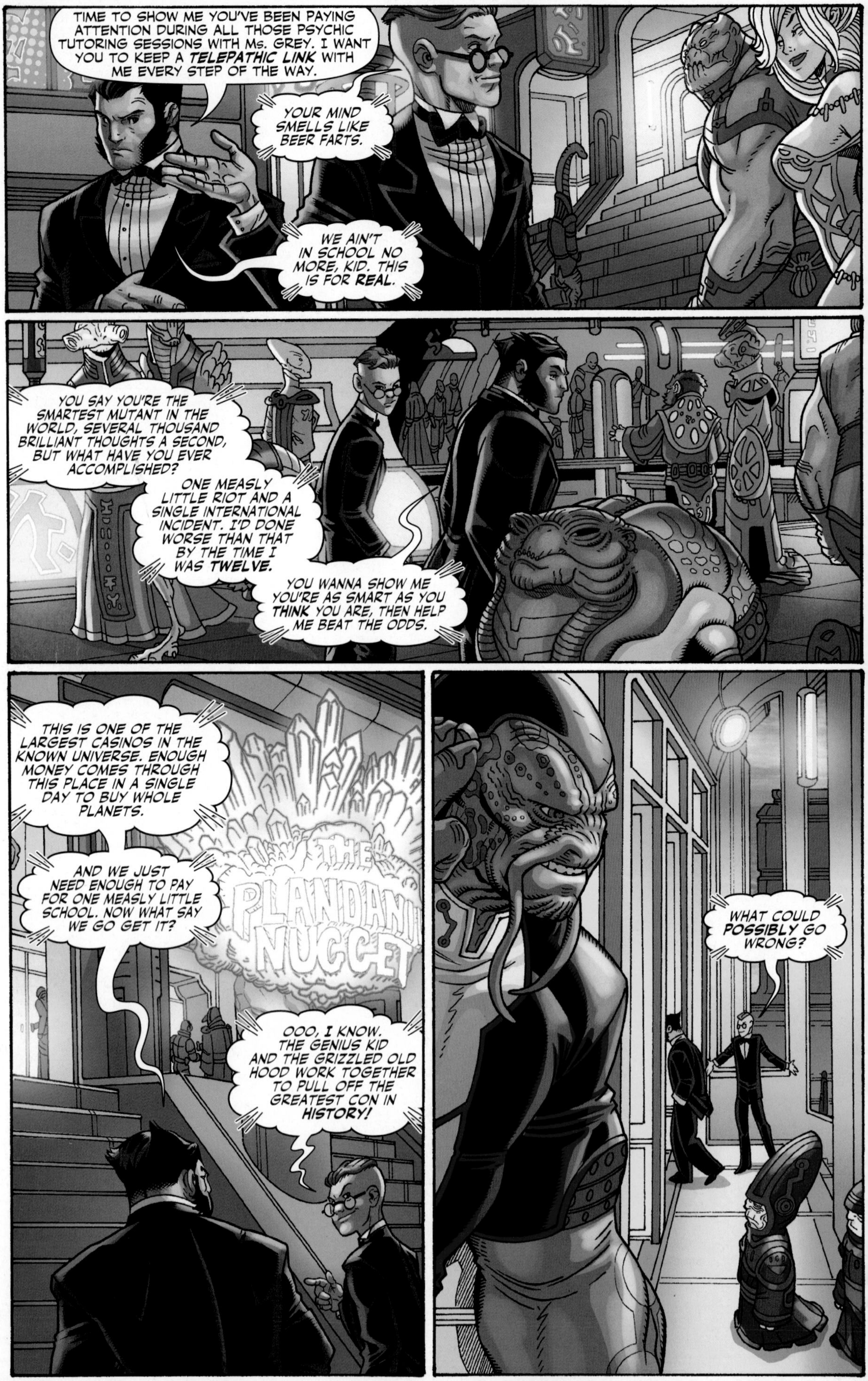

TIME TO SHOW ME YOU'VE BEEN PAYING ATTENTION DURING ALL THOSE PSYCHIC TUTORING SESSIONS WITH Ms. GREY. I WANT YOU TO KEEP A TELEPATHIC LINK WITH ME EVERY STEP OF THE WAY.
YOUR MIND SMELLS LIKE BEER FARTS.
WE AIN'T IN SCHOOL NO MORE, KID. THIS IS FOR REAL.
YOU SAY YOU'RE THE SMARTEST MUTANT IN THE WORLD, SEVERAL THOUSAND BRILLIANT THOUGHTS A SECOND, BUT WHAT HAVE YOU EVER ACCOMPLISHED?
ONE MEASLY LITTLE RIOT AND A SINGLE INTERNATIONAL INCIDENT. I'D DONE WORSE THAN THAT BY THE TIME I WAS TWELVE.
YOU WANNA SHOW ME YOU'RE AS SMART AS YOU THINK YOU ARE, THEN HELP ME BEAT THE ODDS.
THIS IS ONE OF THE LARGEST CASINOS IN THE KNOWN UNIVERSE. ENOUGH MONEY COMES THROUGH THIS PLACE IN A SINGLE DAY TO BUY WHOLE PLANETS.
AND WE JUST NEED ENOUGH TO PAY FOR ONE MEASLY LITTLE SCHOOL. NOW WHAT SAY WE GO GET IT?
OOO, I KNOW. THE GENIUS KID AND THE GRIZZLED OLD HOOD WORK TOGETHER TO PULL OFF THE GREATEST CON IN HISTORY!
WHAT COULD POSSIBLY GO WRONG?

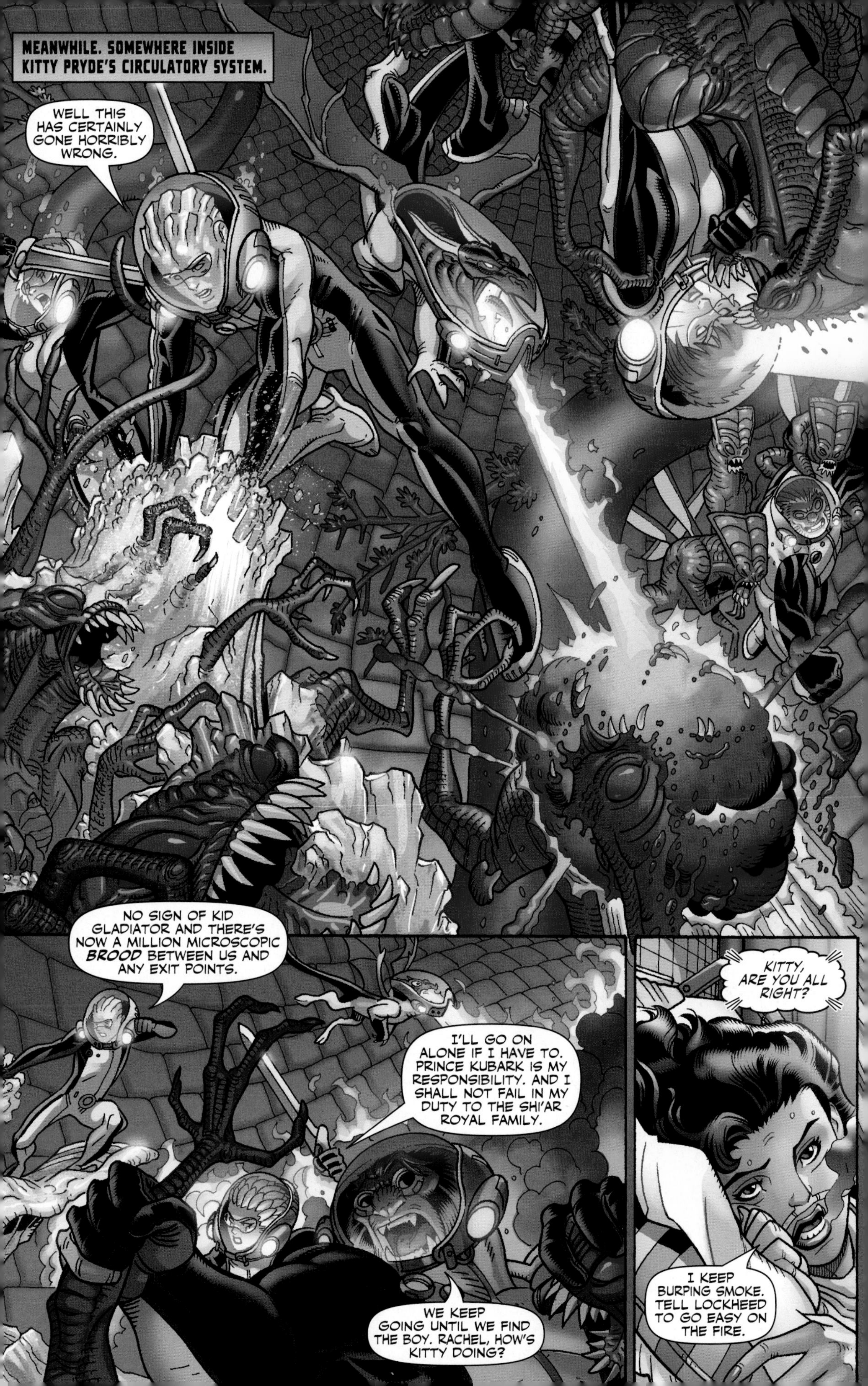
MEANWHILE. SOMEWHERE INSIDE KITTY PRYDE'S CIRCULATORY SYSTEM.
WELL THIS HAS CERTAINLY GONE HORRIBLY WRONG.
NO SIGN OF KID GLADIATOR AND THERE'S NOW A MILLION MICROSCOPIC *BROOD* BETWEEN US AND ANY EXIT POINTS.
I'LL GO ON ALONE IF I HAVE TO. PRINCE KUBARK IS MY RESPONSIBILITY. AND I SHALL NOT FAIL IN MY DUTY TO THE SHI'AR ROYAL FAMILY.
WE KEEP GOING UNTIL WE FIND THE BOY. RACHEL, HOW'S KITTY DOING?
KITTY, ARE YOU ALL RIGHT?
I KEEP BURPING SMOKE. TELL LOCKHEED TO GO EASY ON THE FIRE.

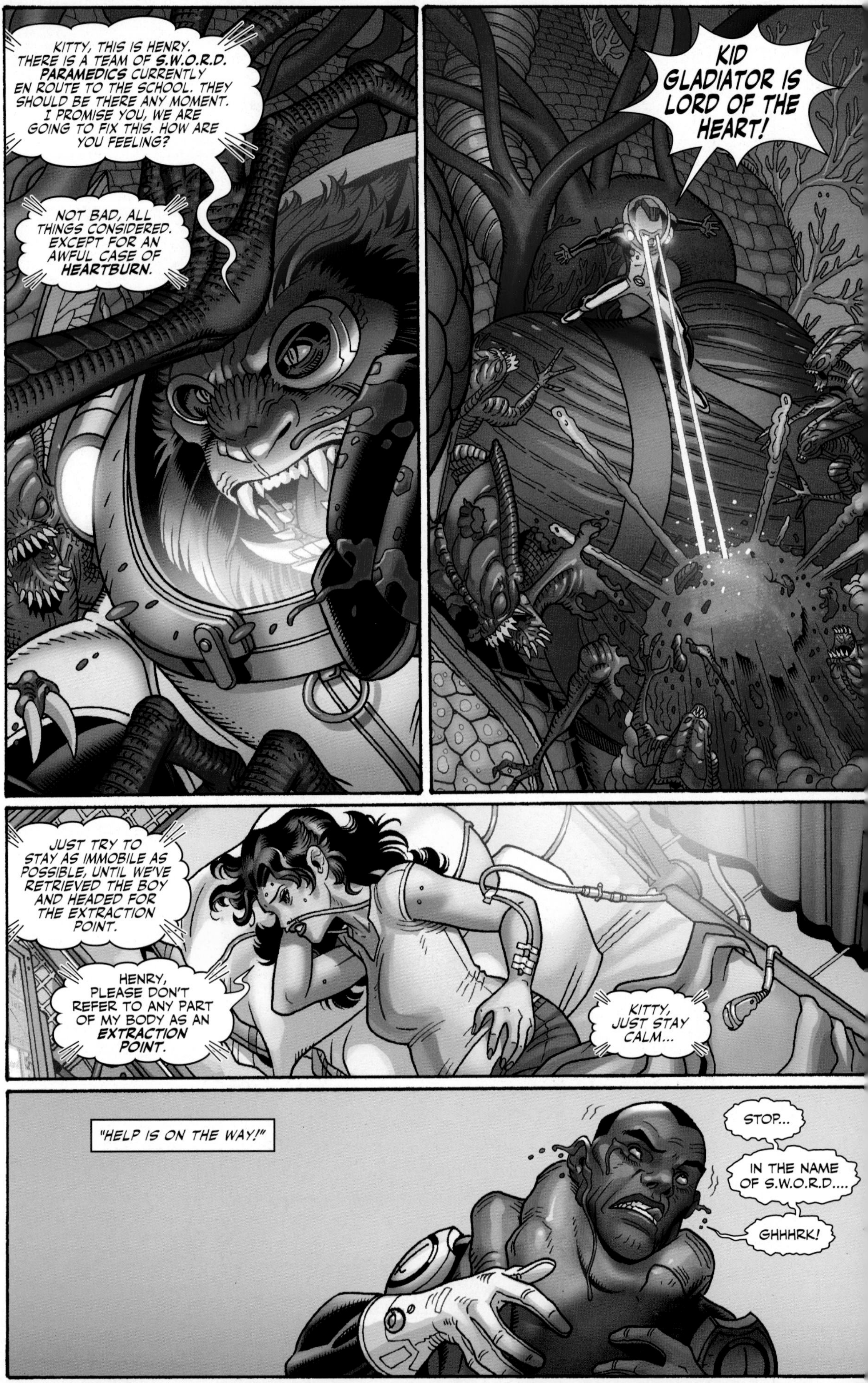
KITTY, THIS IS HENRY. THERE IS A TEAM OF S.W.O.R.D. PARAMEDICS CURRENTLY EN ROUTE TO THE SCHOOL. THEY SHOULD BE THERE ANY MOMENT. I PROMISE YOU, WE ARE GOING TO FIX THIS. HOW ARE YOU FEELING?
NOT BAD, ALL THINGS CONSIDERED. EXCEPT FOR AN AWFUL CASE OF HEARTBURN.
KID GLADIATOR IS LORD OF THE HEART!
JUST TRY TO STAY AS IMMOBILE AS POSSIBLE, UNTIL WE'VE RETRIEVED THE BOY AND HEADED FOR THE EXTRACTION POINT.
HENRY, PLEASE DON'T REFER TO ANY PART OF MY BODY AS AN EXTRACTION POINT.
KITTY, JUST STAY CALM...
"HELP IS ON THE WAY!"
STOP...
IN THE NAME OF S.W.O.R.D....
GHHHRK!

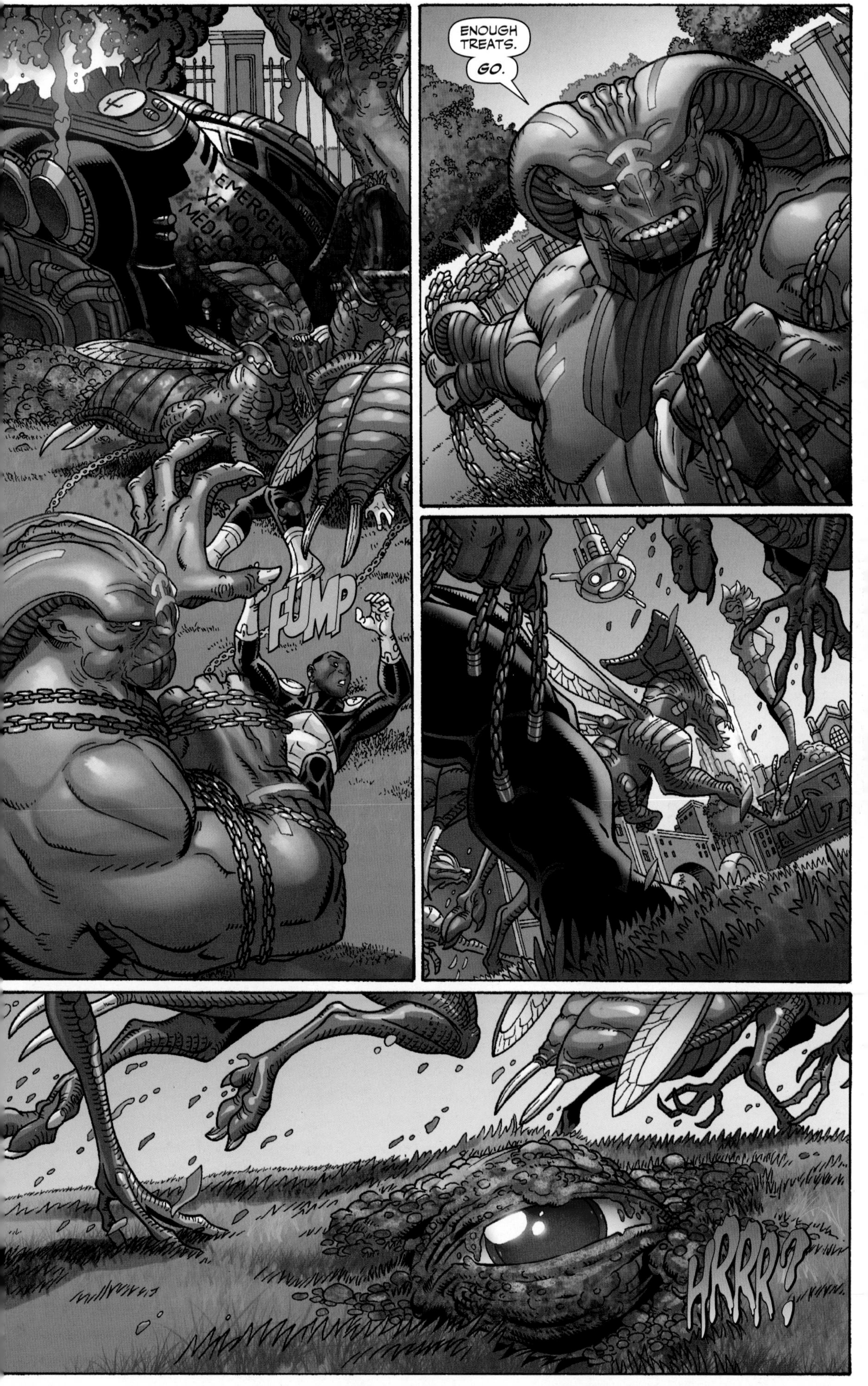
EMERGENCY
XENOLOG
MEDIC
ENOUGH TREATS. GO.
FUMP
HRRR?

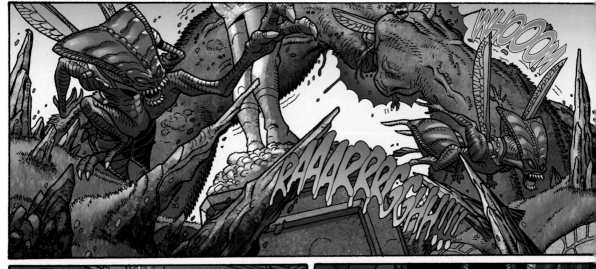

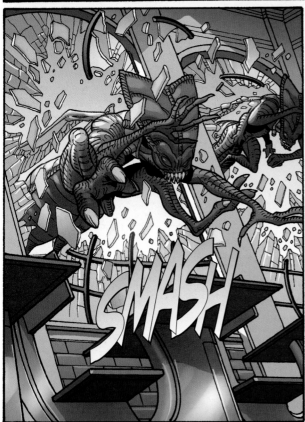

WHOOOM
RAAARRGGAH!!!
SMASH
WARNING: YOU HAVE ILLEGALLY ENTERED THE PREMISES. DANGER ROOM DEFENSES NOW ACTIVATED.
FOOOSH
AAIEEEEEEE!
REPORT.
DEFENSES ANALYZED. TRANSMITTING.

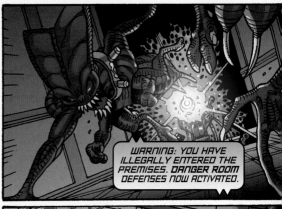

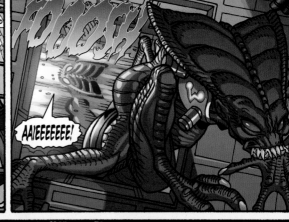

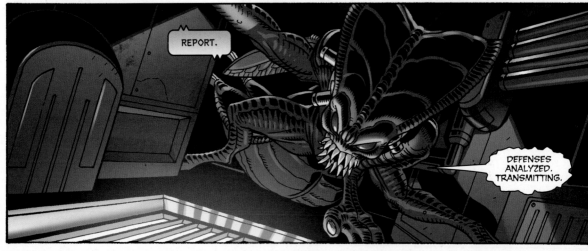

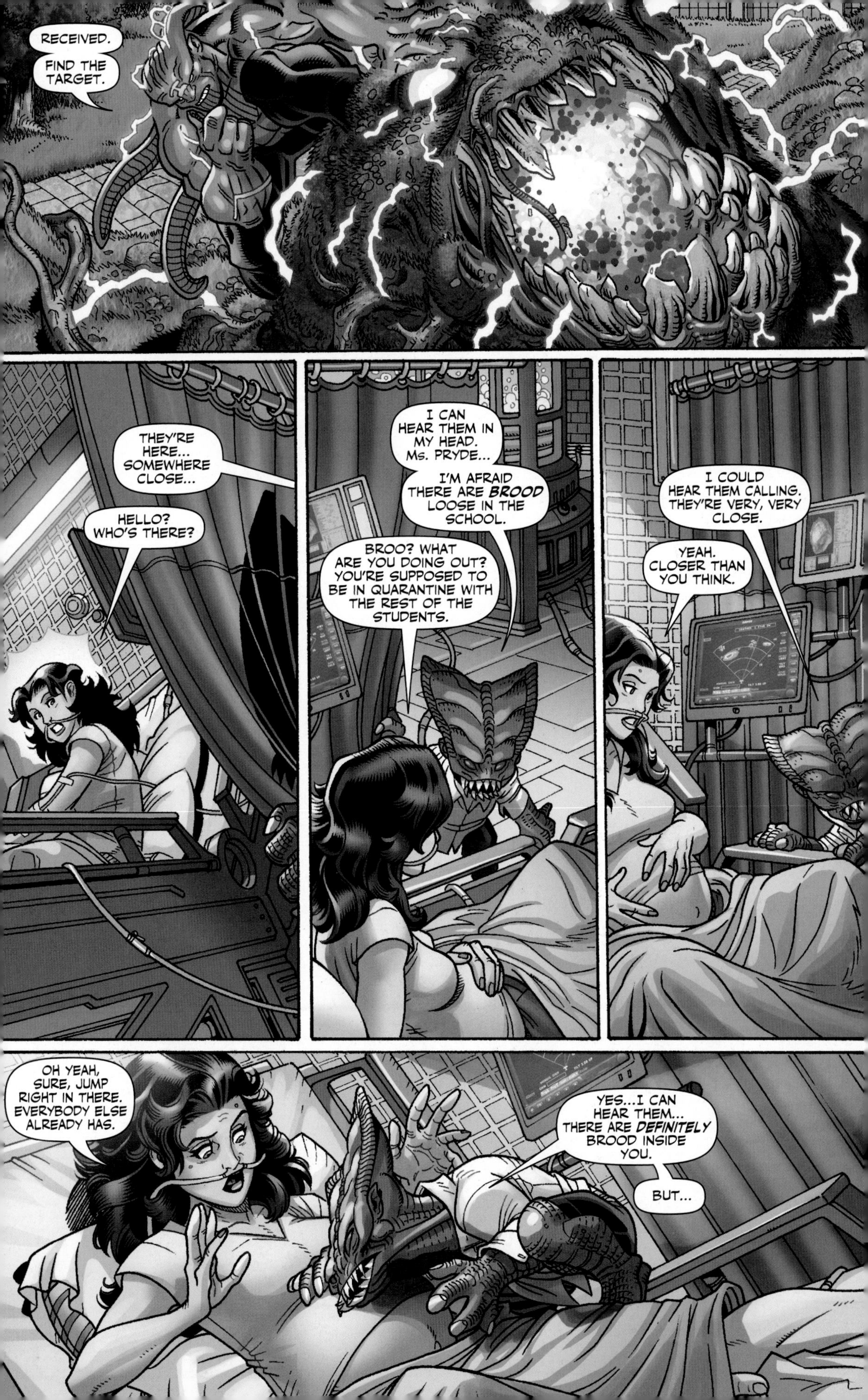
RECEIVED. FIND THE TARGET.
THEY'RE HERE... SOMEWHERE CLOSE...
HELLO? WHO'S THERE?
I CAN HEAR THEM IN MY HEAD. Ms. PRYDE...
I'M AFRAID THERE ARE BROOD LOOSE IN THE SCHOOL.
BROO? WHAT ARE YOU DOING OUT? YOU'RE SUPPOSED TO BE IN QUARANTINE WITH THE REST OF THE STUDENTS.
I COULD HEAR THEM CALLING. THEY'RE VERY, VERY CLOSE.
YEAH. CLOSER THAN YOU THINK.
OH YEAH, SURE, JUMP RIGHT IN THERE. EVERYBODY ELSE ALREADY HAS.
YES...I CAN HEAR THEM... THERE ARE DEFINITELY BROOD INSIDE YOU.
BUT...

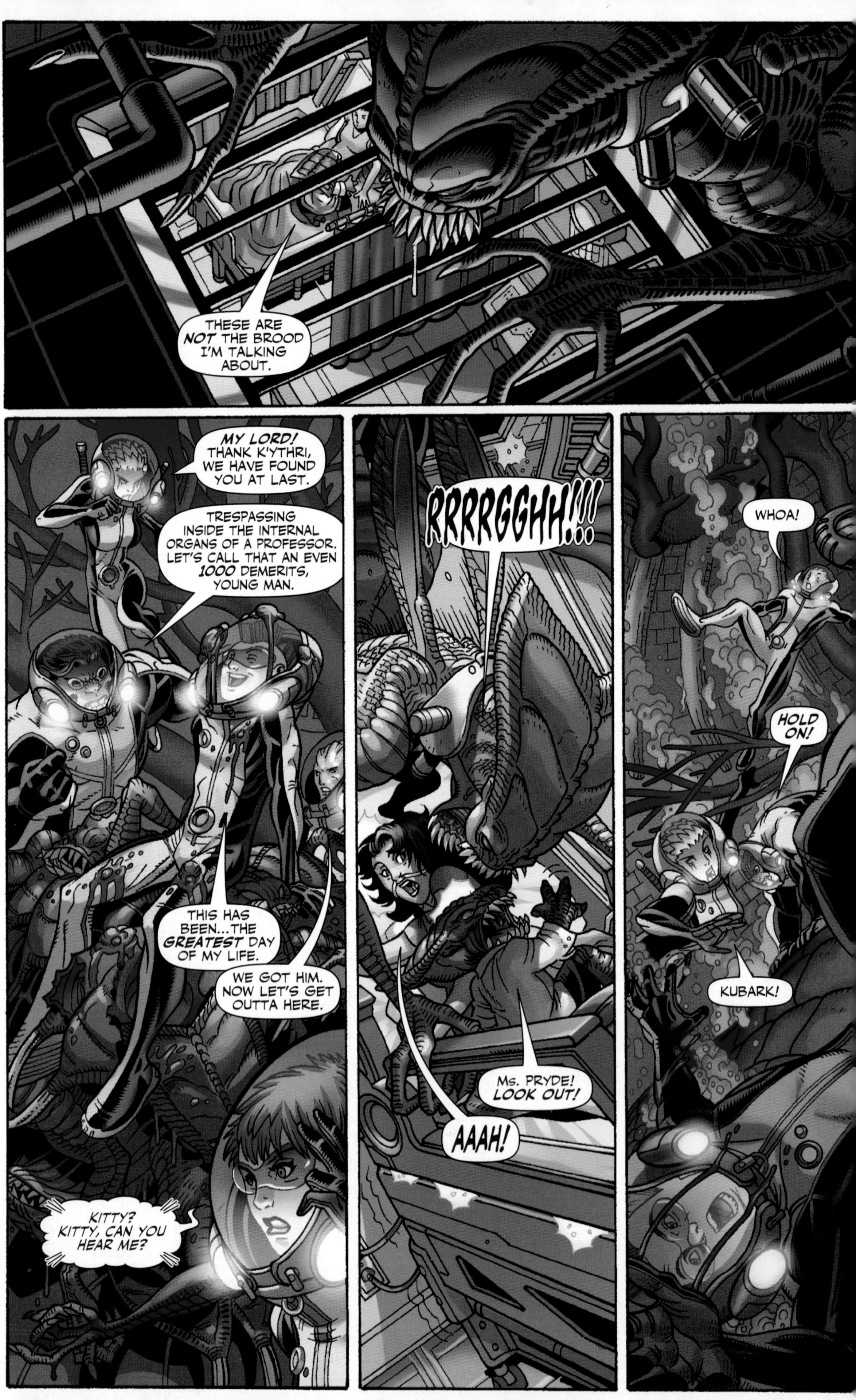

THESE ARE NOT THE BROOD I'M TALKING ABOUT.
MY LORD! THANK K'YTHRI, WE HAVE FOUND YOU AT LAST.
TRESPASSING INSIDE THE INTERNAL ORGANS OF A PROFESSOR. LET'S CALL THAT AN EVEN 1000 DEMERITS, YOUNG MAN.
THIS HAS BEEN...THE GREATEST DAY OF MY LIFE.
WE GOT HIM. NOW LET'S GET OUTTA HERE.
KITTY? KITTY, CAN YOU HEAR ME?
RRRRGGHH!!!
Ms. PRYDE! LOOK OUT!
AAAH!
WHOA!
HOLD ON!
KUBARK!

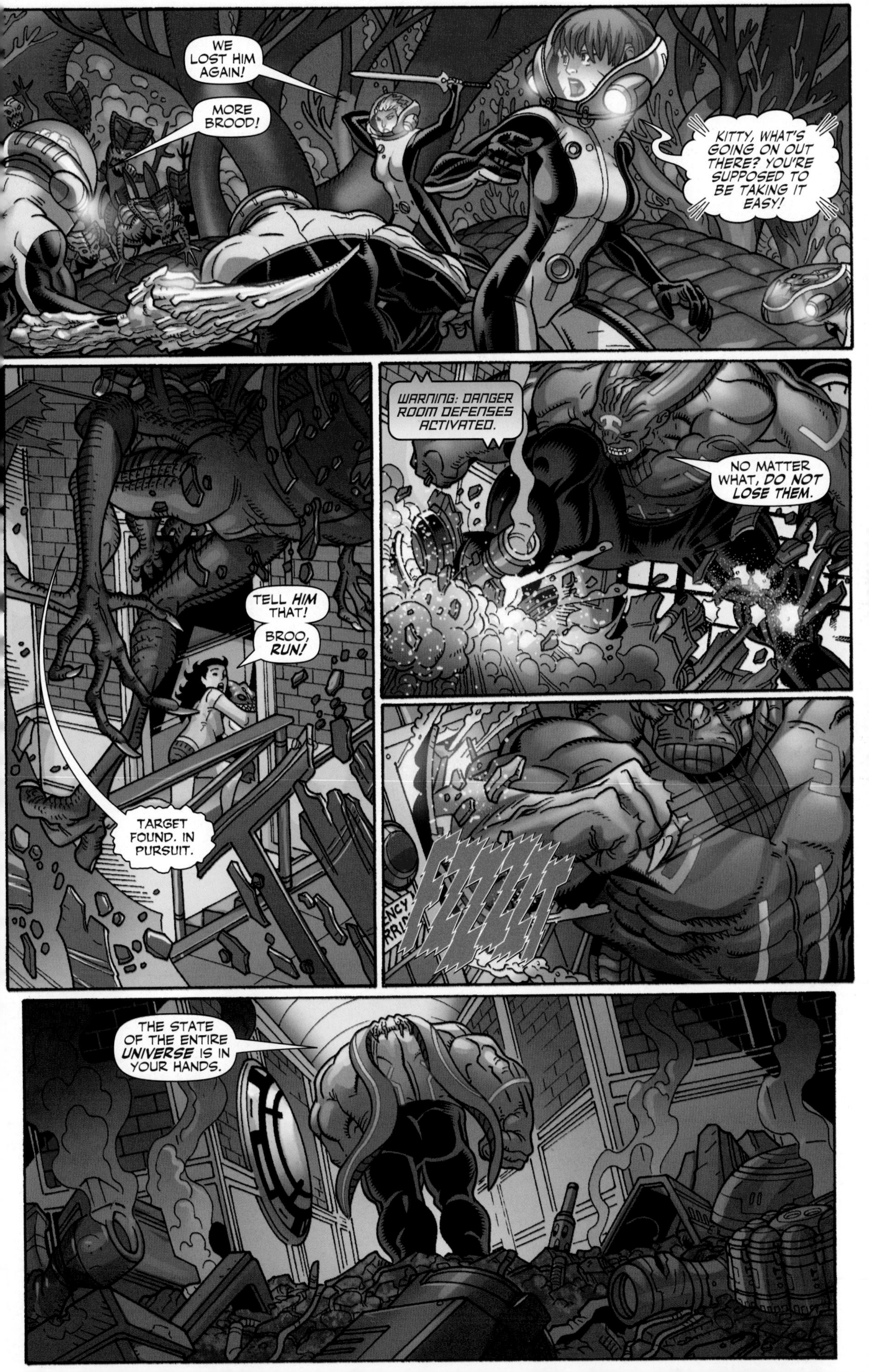
WE LOST HIM AGAIN!
MORE BROOD!
KITTY, WHAT'S GOING ON OUT THERE? YOU'RE SUPPOSED TO BE TAKING IT EASY!
TELL HIM THAT!
BROO, RUN!
TARGET FOUND. IN PURSUIT.
WARNING: DANGER ROOM DEFENSES ACTIVATED.
NO MATTER WHAT, DO NOT LOSE THEM.
FZZZZT
THE STATE OF THE ENTIRE UNIVERSE IS IN YOUR HANDS.

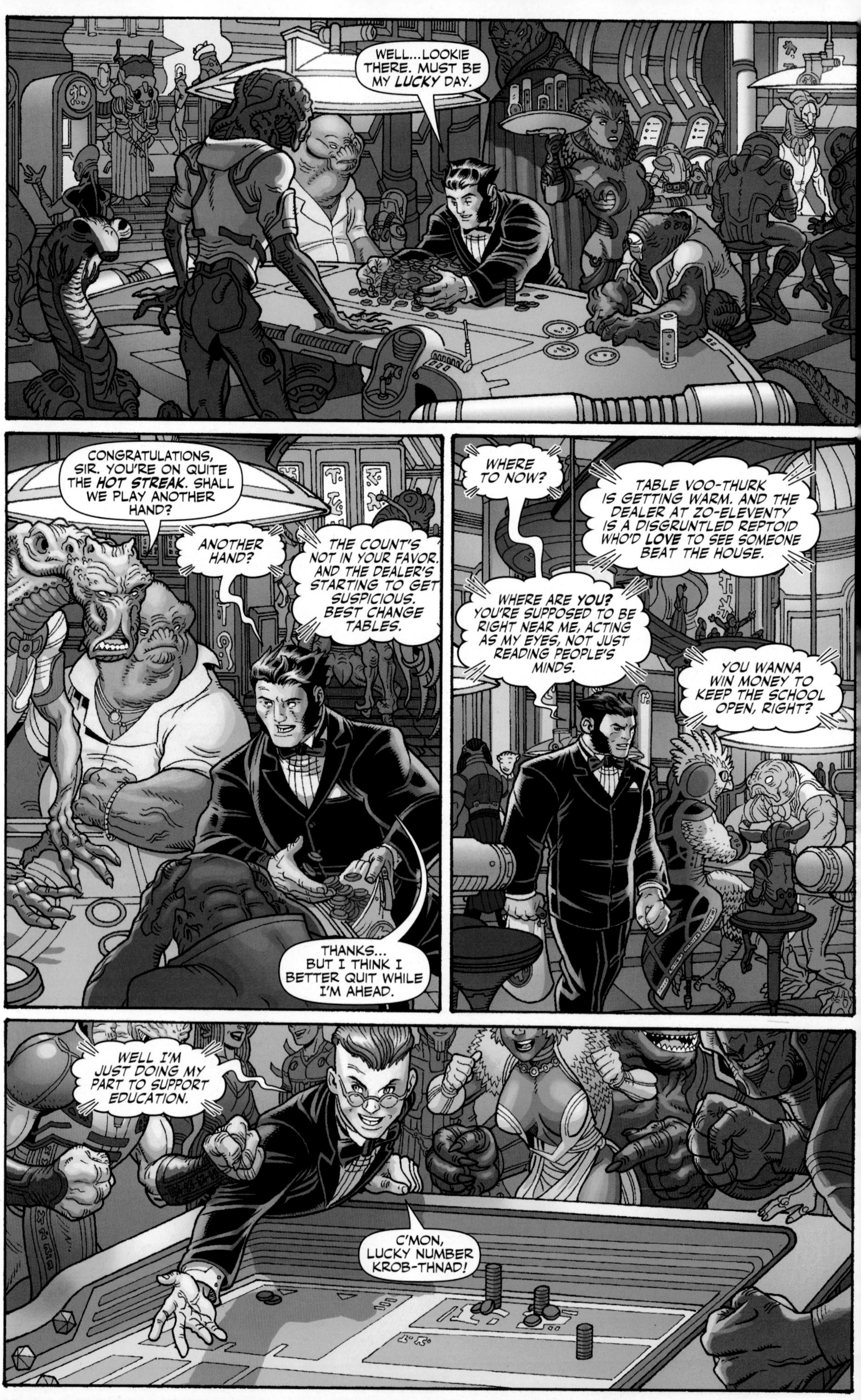
WELL...LOOKIE THERE. MUST BE MY LUCKY DAY.
CONGRATULATIONS, SIR. YOU'RE ON QUITE THE HOT STREAK. SHALL WE PLAY ANOTHER HAND?
ANOTHER HAND?
THE COUNT'S NOT IN YOUR FAVOR. AND THE DEALER'S STARTING TO GET SUSPICIOUS. BEST CHANGE TABLES.
THANKS... BUT I THINK I BETTER QUIT WHILE I'M AHEAD.
WHERE TO NOW?
TABLE VOO-THURK IS GETTING WARM. AND THE DEALER AT ZO-ELEVENTY IS A DISGRUNTLED REPTOID WHO'D LOVE TO SEE SOMEONE BEAT THE HOUSE.
WHERE ARE YOU? YOU'RE SUPPOSED TO BE RIGHT NEAR ME, ACTING AS MY EYES, NOT JUST READING PEOPLE'S MINDS.
YOU WANNA WIN MONEY TO KEEP THE SCHOOL OPEN, RIGHT?
WELL I'M JUST DOING MY PART TO SUPPORT EDUCATION.
C'MON, LUCKY NUMBER KROB-THNAD!

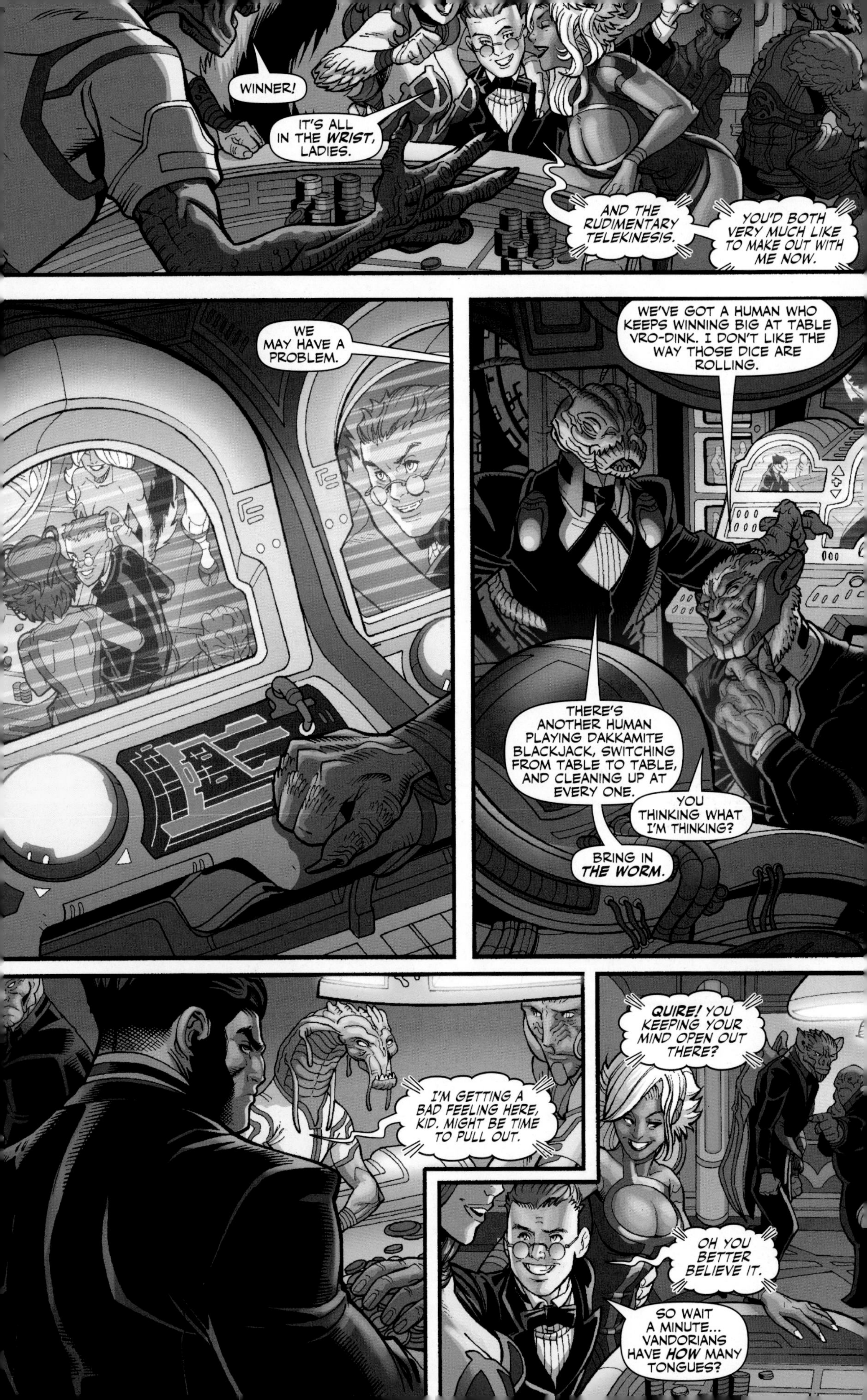
WINNER!
IT'S ALL IN THE WRIST, LADIES.
AND THE RUDIMENTARY TELEKINESIS.
YOU'D BOTH VERY MUCH LIKE TO MAKE OUT WITH ME NOW.
WE MAY HAVE A PROBLEM.
WE'VE GOT A HUMAN WHO KEEPS WINNING BIG AT TABLE VRO-DINK. I DON'T LIKE THE WAY THOSE DICE ARE ROLLING.
THERE'S ANOTHER HUMAN PLAYING DAKKAMITE BLACKJACK, SWITCHING FROM TABLE TO TABLE, AND CLEANING UP AT EVERY ONE.
YOU THINKING WHAT I'M THINKING?
BRING IN THE WORM.
I'M GETTING A BAD FEELING HERE, KID. MIGHT BE TIME TO PULL OUT.
QUIRE! YOU KEEPING YOUR MIND OPEN OUT THERE?
OH YOU BETTER BELIEVE IT.
SO WAIT A MINUTE... VANDORIANS HAVE HOW MANY TONGUES?

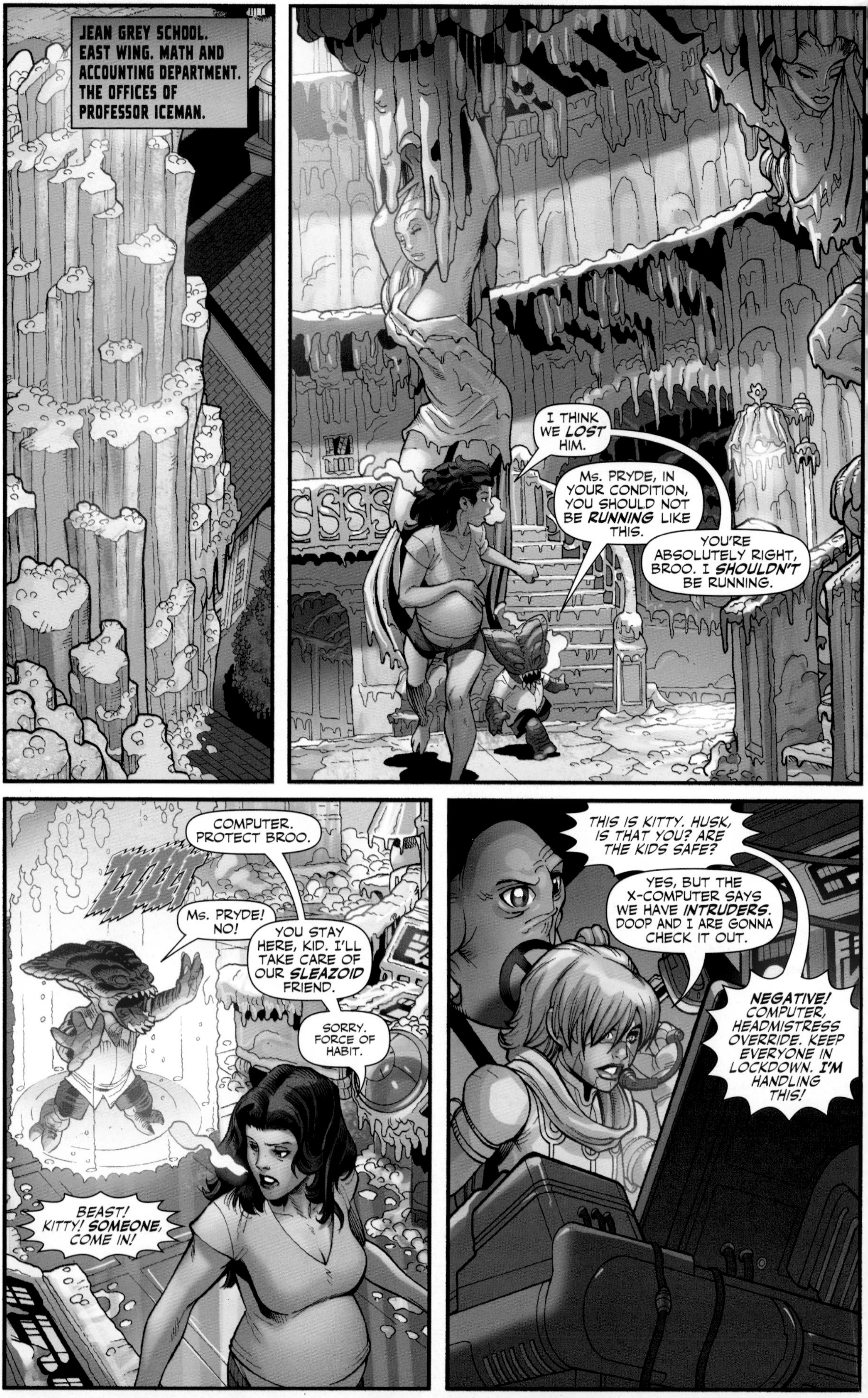
JEAN GREY SCHOOL. EAST WING. MATH AND ACCOUNTING DEPARTMENT. THE OFFICES OF PROFESSOR ICEMAN.
I THINK WE LOST HIM.
Ms. PRYDE, IN YOUR CONDITION, YOU SHOULD NOT BE RUNNING LIKE THIS.
YOU'RE ABSOLUTELY RIGHT, BROO. I SHOULDN'T BE RUNNING.
COMPUTER. PROTECT BROO.
ZZZT
Ms. PRYDE! NO!
YOU STAY HERE, KID. I'LL TAKE CARE OF OUR SLEAZOID FRIEND.
SORRY. FORCE OF HABIT.
BEAST! KITTY! SOMEONE, COME IN!
THIS IS KITTY. HUSK, IS THAT YOU? ARE THE KIDS SAFE?
YES, BUT THE X-COMPUTER SAYS WE HAVE INTRUDERS. DOOP AND I ARE GONNA CHECK IT OUT.
NEGATIVE! COMPUTER, HEADMISTRESS OVERRIDE. KEEP EVERYONE IN LOCKDOWN. I'M HANDLING THIS!

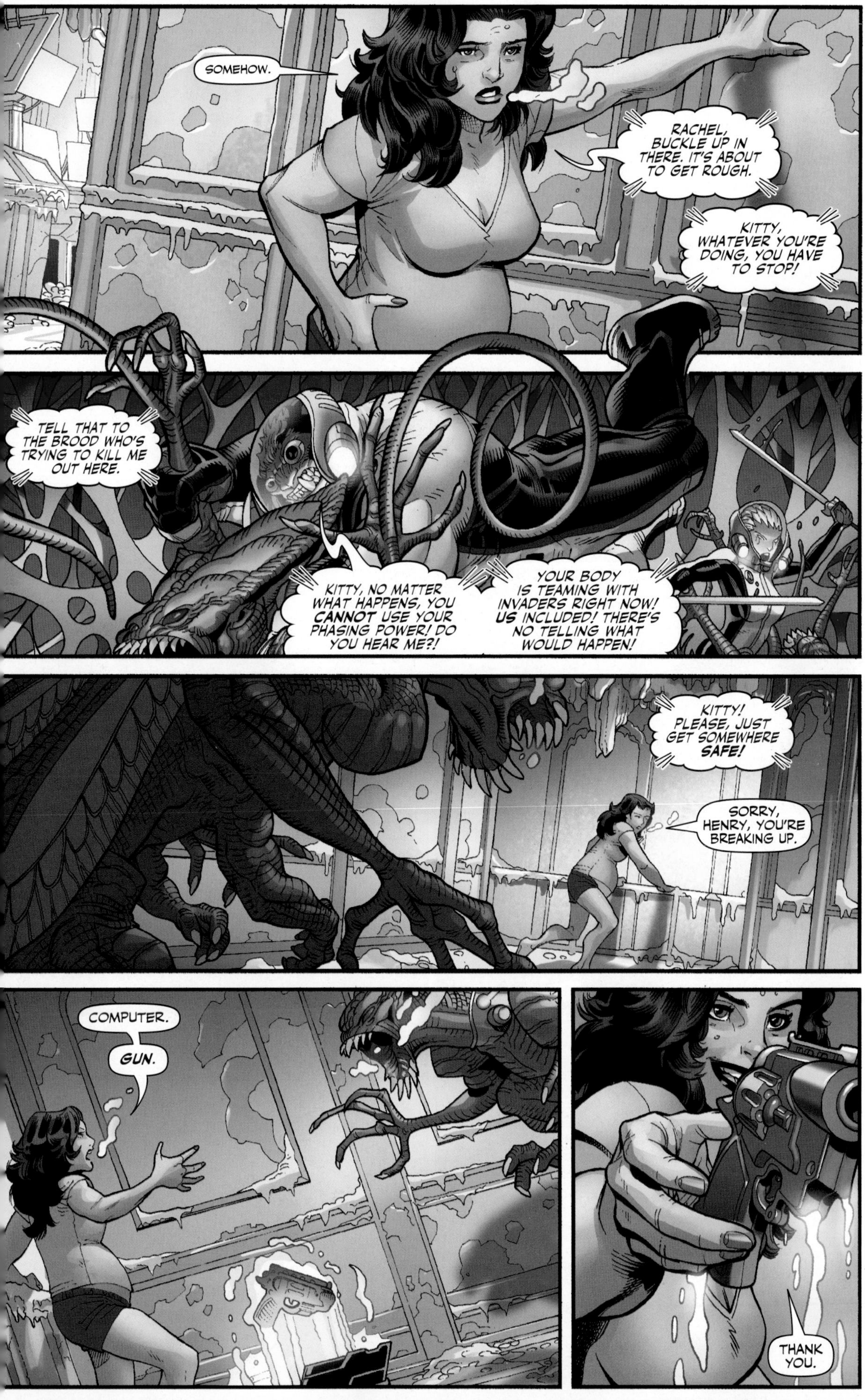
SOMEHOW.
RACHEL, BUCKLE UP IN THERE. IT'S ABOUT TO GET ROUGH.
KITTY, WHATEVER YOU'RE DOING, YOU HAVE TO STOP!
TELL THAT TO THE BROOD WHO'S TRYING TO KILL ME OUT HERE.
KITTY, NO MATTER WHAT HAPPENS, YOU CANNOT USE YOUR PHASING POWER! DO YOU HEAR ME?!
YOUR BODY IS TEAMING WITH INVADERS RIGHT NOW! US INCLUDED! THERE'S NO TELLING WHAT WOULD HAPPEN!
KITTY! PLEASE, JUST GET SOMEWHERE SAFE!
SORRY, HENRY, YOU'RE BREAKING UP.
COMPUTER.
GUN.
THANK YOU.

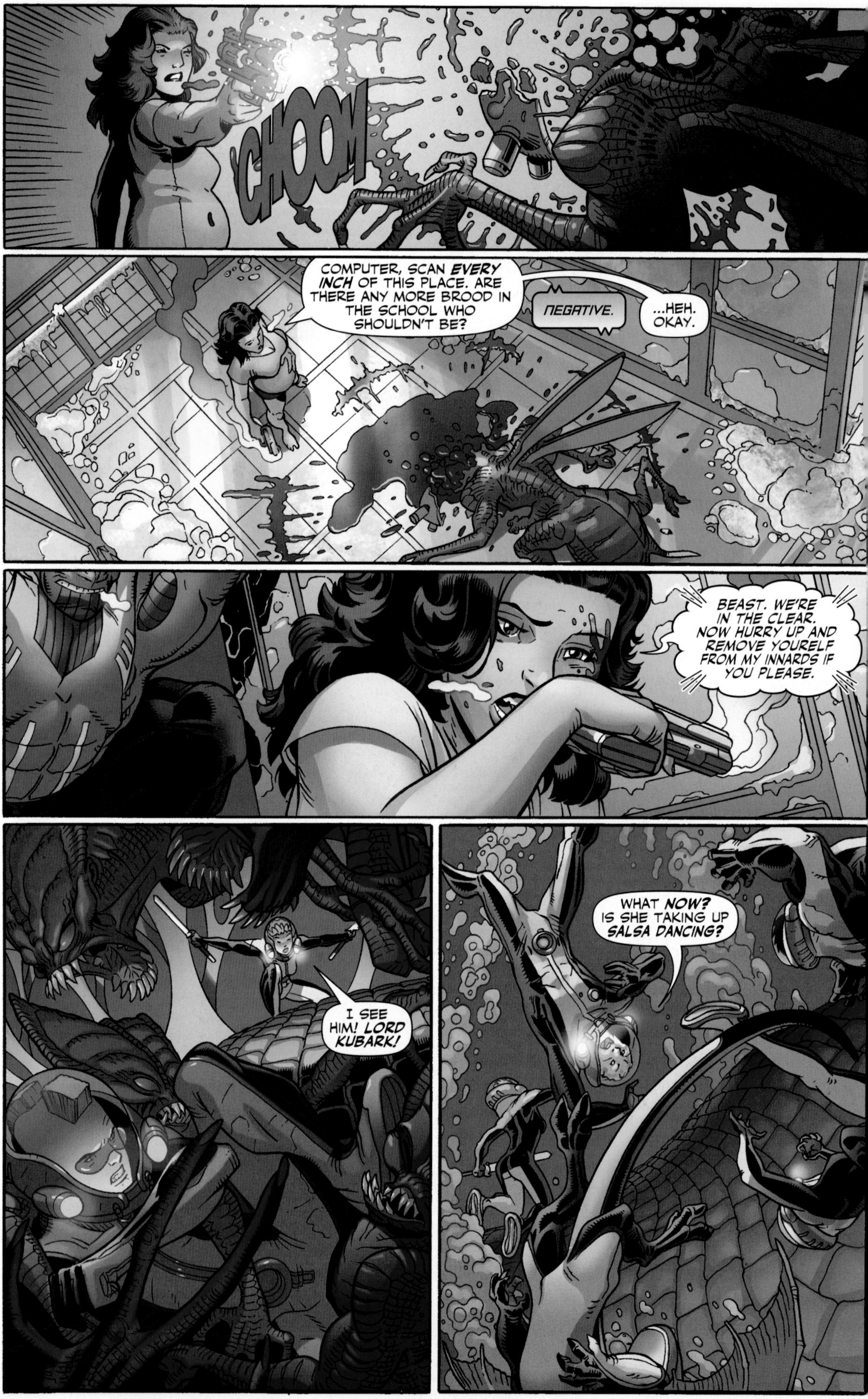
CHOOM
COMPUTER, SCAN EVERY INCH OF THIS PLACE. ARE THERE ANY MORE BROOD IN THE SCHOOL WHO SHOULDN'T BE?
NEGATIVE.
...HEH. OKAY.
BEAST. WE'RE IN THE CLEAR. NOW HURRY UP AND REMOVE YOURELF FROM MY INNARDS IF YOU PLEASE.
I SEE HIM! LORD KUBARK!
WHAT NOW? IS SHE TAKING UP SALSA DANCING?

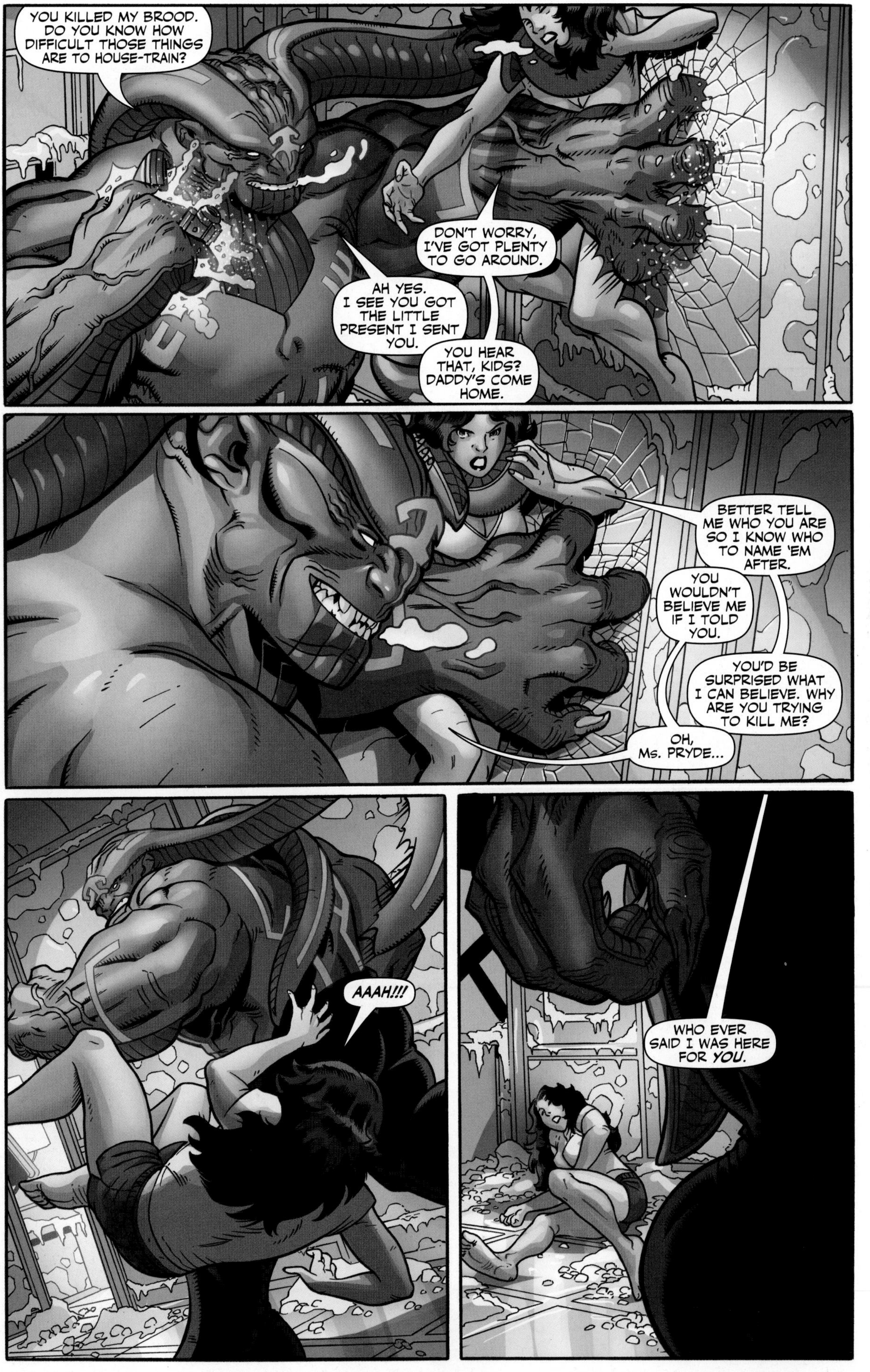

YOU KILLED MY BROOD. DO YOU KNOW HOW DIFFICULT THOSE THINGS ARE TO HOUSE-TRAIN?
DON'T WORRY, I'VE GOT PLENTY TO GO AROUND.
AH YES. I SEE YOU GOT THE LITTLE PRESENT I SENT YOU.
YOU HEAR THAT, KIDS? DADDY'S COME HOME.
BETTER TELL ME WHO YOU ARE SO I KNOW WHO TO NAME 'EM AFTER.
YOU WOULDN'T BELIEVE ME IF I TOLD YOU.
YOU'D BE SURPRISED WHAT I CAN BELIEVE. WHY ARE YOU TRYING TO KILL ME?
OH, Ms. PRYDE...
AAAH!!!
WHO EVER SAID I WAS HERE FOR *YOU*.

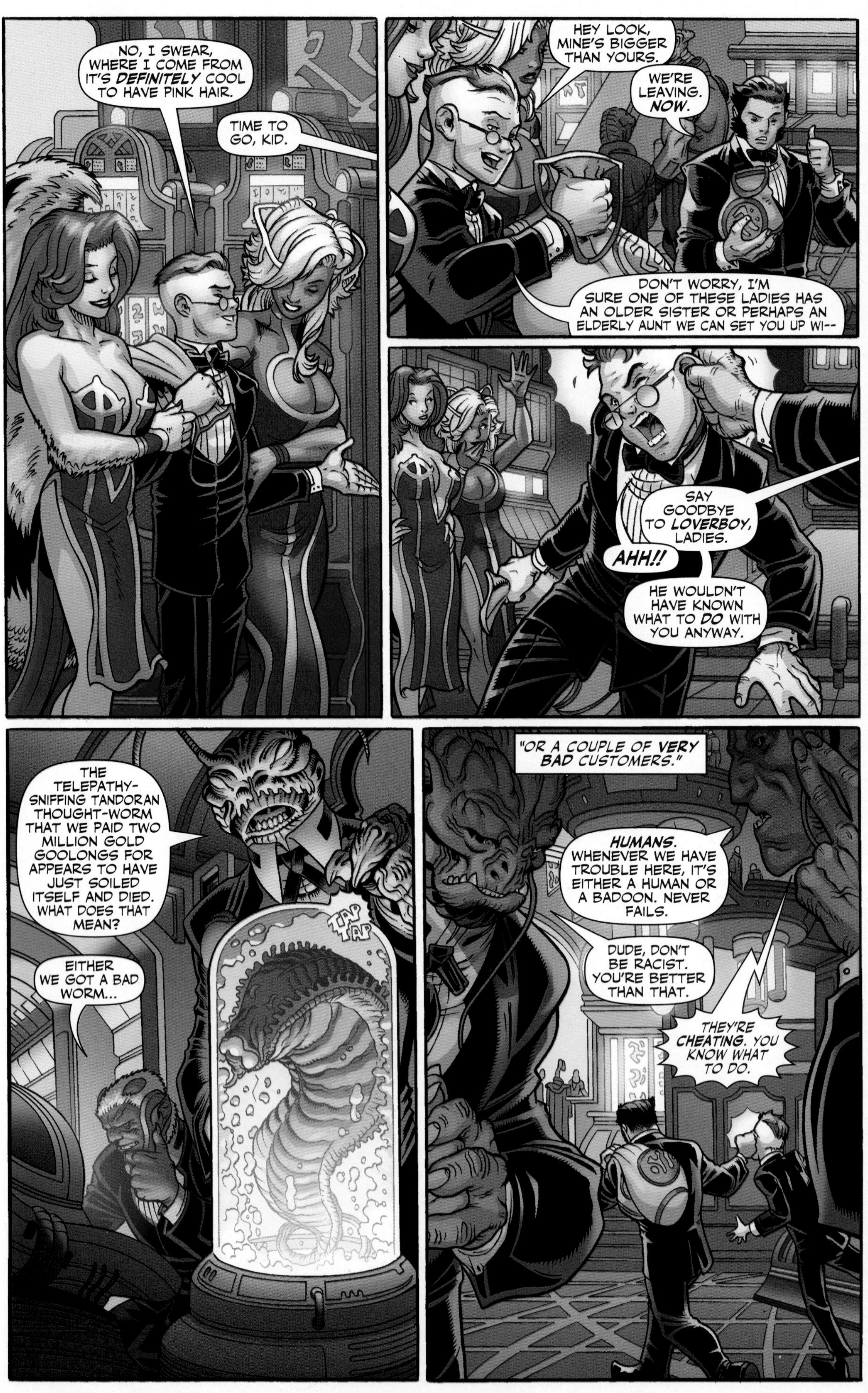
NO, I SWEAR, WHERE I COME FROM IT'S *DEFINITELY* COOL TO HAVE PINK HAIR.
TIME TO GO, KID.
HEY LOOK, MINE'S BIGGER THAN YOURS.
WE'RE LEAVING. *NOW.*
DON'T WORRY, I'M SURE ONE OF THESE LADIES HAS AN OLDER SISTER OR PERHAPS AN ELDERLY AUNT WE CAN SET YOU UP WI--
SAY GOODBYE TO *LOVERBOY*, LADIES.
AHH!!
HE WOULDN'T HAVE KNOWN WHAT TO *DO* WITH YOU ANYWAY.
THE TELEPATHY-SNIFFING TANDORAN THOUGHT-WORM THAT WE PAID TWO MILLION GOLD GOOLONGS FOR APPEARS TO HAVE JUST SOILED ITSELF AND DIED. WHAT DOES THAT MEAN?
TAP TAP
EITHER WE GOT A BAD WORM...
"OR A COUPLE OF *VERY BAD* CUSTOMERS."
HUMANS. WHENEVER WE HAVE TROUBLE HERE, IT'S EITHER A HUMAN OR A BADOON. NEVER FAILS.
DUDE, DON'T BE RACIST. YOU'RE BETTER THAN THAT.
THEY'RE CHEATING. YOU KNOW WHAT TO DO.

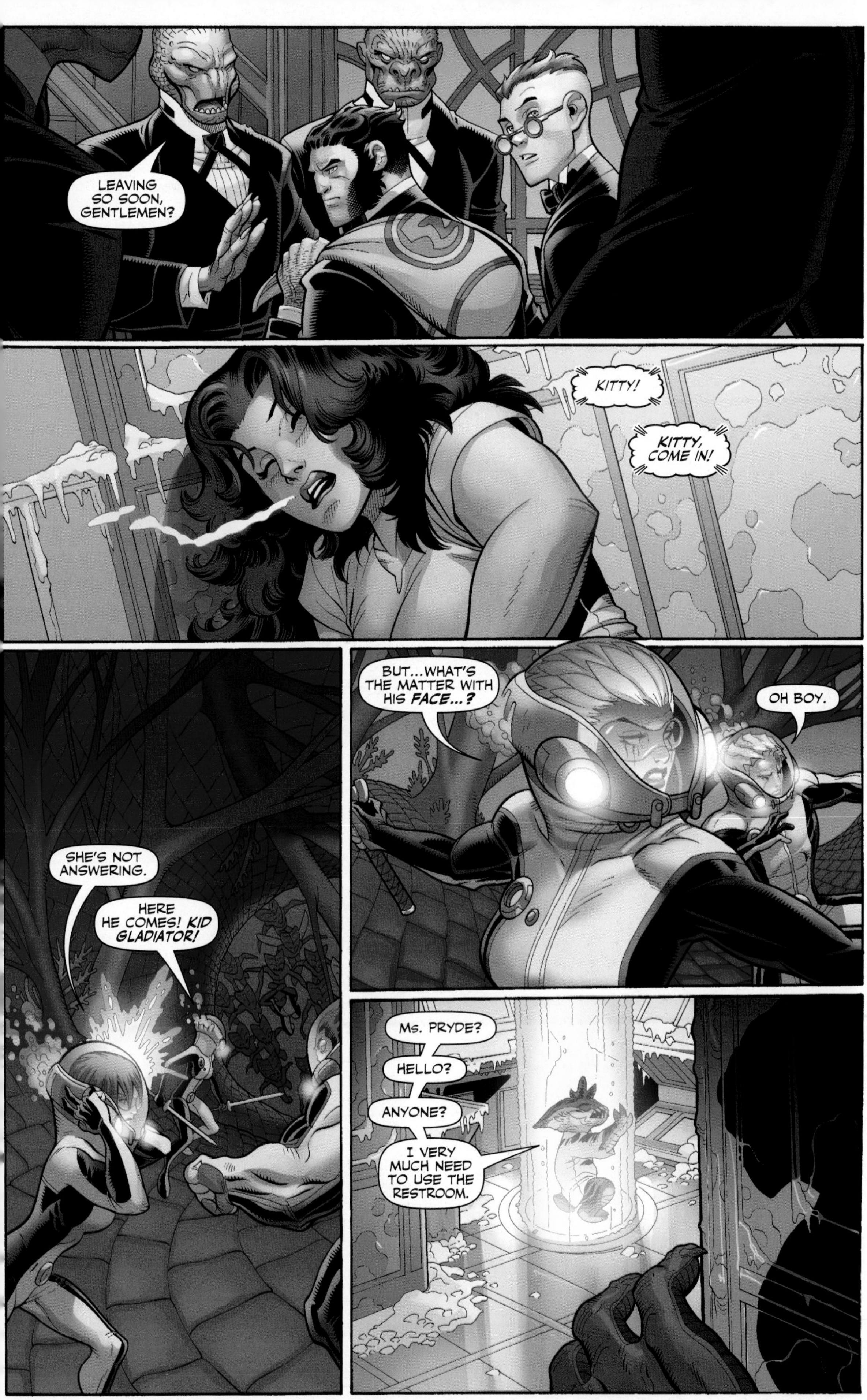
LEAVING SO SOON, GENTLEMEN?
KITTY!
KITTY, COME IN!
SHE'S NOT ANSWERING.
HERE HE COMES! KID GLADIATOR!
BUT...WHAT'S THE MATTER WITH HIS FACE...?
OH BOY.
Ms. PRYDE?
HELLO?
ANYONE?
I VERY MUCH NEED TO USE THE RESTROOM.

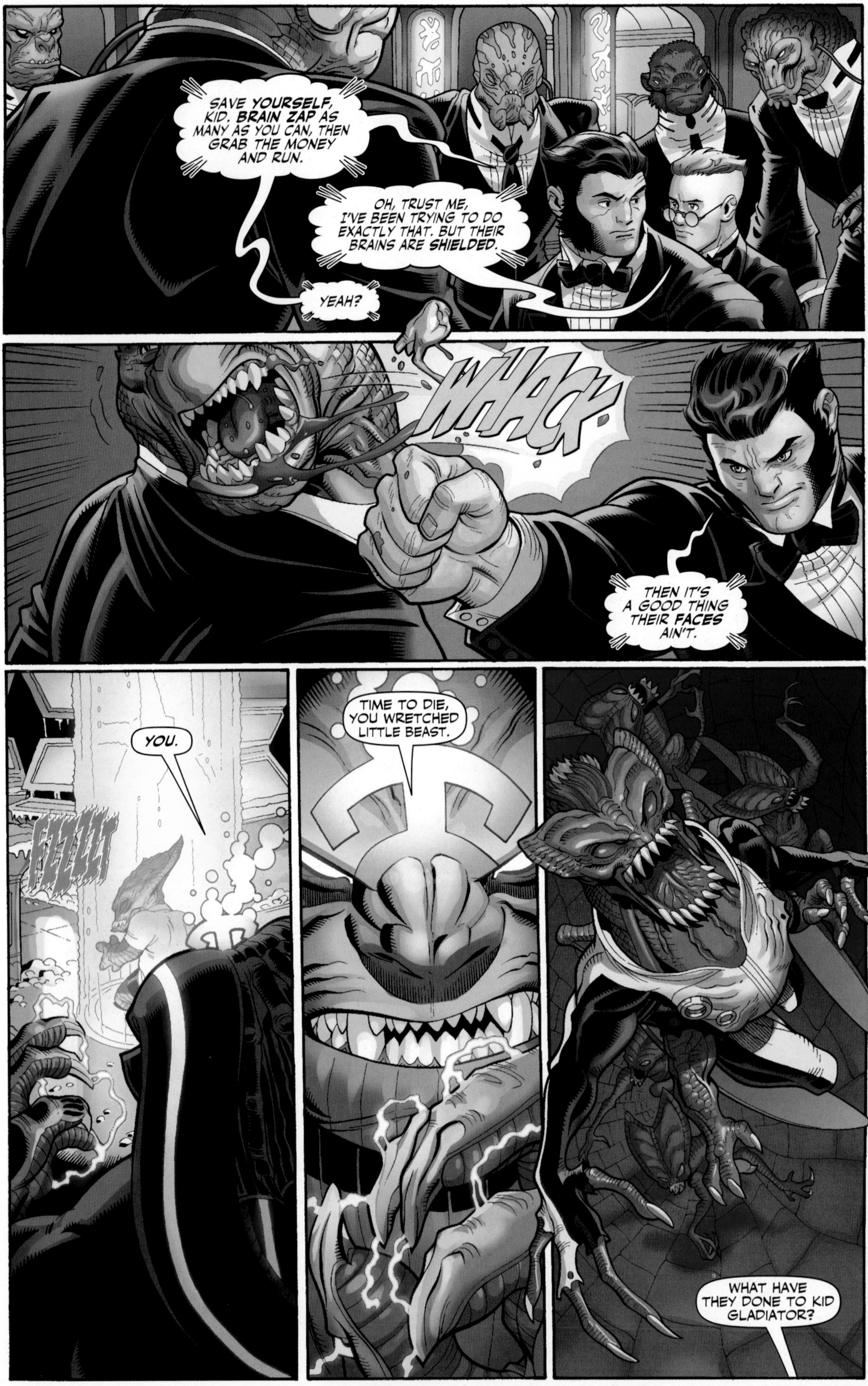
SAVE YOURSELF, KID. BRAIN ZAP AS MANY AS YOU CAN, THEN GRAB THE MONEY AND RUN.
OH, TRUST ME, I'VE BEEN TRYING TO DO EXACTLY THAT. BUT THEIR BRAINS ARE SHIELDED.
YEAH?
WHACK
THEN IT'S A GOOD THING THEIR FACES AIN'T.
YOU.
FZZZZT
TIME TO DIE, YOU WRETCHED LITTLE BEAST.
WHAT HAVE THEY DONE TO KID GLADIATOR?

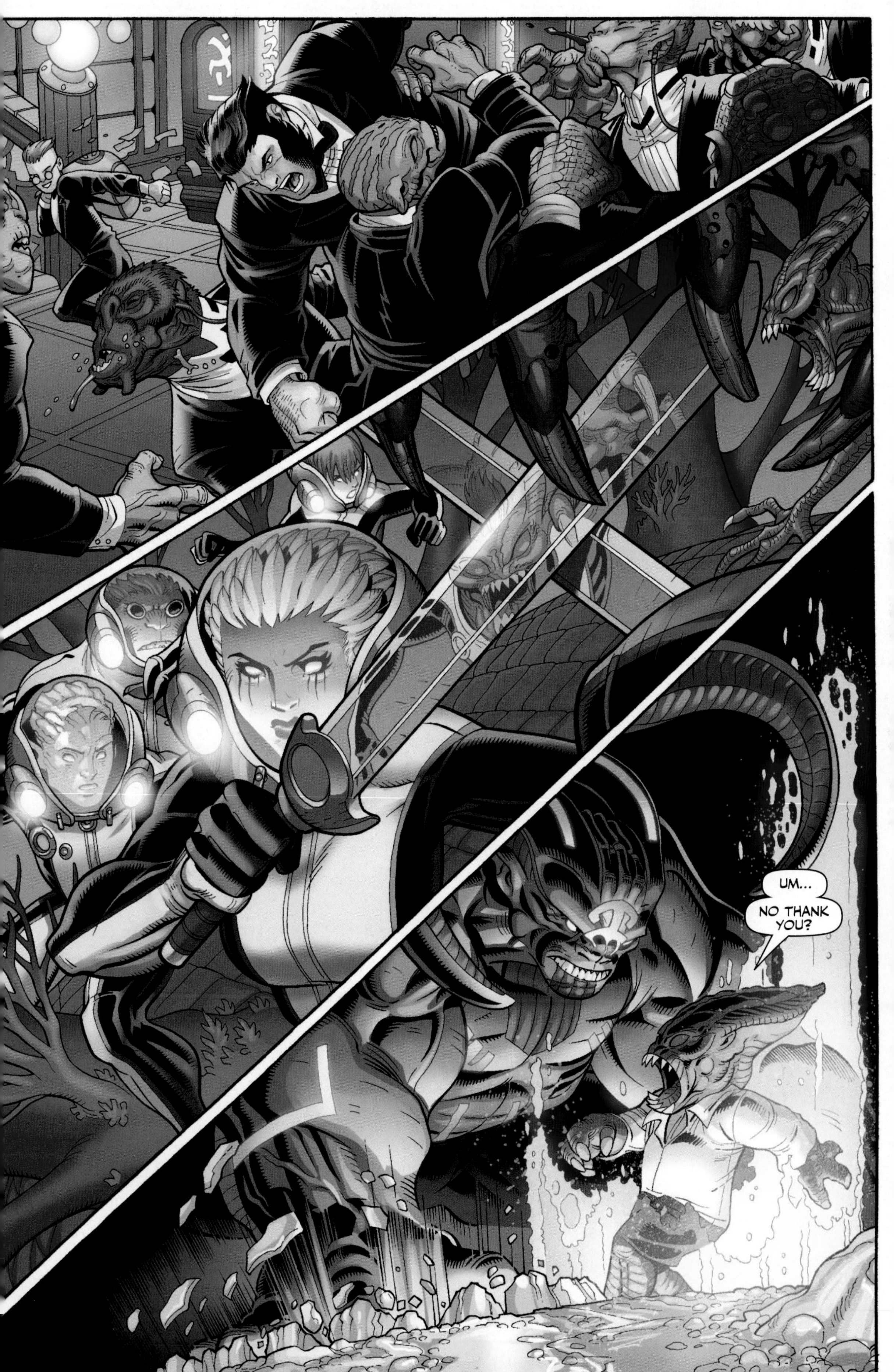
UM...
NO THANK YOU?

7 "MUTATIS MUTANDIS"
CONCLUSION: IT AIN'T EASY BEIN' BROOD

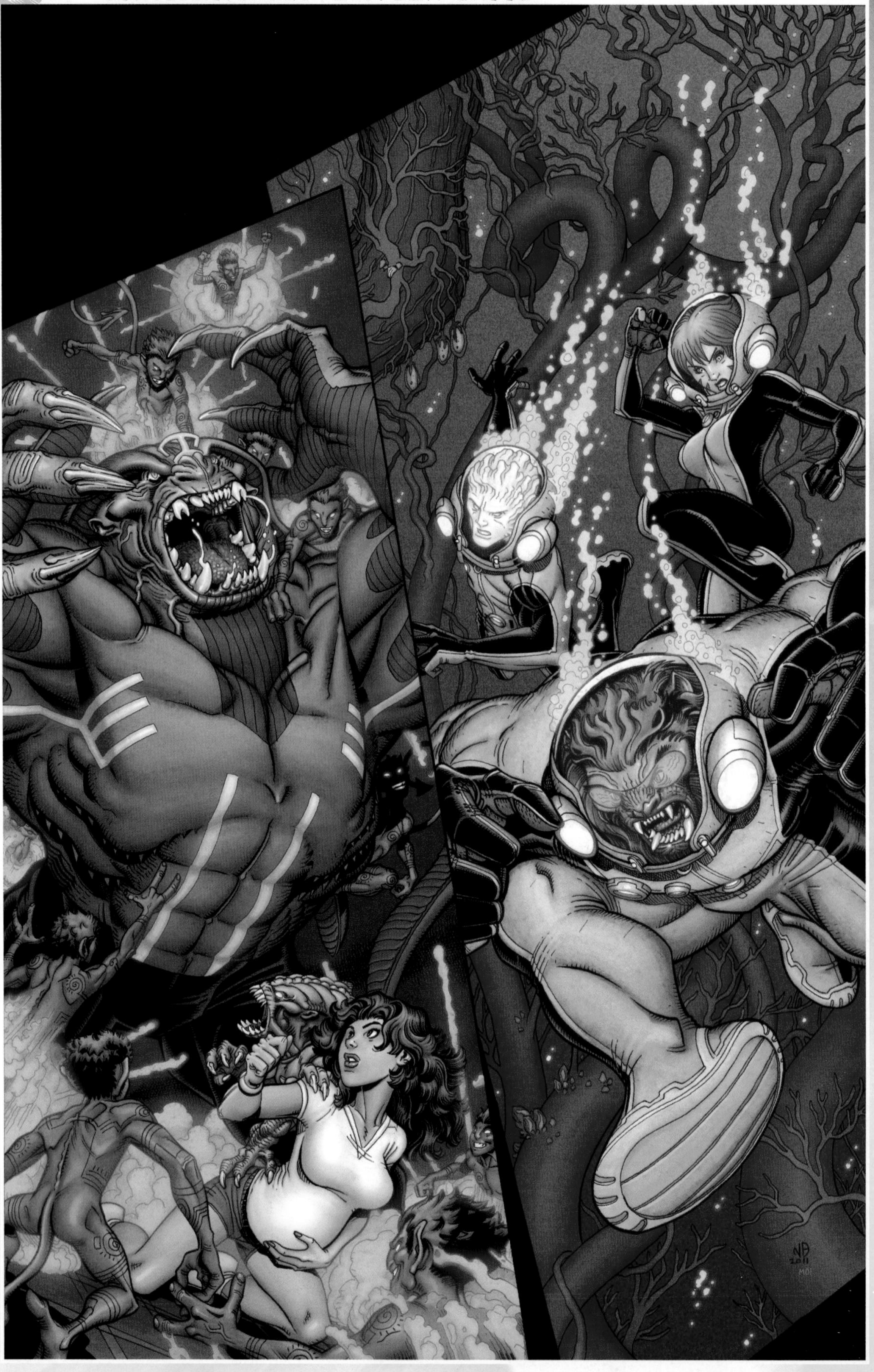

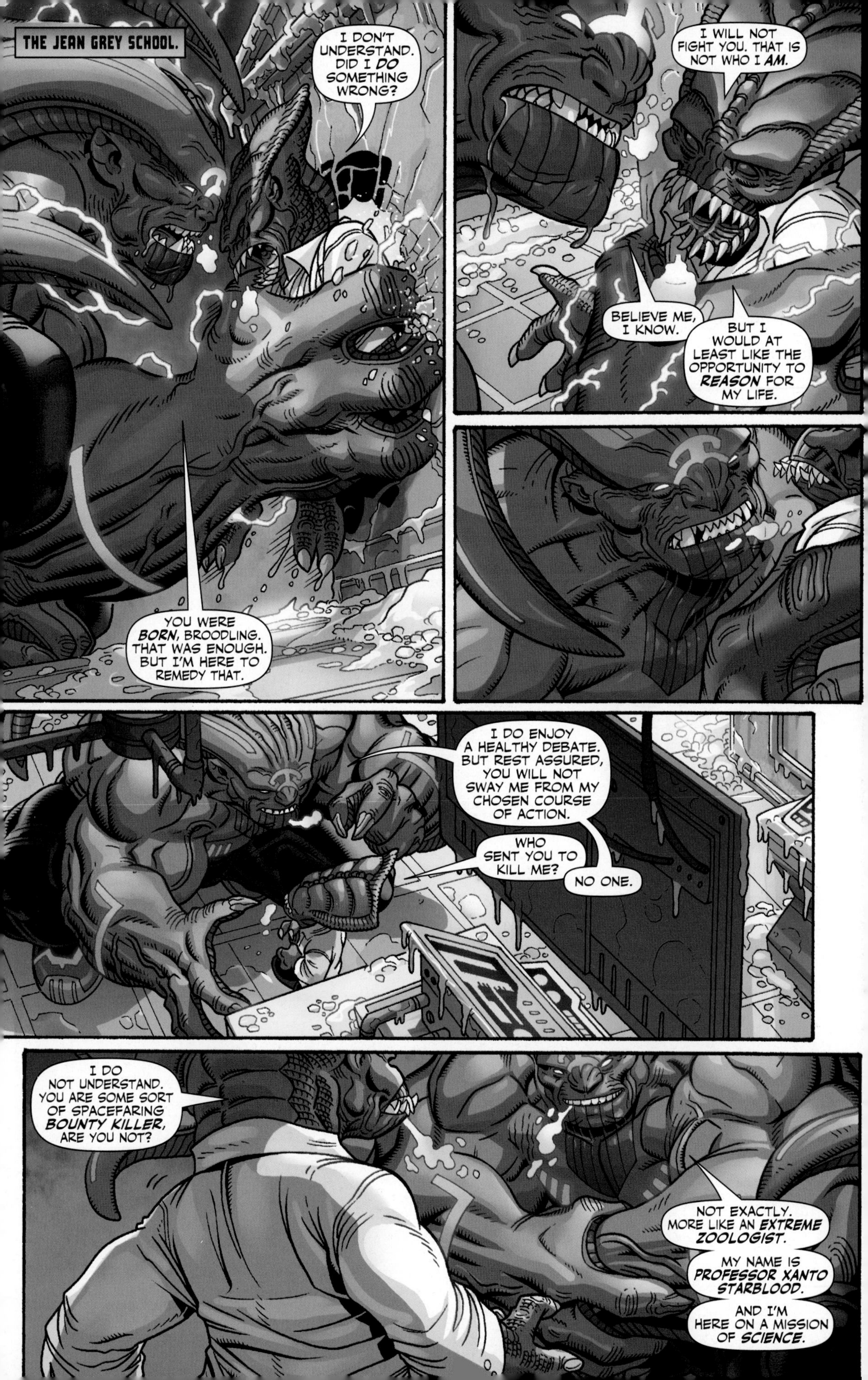
THE JEAN GREY SCHOOL.
I DON'T UNDERSTAND. DID I *DO* SOMETHING WRONG?
YOU WERE *BORN*, BROODLING. THAT WAS ENOUGH. BUT I'M HERE TO REMEDY THAT.
I WILL NOT FIGHT YOU. THAT IS NOT WHO I *AM*.
BELIEVE ME, I KNOW.
BUT I WOULD AT LEAST LIKE THE OPPORTUNITY TO *REASON* FOR MY LIFE.
I DO ENJOY A HEALTHY DEBATE. BUT REST ASSURED, YOU WILL NOT SWAY ME FROM MY CHOSEN COURSE OF ACTION.
WHO SENT YOU TO KILL ME?
NO ONE.
I DO NOT UNDERSTAND. YOU ARE SOME SORT OF SPACEFARING *BOUNTY KILLER*, ARE YOU NOT?
NOT EXACTLY. MORE LIKE AN *EXTREME ZOOLOGIST*.
MY NAME IS *PROFESSOR XANTO STARBLOOD*.
AND I'M HERE ON A MISSION OF *SCIENCE*.

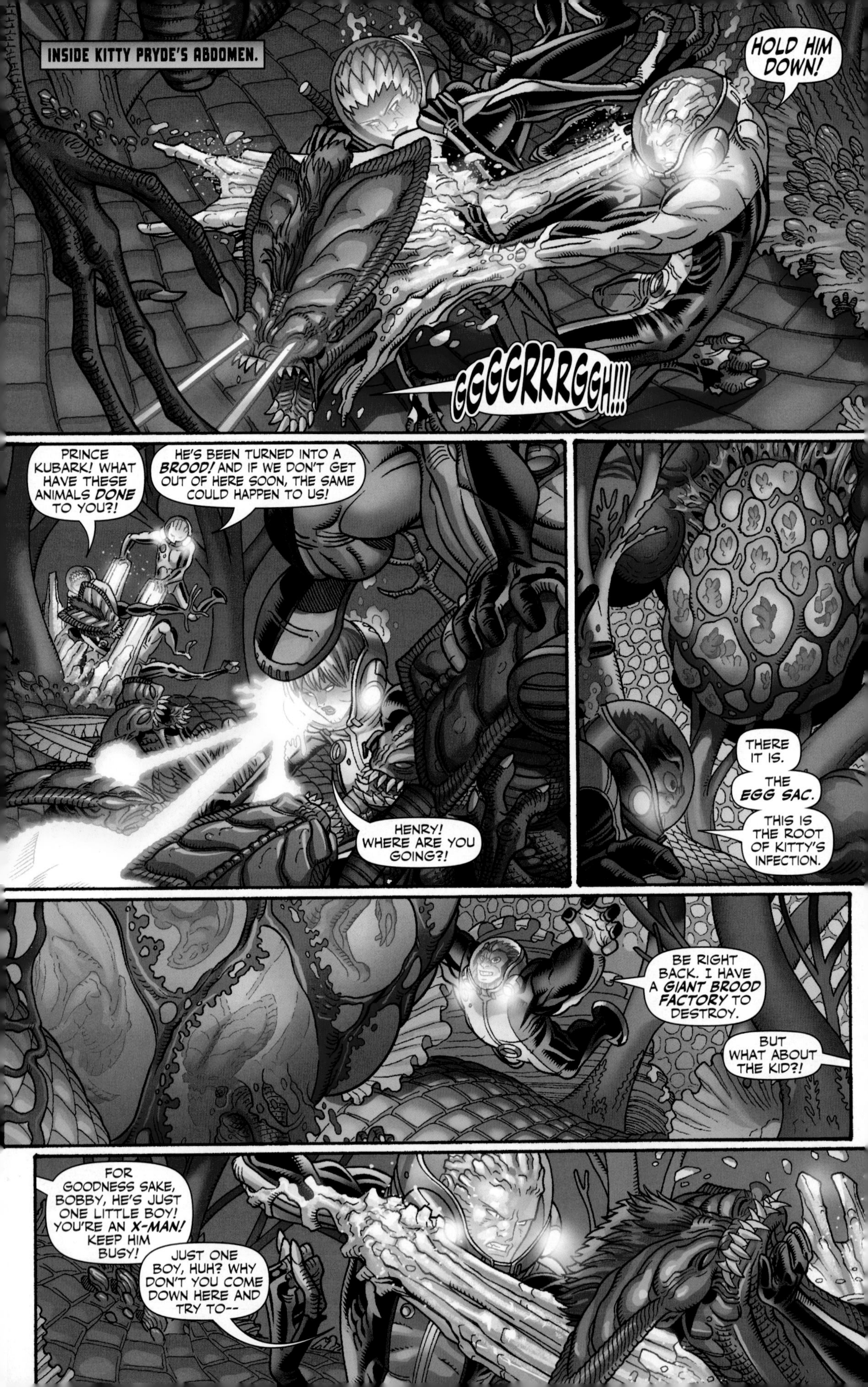

INSIDE KITTY PRYDE'S ABDOMEN.
HOLD HIM DOWN!
GGGGRRRGGH!!!
PRINCE KUBARK! WHAT HAVE THESE ANIMALS DONE TO YOU?!
HE'S BEEN TURNED INTO A BROOD! AND IF WE DON'T GET OUT OF HERE SOON, THE SAME COULD HAPPEN TO US!
HENRY! WHERE ARE YOU GOING?!
THERE IT IS.
THE EGG SAC.
THIS IS THE ROOT OF KITTY'S INFECTION.
BE RIGHT BACK. I HAVE A GIANT BROOD FACTORY TO DESTROY.
BUT WHAT ABOUT THE KID?!
FOR GOODNESS SAKE, BOBBY, HE'S JUST ONE LITTLE BOY! YOU'RE AN X-MAN! KEEP HIM BUSY!
JUST ONE BOY, HUH? WHY DON'T YOU COME DOWN HERE AND TRY TO--

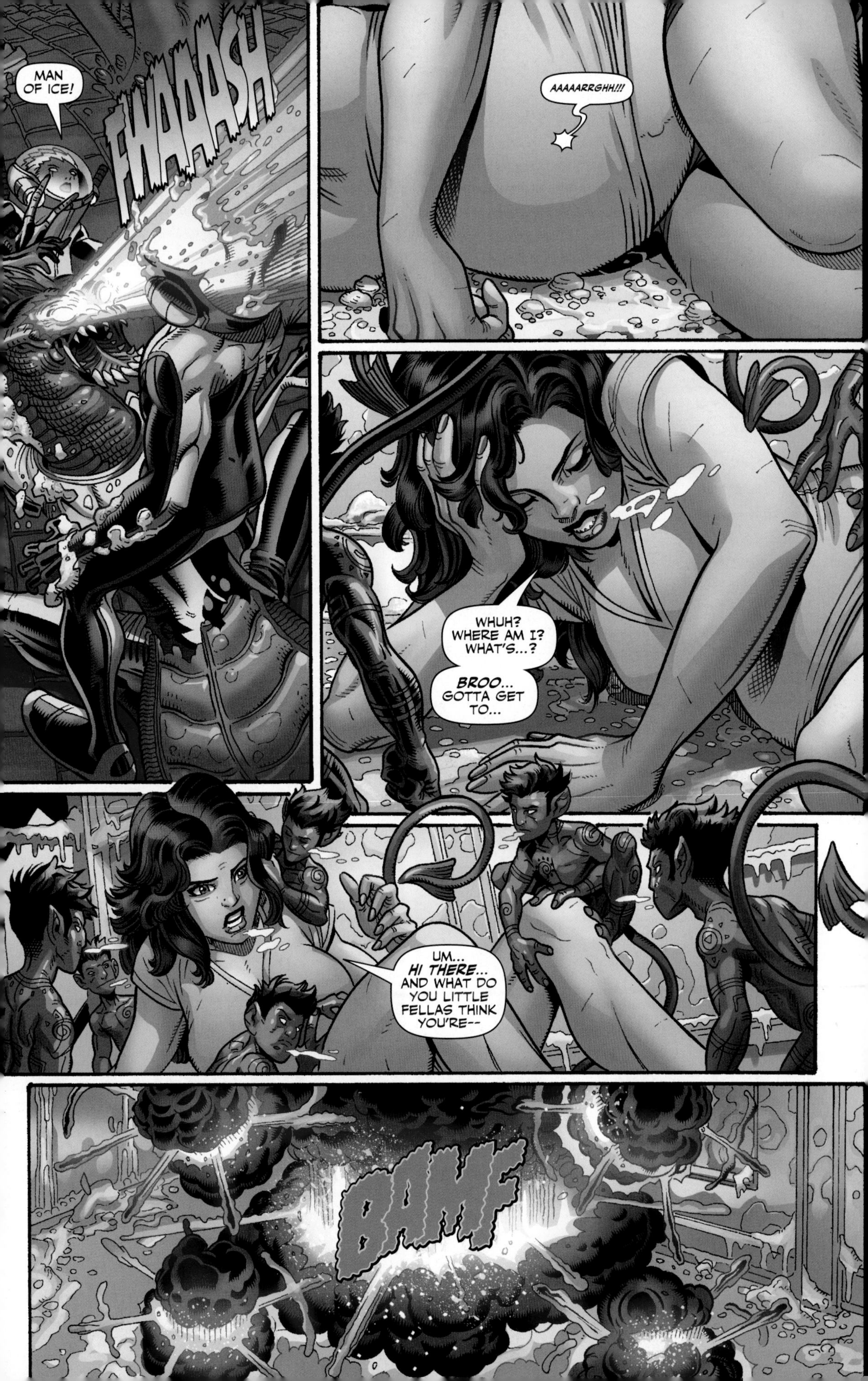
MAN OF ICE!
FWAAASH
AAAAARRGHH!!!
WHUH? WHERE AM I? WHAT'S...?
BROO... GOTTA GET TO...
UM... HI THERE... AND WHAT DO YOU LITTLE FELLAS THINK YOU'RE--
BAMF

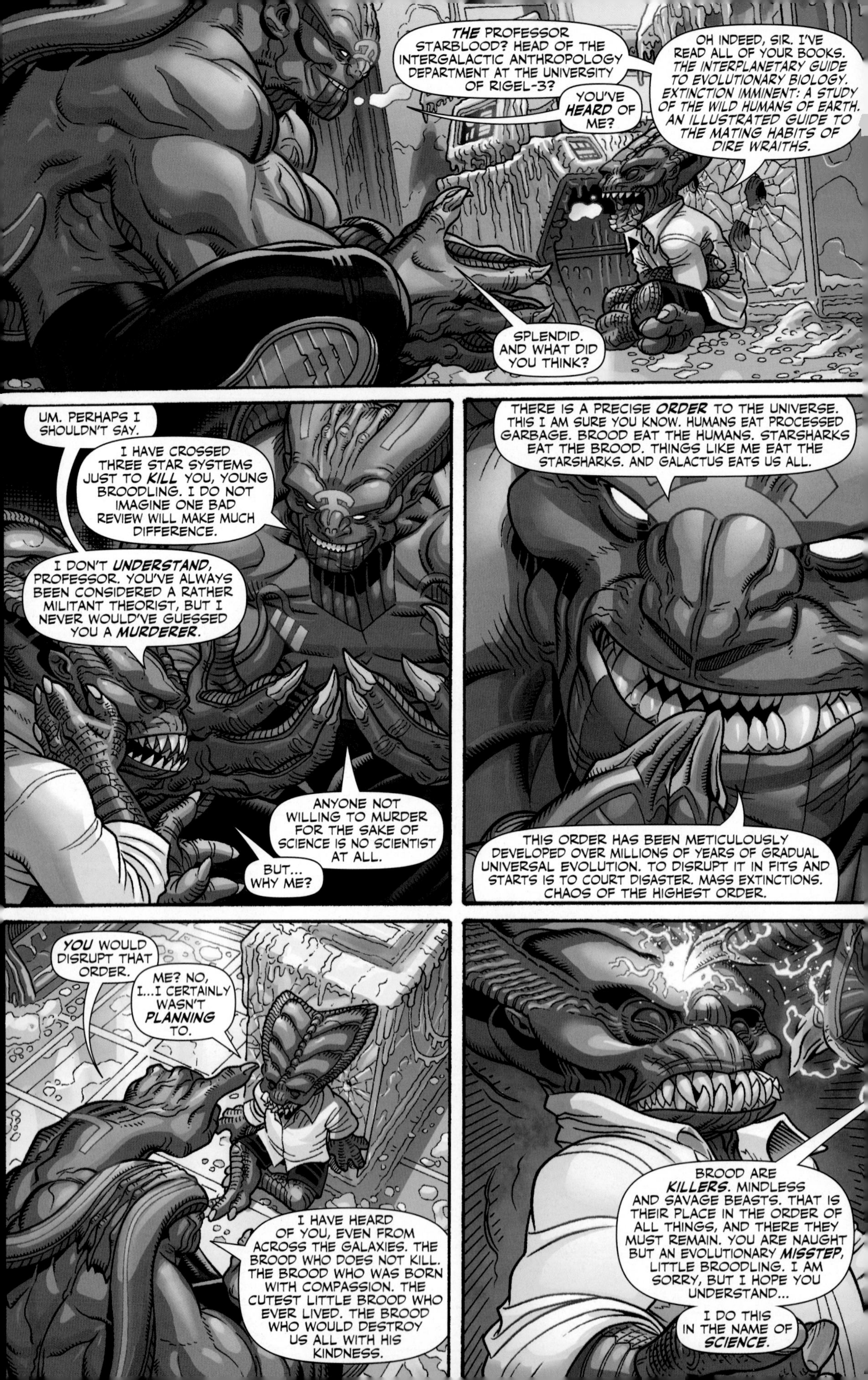
THE PROFESSOR STARBLOOD? HEAD OF THE INTERGALACTIC ANTHROPOLOGY DEPARTMENT AT THE UNIVERSITY OF RIGEL-3?
YOU'VE HEARD OF ME?
OH INDEED, SIR. I'VE READ ALL OF YOUR BOOKS. THE INTERPLANETARY GUIDE TO EVOLUTIONARY BIOLOGY. EXTINCTION IMMINENT: A STUDY OF THE WILD HUMANS OF EARTH. AN ILLUSTRATED GUIDE TO THE MATING HABITS OF DIRE WRAITHS.
SPLENDID. AND WHAT DID YOU THINK?
UM. PERHAPS I SHOULDN'T SAY.
I HAVE CROSSED THREE STAR SYSTEMS JUST TO KILL YOU, YOUNG BROODLING. I DO NOT IMAGINE ONE BAD REVIEW WILL MAKE MUCH DIFFERENCE.
I DON'T UNDERSTAND, PROFESSOR. YOU'VE ALWAYS BEEN CONSIDERED A RATHER MILITANT THEORIST, BUT I NEVER WOULD'VE GUESSED YOU A MURDERER.
ANYONE NOT WILLING TO MURDER FOR THE SAKE OF SCIENCE IS NO SCIENTIST AT ALL.
BUT... WHY ME?
THERE IS A PRECISE ORDER TO THE UNIVERSE. THIS I AM SURE YOU KNOW. HUMANS EAT PROCESSED GARBAGE. BROOD EAT THE HUMANS. STARSHARKS EAT THE BROOD. THINGS LIKE ME EAT THE STARSHARKS. AND GALACTUS EATS US ALL.
THIS ORDER HAS BEEN METICULOUSLY DEVELOPED OVER MILLIONS OF YEARS OF GRADUAL UNIVERSAL EVOLUTION. TO DISRUPT IT IN FITS AND STARTS IS TO COURT DISASTER. MASS EXTINCTIONS. CHAOS OF THE HIGHEST ORDER.
YOU WOULD DISRUPT THAT ORDER.
ME? NO, I...I CERTAINLY WASN'T PLANNING TO.
I HAVE HEARD OF YOU, EVEN FROM ACROSS THE GALAXIES. THE BROOD WHO DOES NOT KILL. THE BROOD WHO WAS BORN WITH COMPASSION. THE CUTEST LITTLE BROOD WHO EVER LIVED. THE BROOD WHO WOULD DESTROY US ALL WITH HIS KINDNESS.
BROOD ARE KILLERS. MINDLESS AND SAVAGE BEASTS. THAT IS THEIR PLACE IN THE ORDER OF ALL THINGS, AND THERE THEY MUST REMAIN. YOU ARE NAUGHT BUT AN EVOLUTIONARY MISSTEP, LITTLE BROODLING. I AM SORRY, BUT I HOPE YOU UNDERSTAND...
I DO THIS IN THE NAME OF SCIENCE.

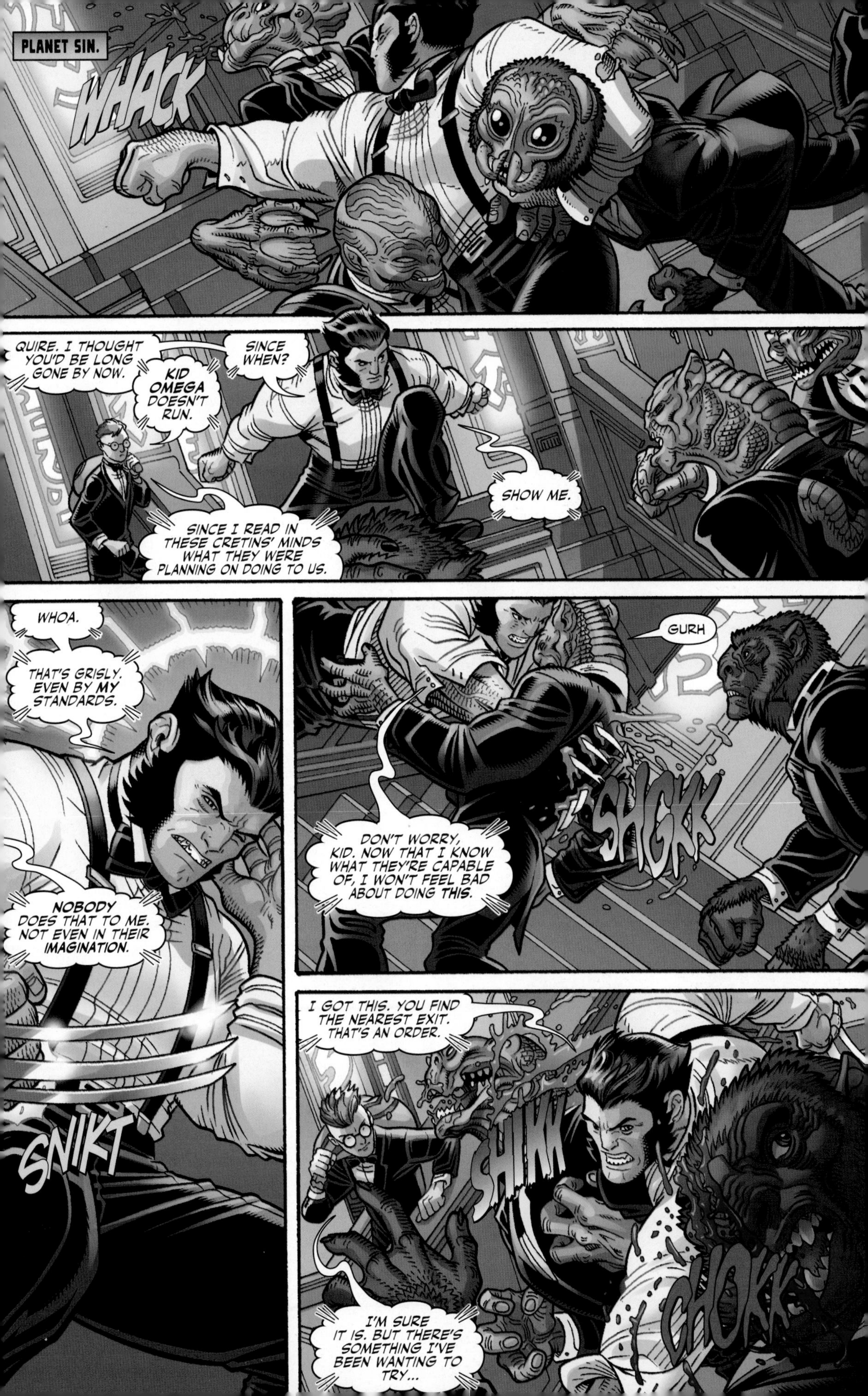
PLANET SIN.
WHACK
QUIRE. I THOUGHT YOU'D BE LONG GONE BY NOW.
SINCE WHEN?
KID OMEGA DOESN'T RUN.
SINCE I READ IN THESE CRETINS' MINDS WHAT THEY WERE PLANNING ON DOING TO US.
SHOW ME.
WHOA.
THAT'S GRISLY. EVEN BY MY STANDARDS.
NOBODY DOES THAT TO ME. NOT EVEN IN THEIR IMAGINATION.
SNIKT
GURH
DON'T WORRY, KID. NOW THAT I KNOW WHAT THEY'RE CAPABLE OF, I WON'T FEEL BAD ABOUT DOING THIS.
SHGKK
I GOT THIS. YOU FIND THE NEAREST EXIT. THAT'S AN ORDER.
SHIKK
I'M SURE IT IS. BUT THERE'S SOMETHING I'VE BEEN WANTING TO TRY...
CHOKK

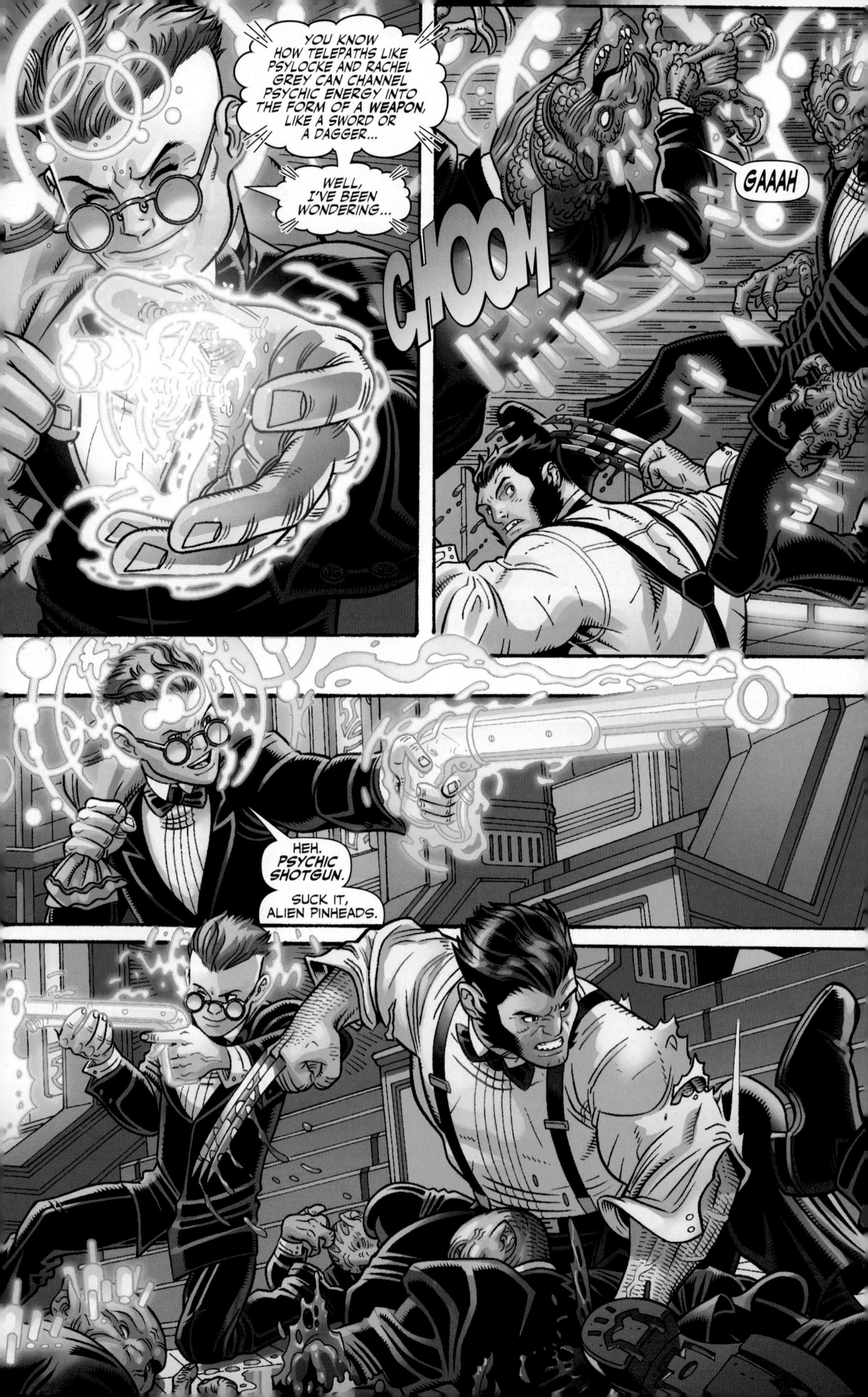

YOU KNOW HOW TELEPATHS LIKE PSYLOCKE AND RACHEL GREY CAN CHANNEL PSYCHIC ENERGY INTO THE FORM OF A WEAPON, LIKE A SWORD OR A DAGGER...
WELL, I'VE BEEN WONDERING...
CHOOM
GAAAH
HEH. PSYCHIC SHOTGUN.
SUCK IT, ALIEN PINHEADS.

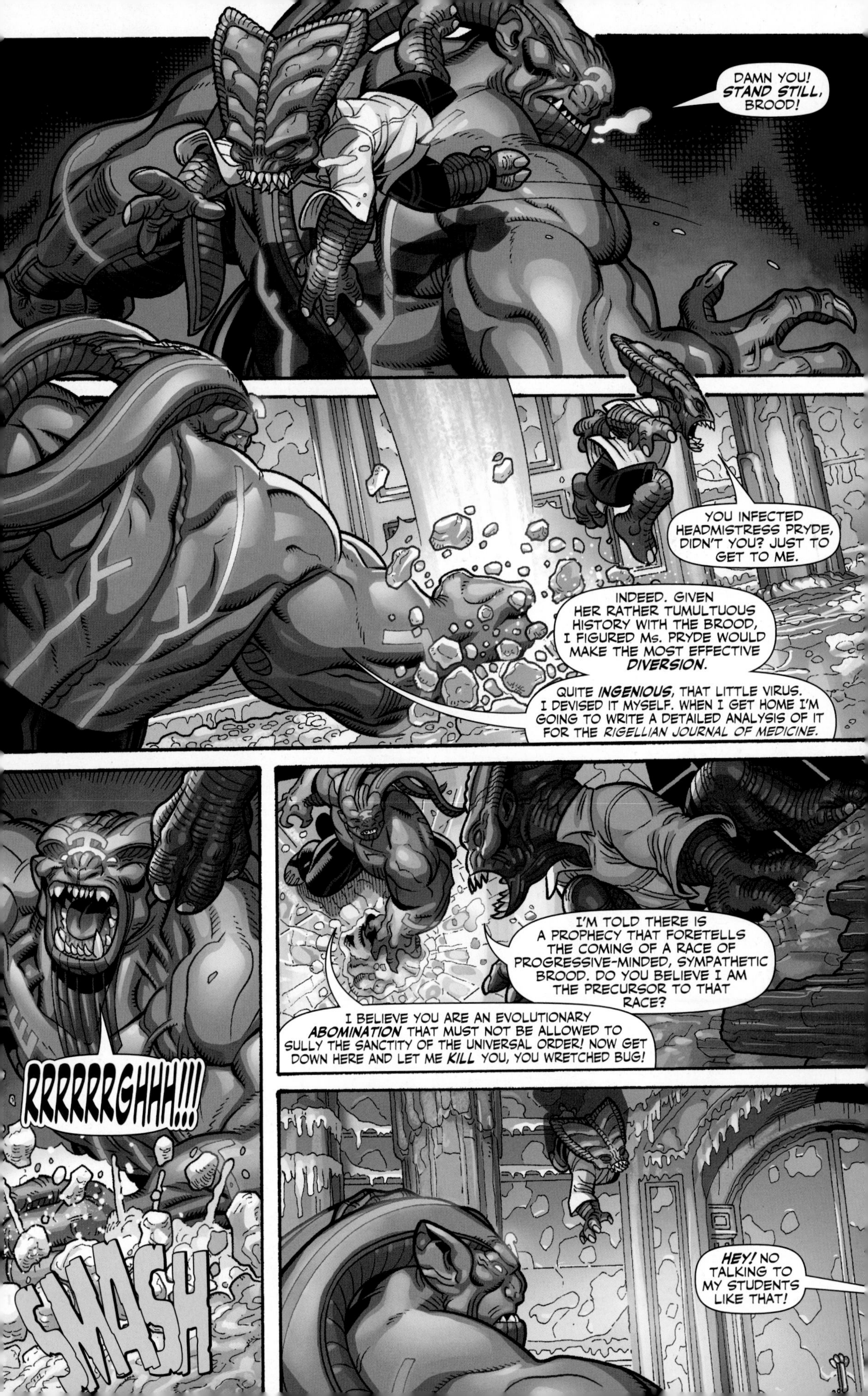
DAMN YOU! STAND STILL, BROOD!
YOU INFECTED HEADMISTRESS PRYDE, DIDN'T YOU? JUST TO GET TO ME.
INDEED. GIVEN HER RATHER TUMULTUOUS HISTORY WITH THE BROOD, I FIGURED Ms. PRYDE WOULD MAKE THE MOST EFFECTIVE DIVERSION.
QUITE INGENIOUS, THAT LITTLE VIRUS. I DEVISED IT MYSELF. WHEN I GET HOME I'M GOING TO WRITE A DETAILED ANALYSIS OF IT FOR THE RIGELLIAN JOURNAL OF MEDICINE.
RRRRRRGHHH!!!
SMASH
I'M TOLD THERE IS A PROPHECY THAT FORETELLS THE COMING OF A RACE OF PROGRESSIVE-MINDED, SYMPATHETIC BROOD. DO YOU BELIEVE I AM THE PRECURSOR TO THAT RACE?
I BELIEVE YOU ARE AN EVOLUTIONARY ABOMINATION THAT MUST NOT BE ALLOWED TO SULLY THE SANCTITY OF THE UNIVERSAL ORDER! NOW GET DOWN HERE AND LET ME KILL YOU, YOU WRETCHED BUG!
HEY! NO TALKING TO MY STUDENTS LIKE THAT!

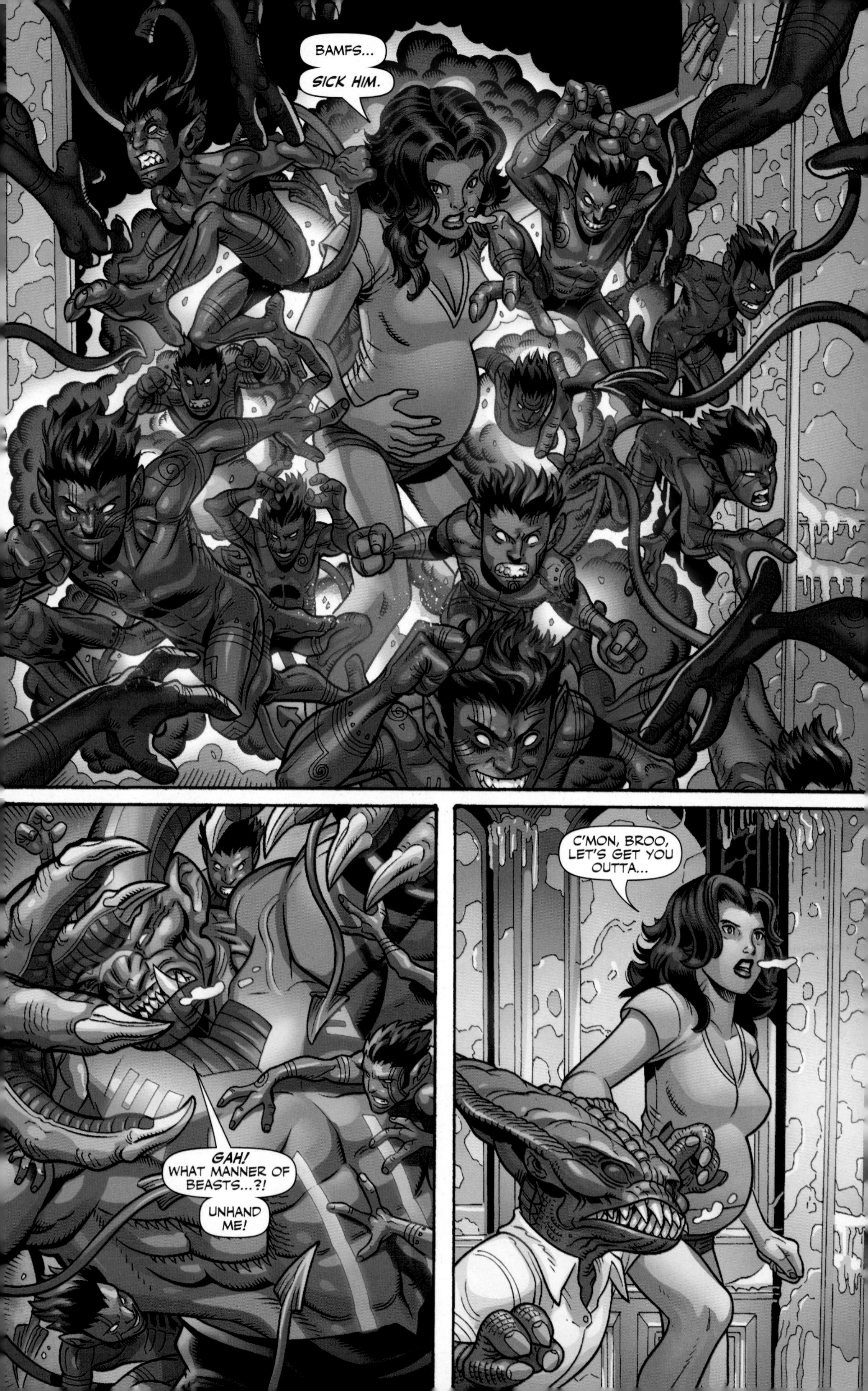
BAMFS...
SICK HIM.
GAH! WHAT MANNER OF BEASTS...?!
UNHAND ME!
C'MON, BROO, LET'S GET YOU OUTTA...

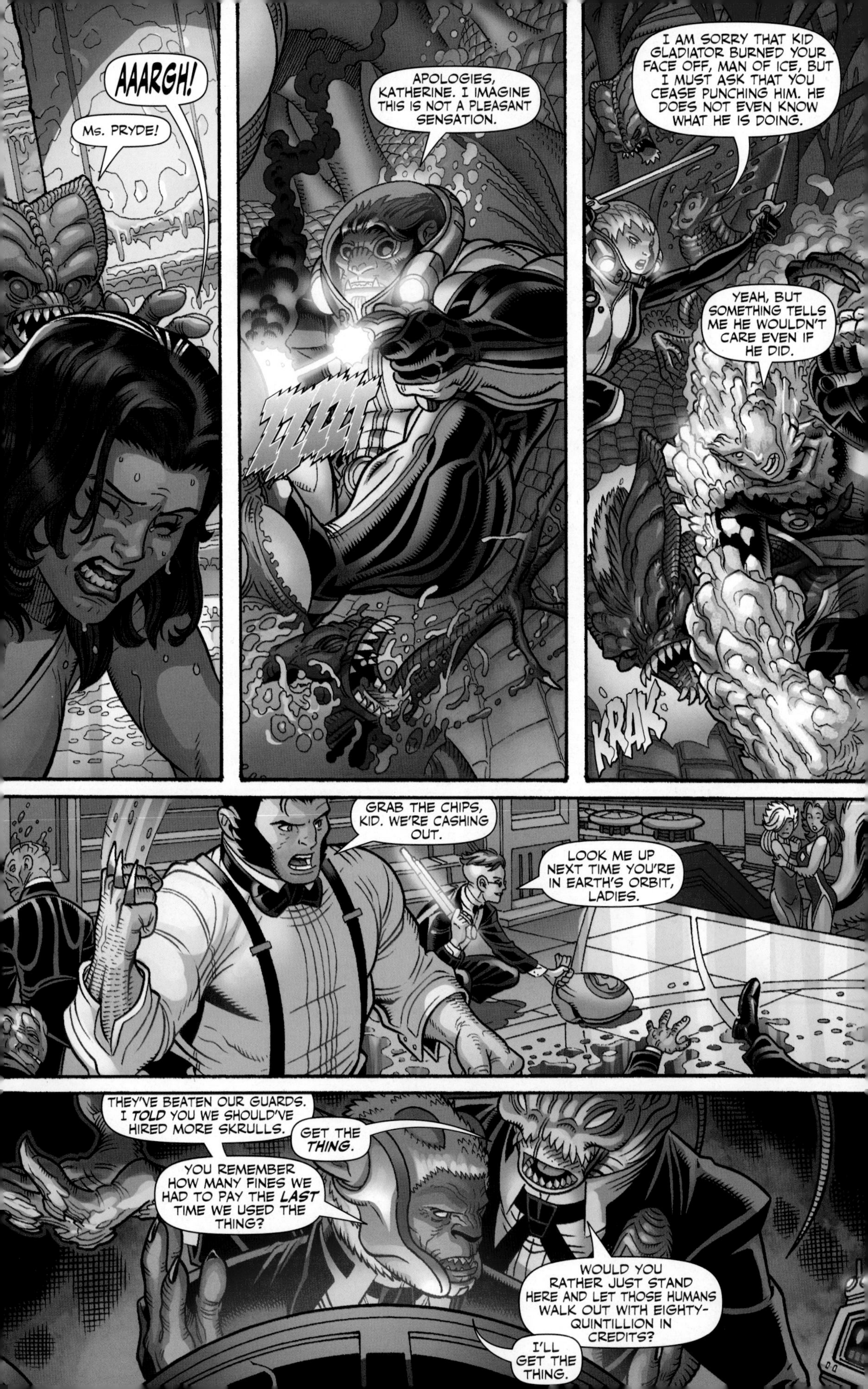
AAARGH!
Ms. PRYDE!
APOLOGIES, KATHERINE. I IMAGINE THIS IS NOT A PLEASANT SENSATION.
ZZZZT
I AM SORRY THAT KID GLADIATOR BURNED YOUR FACE OFF, MAN OF ICE, BUT I MUST ASK THAT YOU CEASE PUNCHING HIM. HE DOES NOT EVEN KNOW WHAT HE IS DOING.
YEAH, BUT SOMETHING TELLS ME HE WOULDN'T CARE EVEN IF HE DID.
KRAK
GRAB THE CHIPS, KID. WE'RE CASHING OUT.
LOOK ME UP NEXT TIME YOU'RE IN EARTH'S ORBIT, LADIES.
THEY'VE BEATEN OUR GUARDS. I TOLD YOU WE SHOULD'VE HIRED MORE SKRULLS.
GET THE THING.
YOU REMEMBER HOW MANY FINES WE HAD TO PAY THE LAST TIME WE USED THE THING?
WOULD YOU RATHER JUST STAND HERE AND LET THOSE HUMANS WALK OUT WITH EIGHTY-QUINTILLION IN CREDITS?
I'LL GET THE THING.

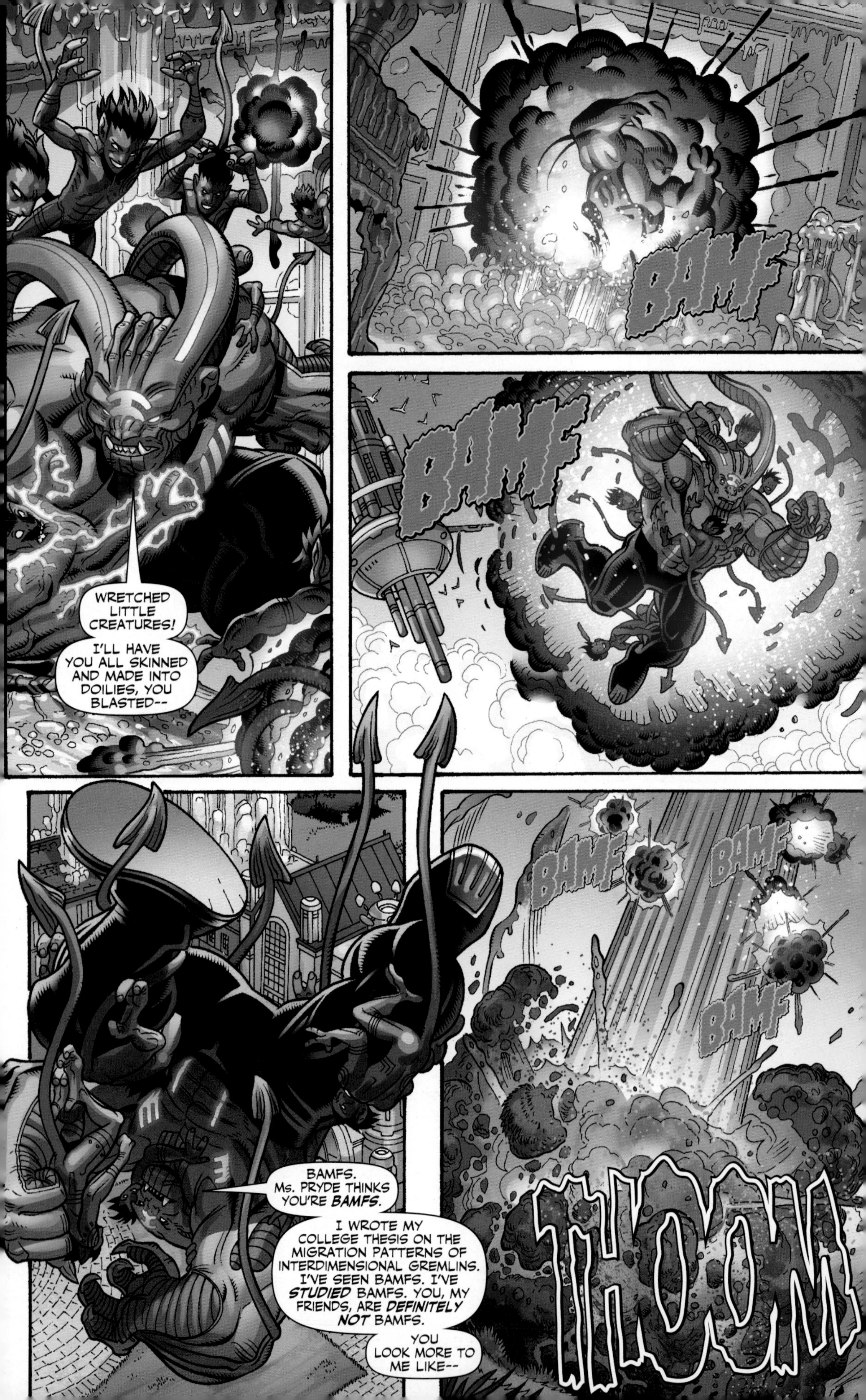

WRETCHED LITTLE CREATURES!
I'LL HAVE YOU ALL SKINNED AND MADE INTO DOILIES, YOU BLASTED--
BAMF
BAMF
BAMFS. Ms. PRYDE THINKS YOU'RE BAMFS.
I WROTE MY COLLEGE THESIS ON THE MIGRATION PATTERNS OF INTERDIMENSIONAL GREMLINS. I'VE SEEN BAMFS. I'VE STUDIED BAMFS. YOU, MY FRIENDS, ARE DEFINITELY NOT BAMFS.
YOU LOOK MORE TO ME LIKE--
BAMF
BAMF
BAMF
THOOM

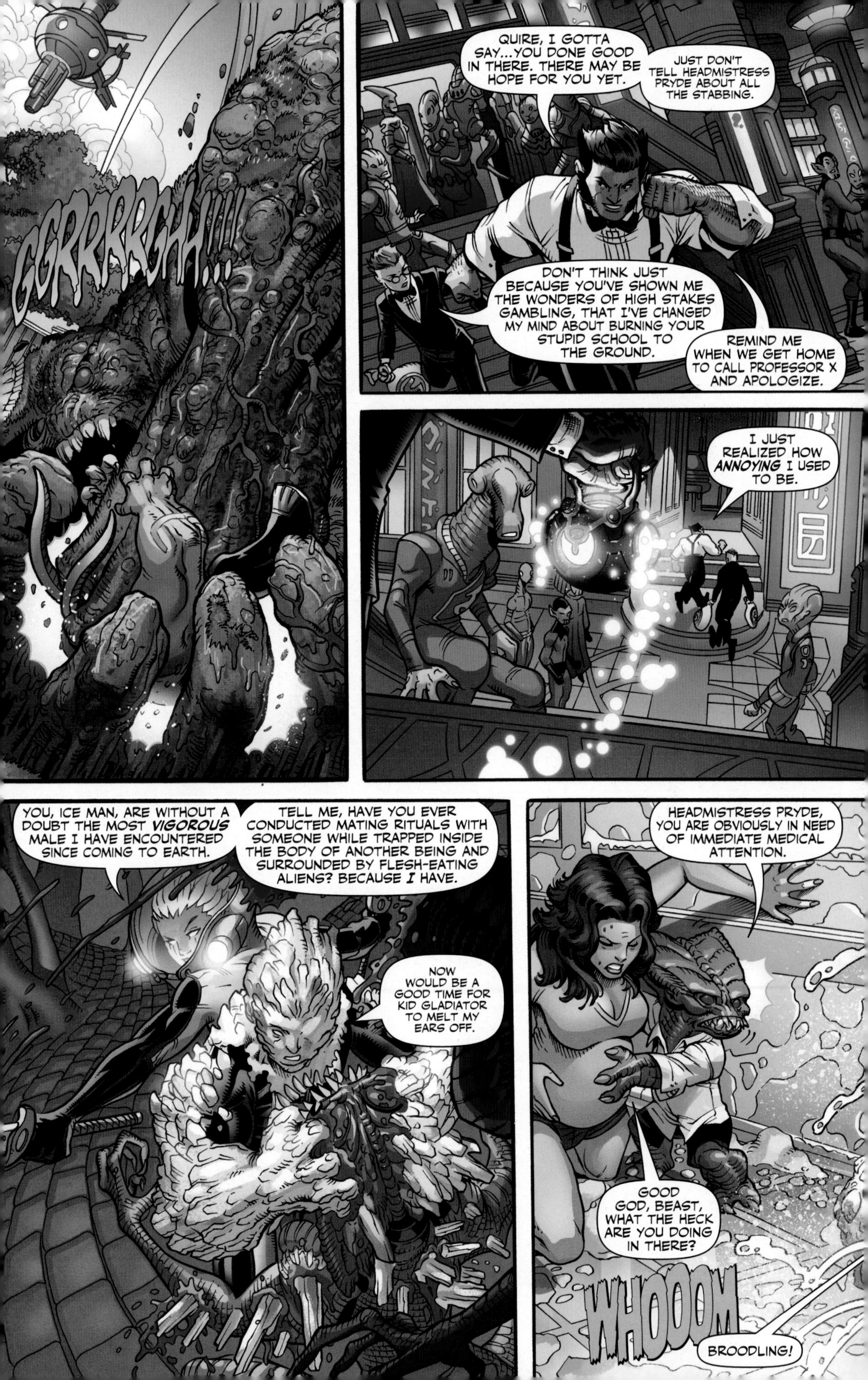
GGRRRGH!!!
QUIRE, I GOTTA SAY...YOU DONE GOOD IN THERE. THERE MAY BE HOPE FOR YOU YET.
JUST DON'T TELL HEADMISTRESS PRYDE ABOUT ALL THE STABBING.
DON'T THINK JUST BECAUSE YOU'VE SHOWN ME THE WONDERS OF HIGH STAKES GAMBLING, THAT I'VE CHANGED MY MIND ABOUT BURNING YOUR STUPID SCHOOL TO THE GROUND.
REMIND ME WHEN WE GET HOME TO CALL PROFESSOR X AND APOLOGIZE.
I JUST REALIZED HOW ANNOYING I USED TO BE.
YOU, ICE MAN, ARE WITHOUT A DOUBT THE MOST VIGOROUS MALE I HAVE ENCOUNTERED SINCE COMING TO EARTH.
TELL ME, HAVE YOU EVER CONDUCTED MATING RITUALS WITH SOMEONE WHILE TRAPPED INSIDE THE BODY OF ANOTHER BEING AND SURROUNDED BY FLESH-EATING ALIENS? BECAUSE I HAVE.
NOW WOULD BE A GOOD TIME FOR KID GLADIATOR TO MELT MY EARS OFF.
HEADMISTRESS PRYDE, YOU ARE OBVIOUSLY IN NEED OF IMMEDIATE MEDICAL ATTENTION.
GOOD GOD, BEAST, WHAT THE HECK ARE YOU DOING IN THERE?
WHOOOM
BROODLING!

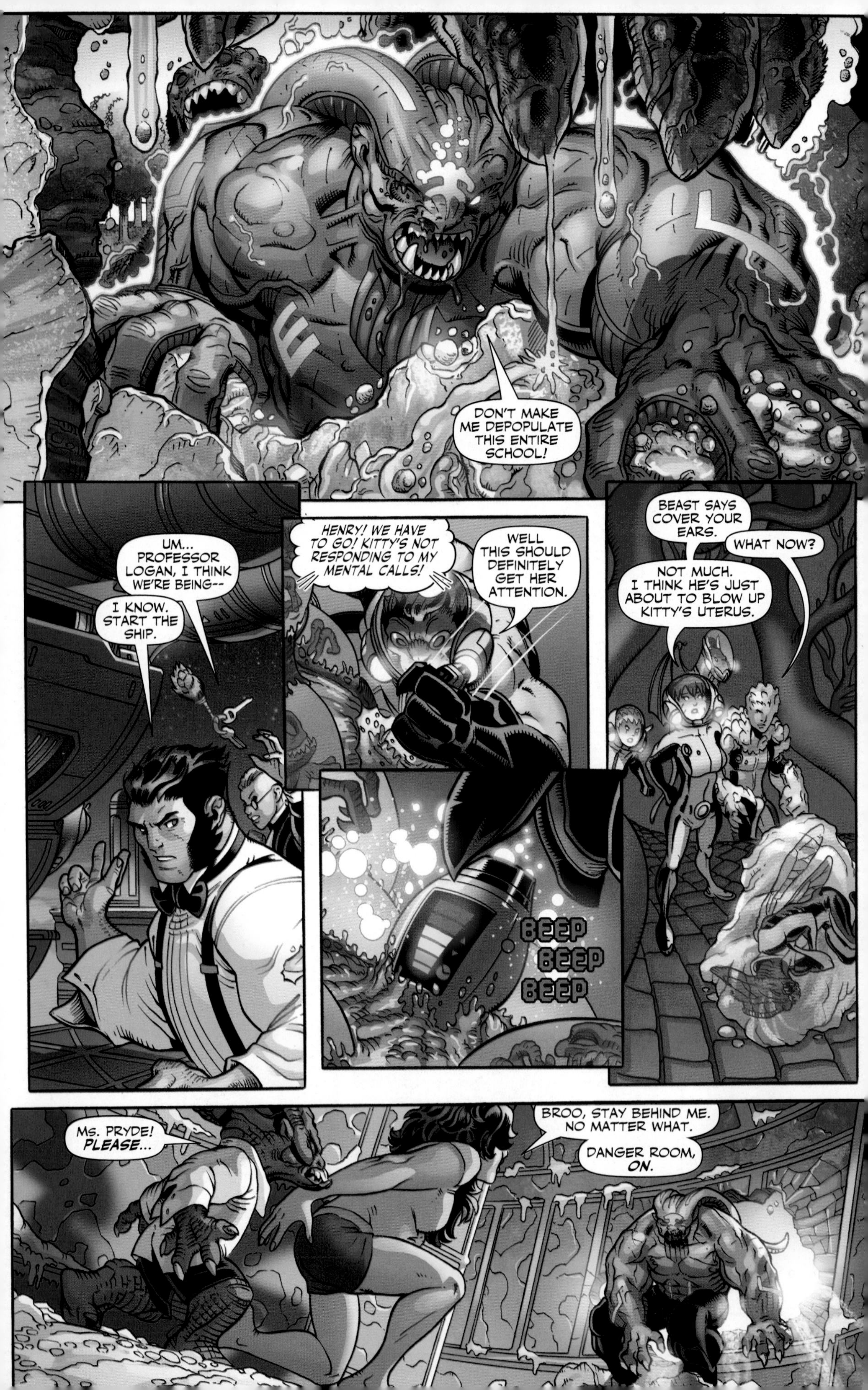
DON'T MAKE ME DEPOPULATE THIS ENTIRE SCHOOL!
UM... PROFESSOR LOGAN, I THINK WE'RE BEING--
I KNOW. START THE SHIP.
HENRY! WE HAVE TO GO! KITTY'S NOT RESPONDING TO MY MENTAL CALLS!
WELL THIS SHOULD DEFINITELY GET HER ATTENTION.
BEEP BEEP BEEP
BEAST SAYS COVER YOUR EARS.
WHAT NOW?
NOT MUCH. I THINK HE'S JUST ABOUT TO BLOW UP KITTY'S UTERUS.
Ms. PRYDE! PLEASE...
BROO, STAY BEHIND ME. NO MATTER WHAT.
DANGER ROOM, ON.

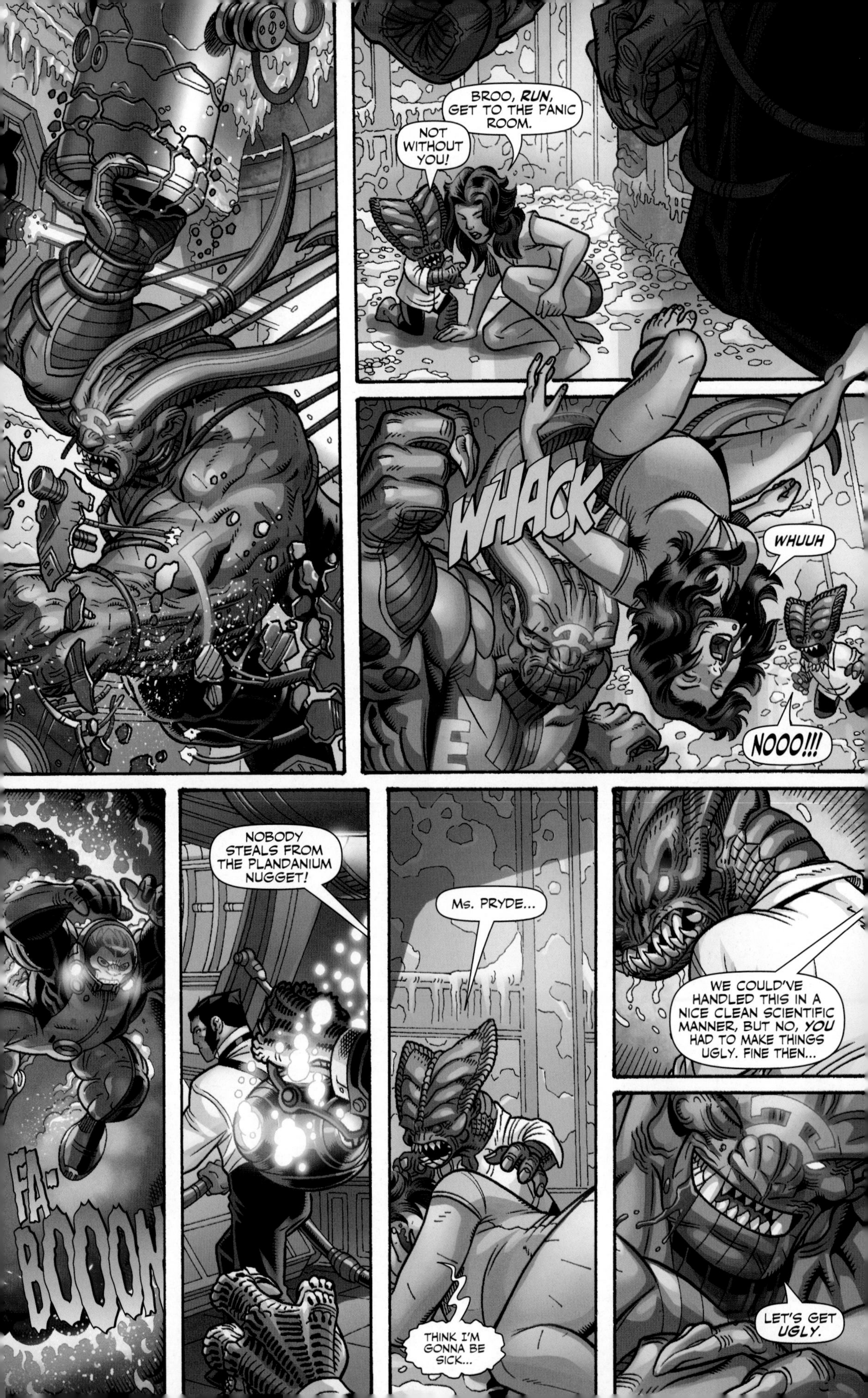
BROO, RUN, GET TO THE PANIC ROOM.
NOT WITHOUT YOU!
WHACK
WHUUH
NOOO!!!
FA-BOOOM
NOBODY STEALS FROM THE PLANDANIUM NUGGET!
Ms. PRYDE...
THINK I'M GONNA BE SICK...
WE COULD'VE HANDLED THIS IN A NICE CLEAN SCIENTIFIC MANNER, BUT NO, YOU HAD TO MAKE THINGS UGLY. FINE THEN...
LET'S GET UGLY.

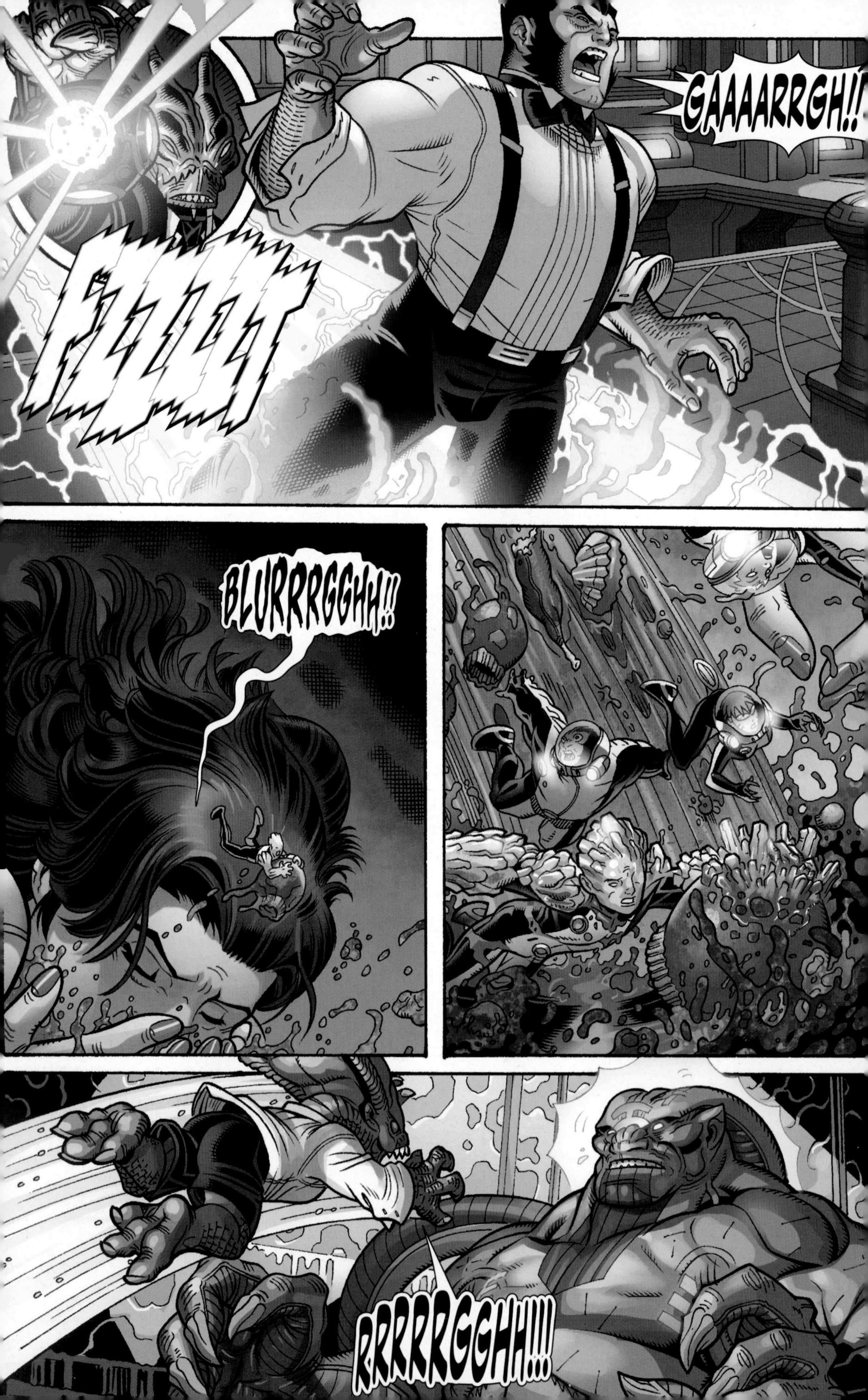
GAAAARRGH!!
FZZZT
BLURRRGGHH!!
RRRRRGGHH!!!!

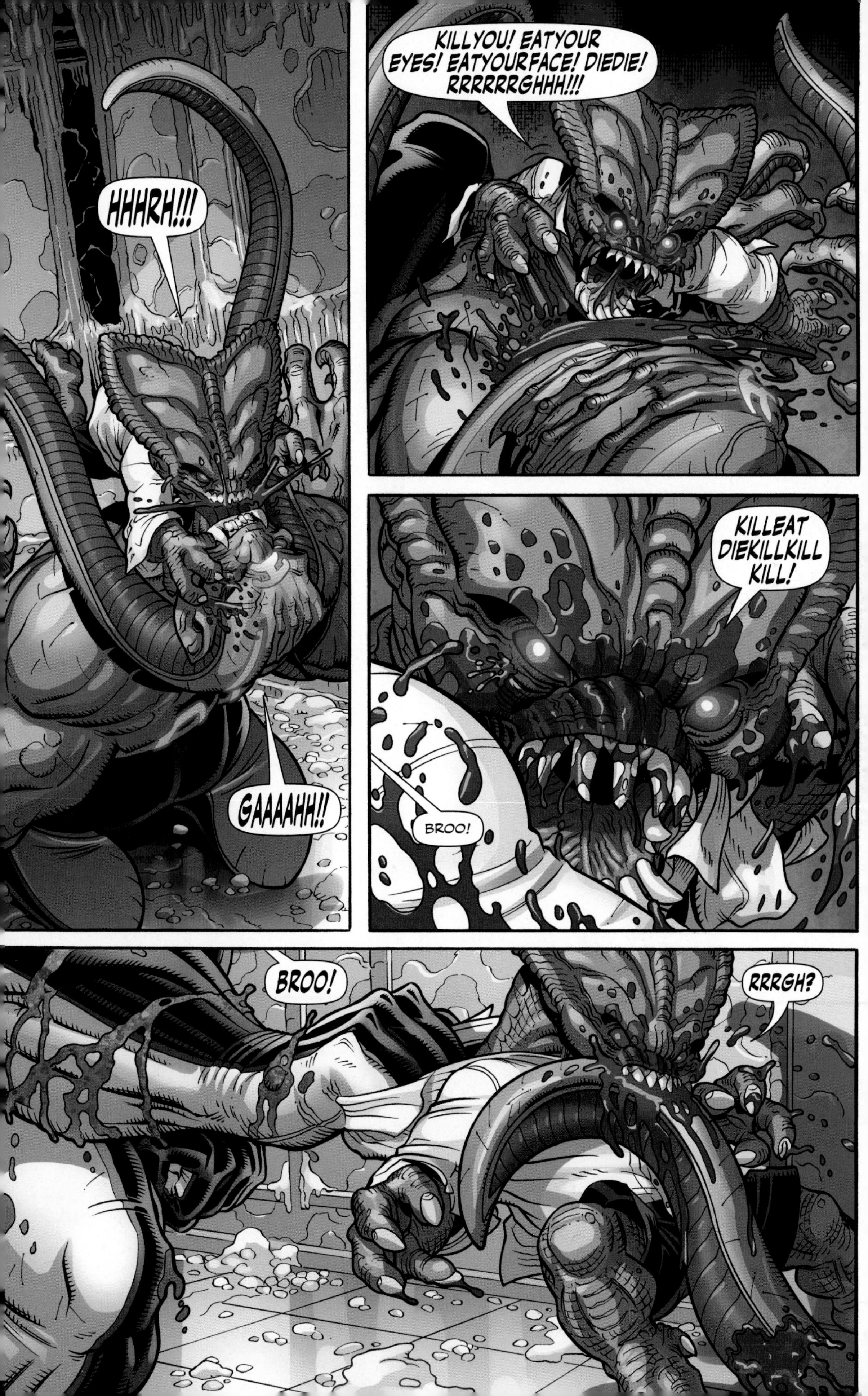
HHHRH!!!
GAAAAHH!!
KILLYOU! EATYOUR EYES! EATYOURFACE! DIEDIE! RRRRRRGHHH!!!
KILLEAT DIEKILLKILL KILL!
BROO!
BROO!
RRRGH?

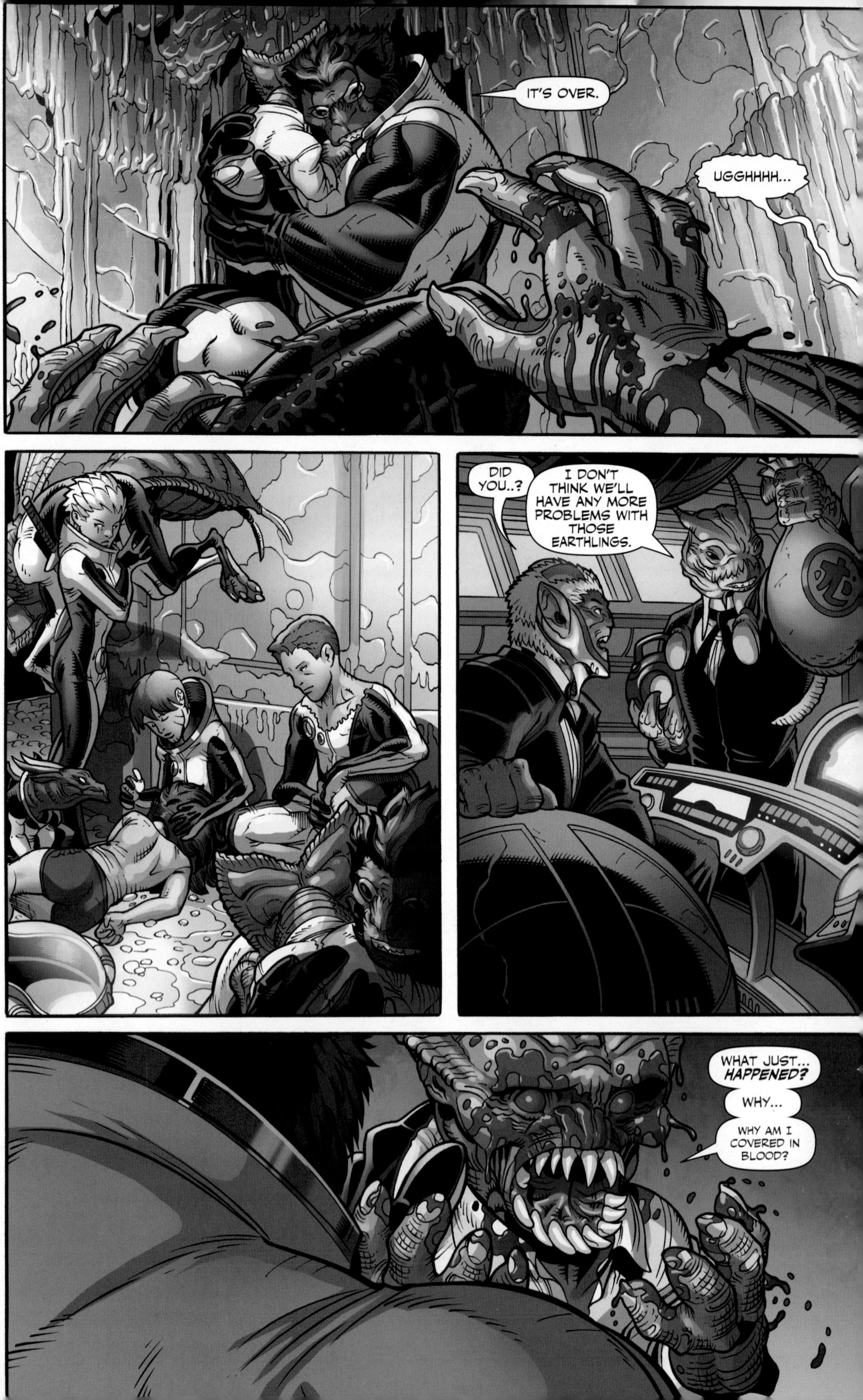
IT'S OVER.
UGGHHHH...
DID YOU..?
I DON'T THINK WE'LL HAVE ANY MORE PROBLEMS WITH THOSE EARTHLINGS.
WHAT JUST... HAPPENED?
WHY...
WHY AM I COVERED IN BLOOD?

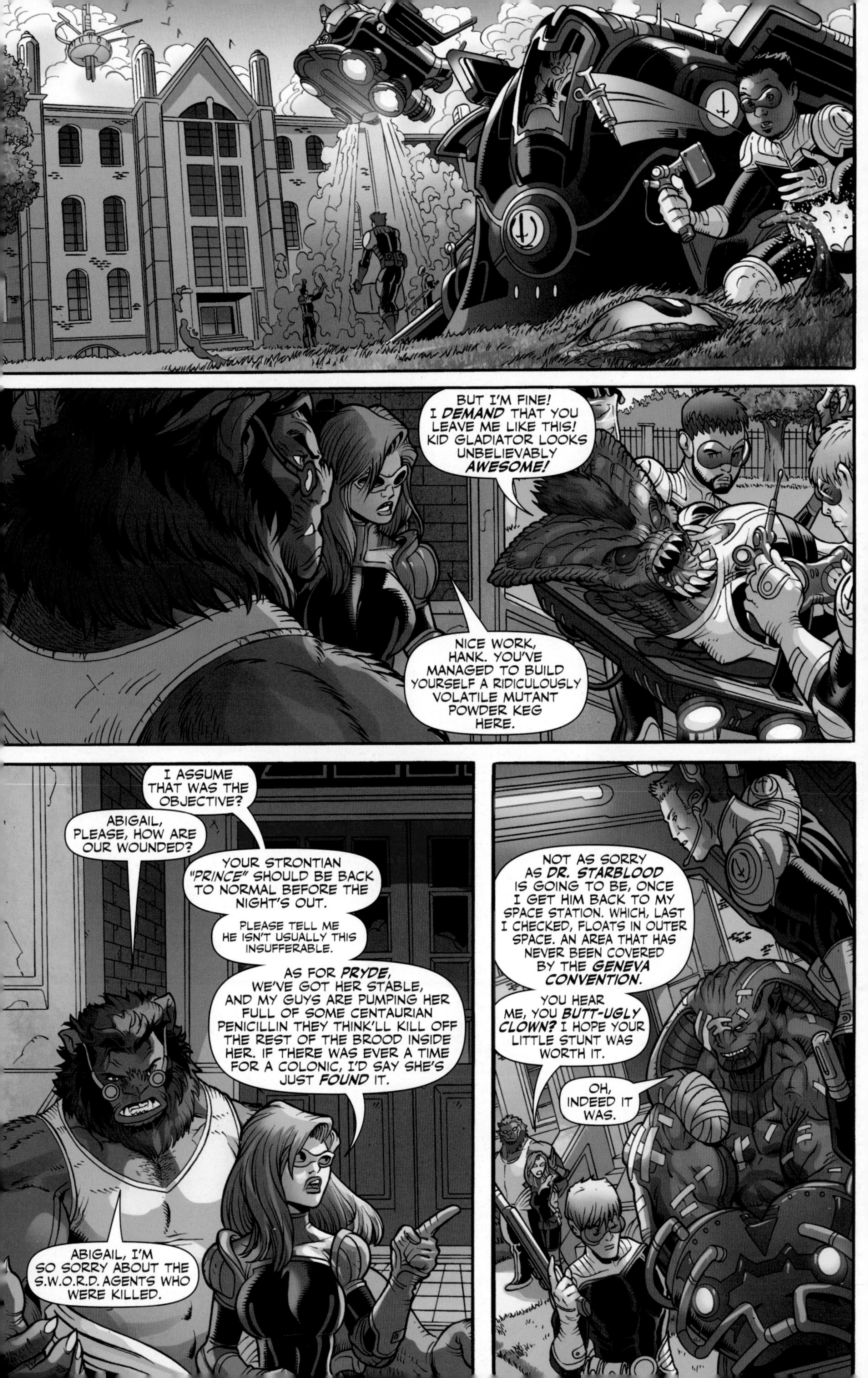
BUT I'M FINE! I DEMAND THAT YOU LEAVE ME LIKE THIS! KID GLADIATOR LOOKS UNBELIEVABLY AWESOME!
NICE WORK, HANK. YOU'VE MANAGED TO BUILD YOURSELF A RIDICULOUSLY VOLATILE MUTANT POWDER KEG HERE.
I ASSUME THAT WAS THE OBJECTIVE?
ABIGAIL, PLEASE, HOW ARE OUR WOUNDED?
YOUR STRONTIAN "PRINCE" SHOULD BE BACK TO NORMAL BEFORE THE NIGHT'S OUT.
PLEASE TELL ME HE ISN'T USUALLY THIS INSUFFERABLE.
AS FOR PRYDE, WE'VE GOT HER STABLE, AND MY GUYS ARE PUMPING HER FULL OF SOME CENTAURIAN PENICILLIN THEY THINK'LL KILL OFF THE REST OF THE BROOD INSIDE HER. IF THERE WAS EVER A TIME FOR A COLONIC, I'D SAY SHE'S JUST FOUND IT.
ABIGAIL, I'M SO SORRY ABOUT THE S.W.O.R.D. AGENTS WHO WERE KILLED.
NOT AS SORRY AS DR. STARBLOOD IS GOING TO BE, ONCE I GET HIM BACK TO MY SPACE STATION. WHICH, LAST I CHECKED, FLOATS IN OUTER SPACE. AN AREA THAT HAS NEVER BEEN COVERED BY THE GENEVA CONVENTION.
YOU HEAR ME, YOU BUTT-UGLY CLOWN? I HOPE YOUR LITTLE STUNT WAS WORTH IT.
OH, INDEED IT WAS.

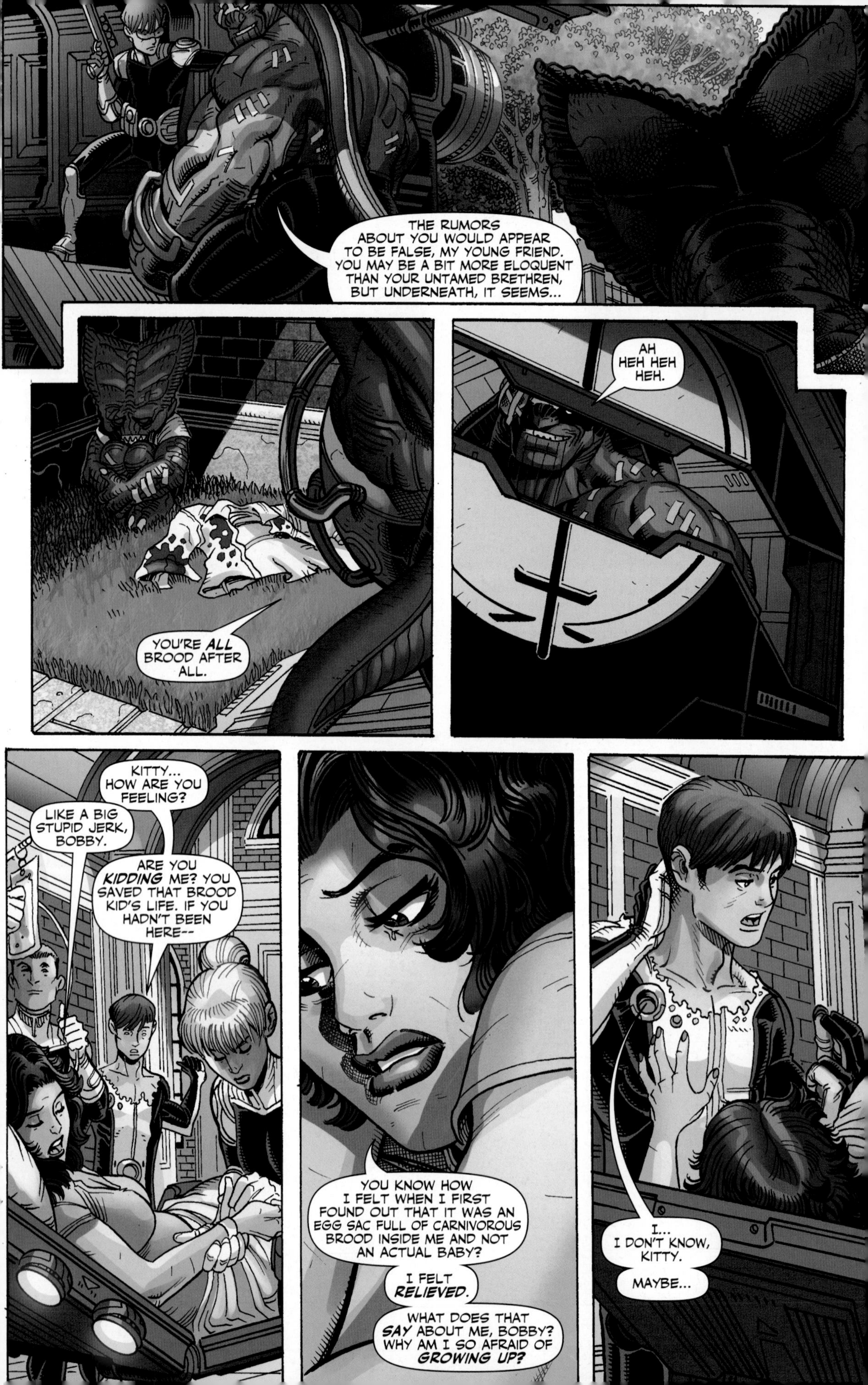
THE RUMORS ABOUT YOU WOULD APPEAR TO BE FALSE, MY YOUNG FRIEND. YOU MAY BE A BIT MORE ELOQUENT THAN YOUR UNTAMED BRETHREN, BUT UNDERNEATH, IT SEEMS...
YOU'RE ALL BROOD AFTER ALL.
AH HEH HEH HEH.
KITTY... HOW ARE YOU FEELING?
LIKE A BIG STUPID JERK, BOBBY.
ARE YOU KIDDING ME? YOU SAVED THAT BROOD KID'S LIFE. IF YOU HADN'T BEEN HERE--
YOU KNOW HOW I FELT WHEN I FIRST FOUND OUT THAT IT WAS AN EGG SAC FULL OF CARNIVOROUS BROOD INSIDE ME AND NOT AN ACTUAL BABY?
I FELT RELIEVED.
WHAT DOES THAT SAY ABOUT ME, BOBBY? WHY AM I SO AFRAID OF GROWING UP?
I... I DON'T KNOW, KITTY.
MAYBE...

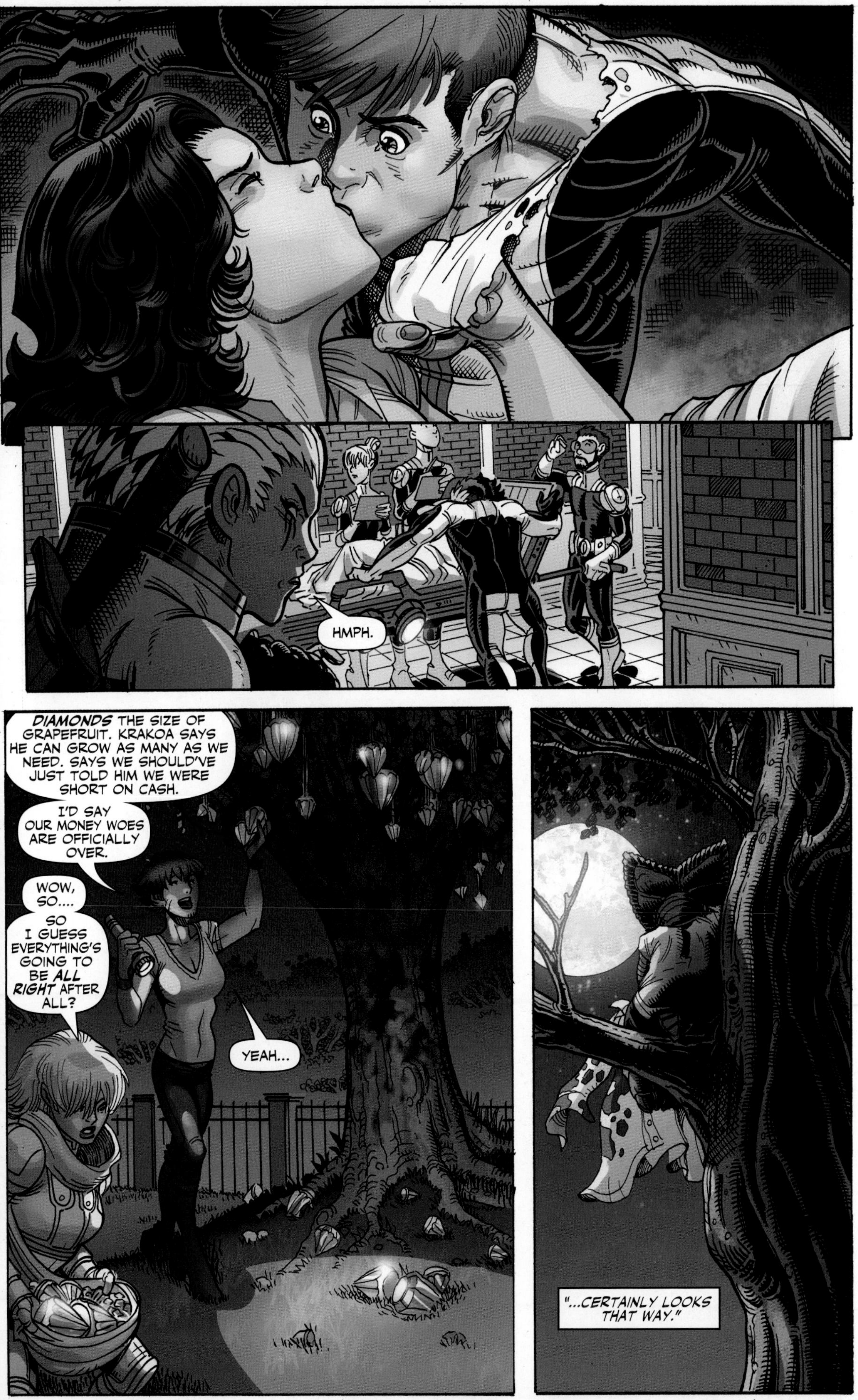
HMPH.
DIAMONDS THE SIZE OF GRAPEFRUIT. KRAKOA SAYS HE CAN GROW AS MANY AS WE NEED. SAYS WE SHOULD'VE JUST TOLD HIM WE WERE SHORT ON CASH.
I'D SAY OUR MONEY WOES ARE OFFICIALLY OVER.
WOW, SO....
SO I GUESS EVERYTHING'S GOING TO BE ALL RIGHT AFTER ALL?
YEAH...
"...CERTAINLY LOOKS THAT WAY."

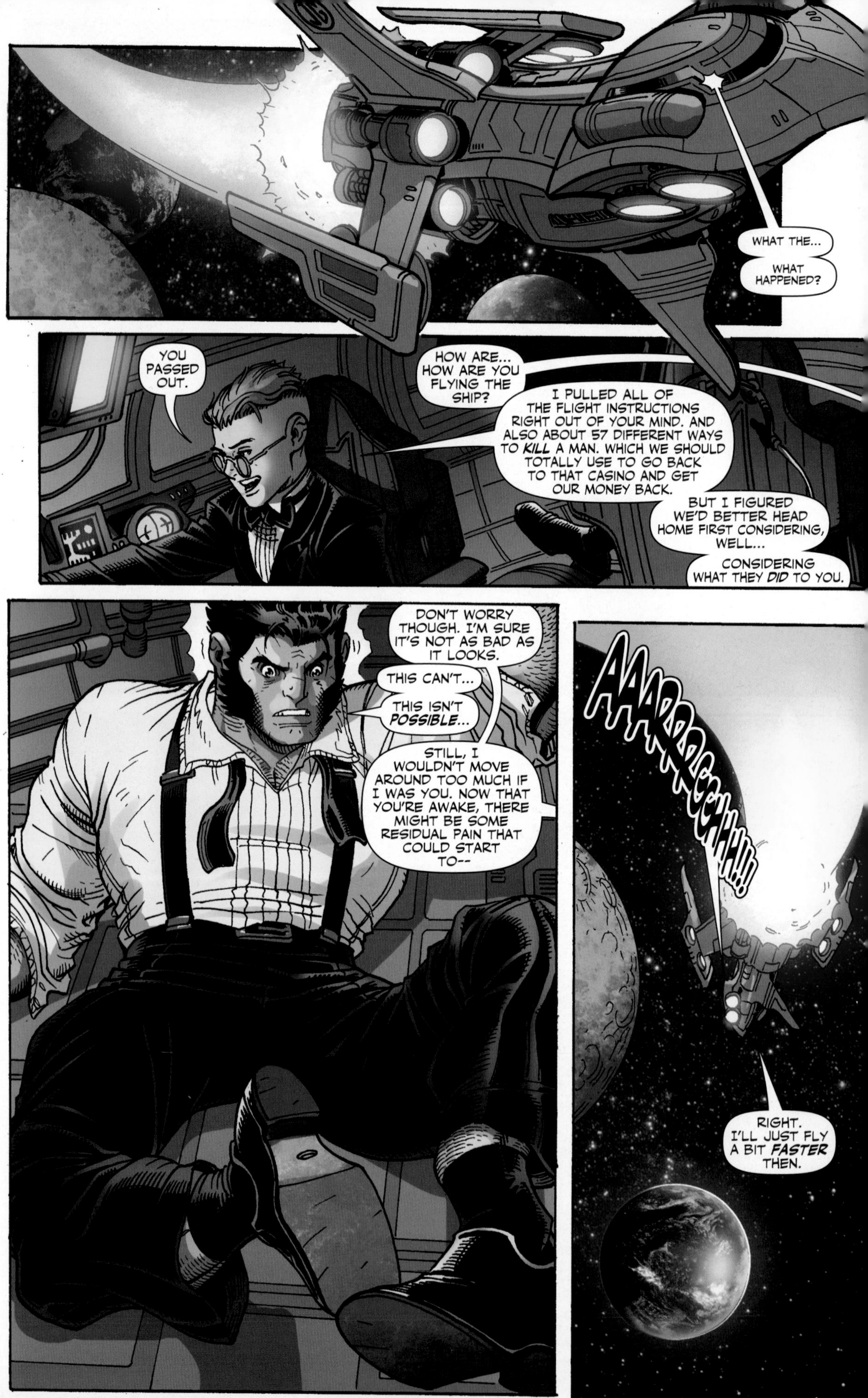
WHAT THE...
WHAT HAPPENED?
YOU PASSED OUT.
HOW ARE... HOW ARE YOU FLYING THE SHIP?
I PULLED ALL OF THE FLIGHT INSTRUCTIONS RIGHT OUT OF YOUR MIND. AND ALSO ABOUT 57 DIFFERENT WAYS TO KILL A MAN. WHICH WE SHOULD TOTALLY USE TO GO BACK TO THAT CASINO AND GET OUR MONEY BACK.
BUT I FIGURED WE'D BETTER HEAD HOME FIRST CONSIDERING, WELL...
CONSIDERING WHAT THEY DID TO YOU.
DON'T WORRY THOUGH. I'M SURE IT'S NOT AS BAD AS IT LOOKS.
THIS CAN'T...
THIS ISN'T POSSIBLE...
STILL, I WOULDN'T MOVE AROUND TOO MUCH IF I WAS YOU. NOW THAT YOU'RE AWAKE, THERE MIGHT BE SOME RESIDUAL PAIN THAT COULD START TO--
AAARRRGGHHH!!!
RIGHT. I'LL JUST FLY A BIT FASTER THEN.

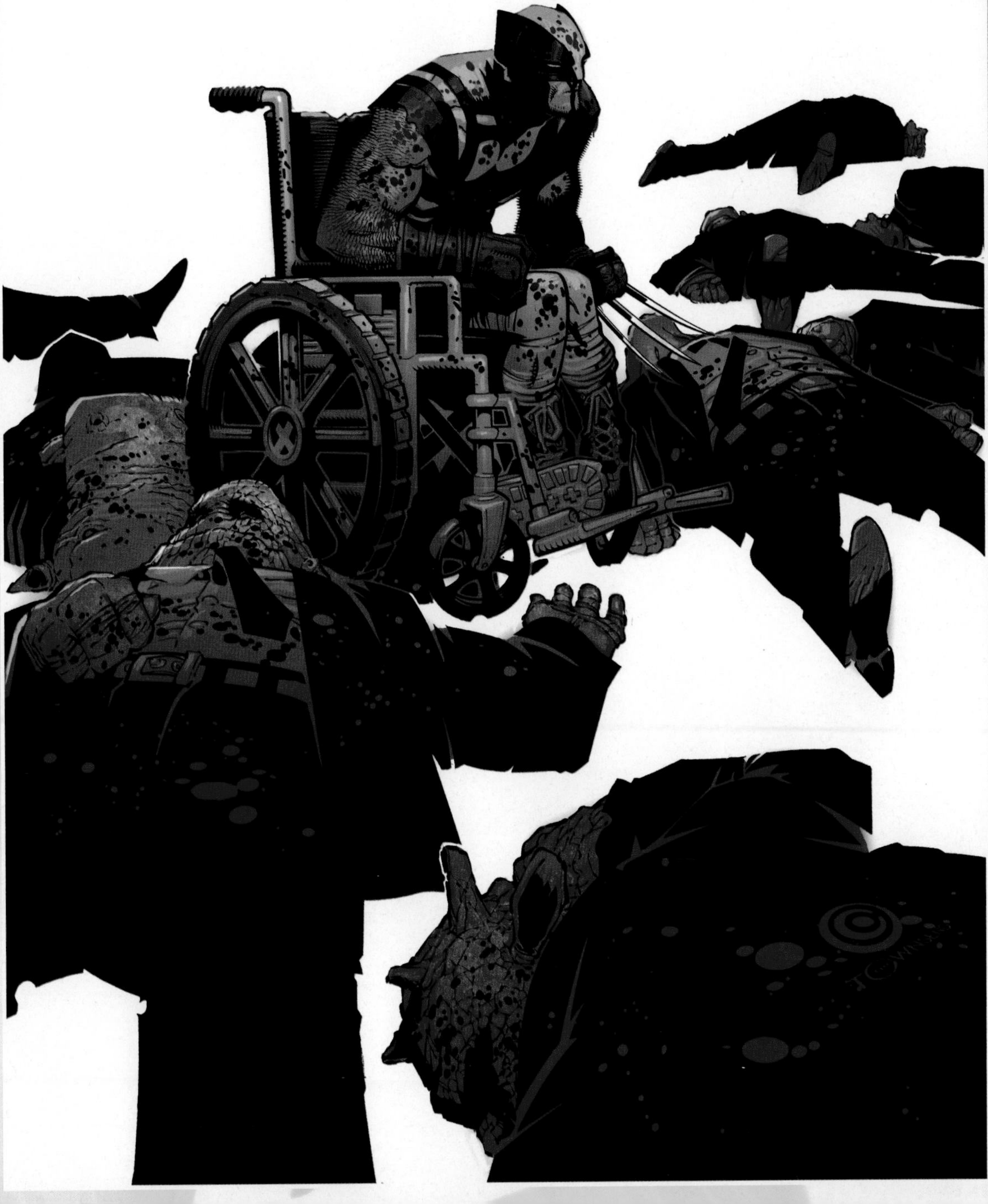

CORPORATE HEADQUARTERS OF KILGORE ARMS, THE C.E.O.'S PRIVATE PENTHOUSE.
PRETEND I'M THE THING YOU HATE *MOST* IN THE WORLD.
I'M *WOLVERINE'S SCHOOL*.
AND YOU WANNA SHUT ME DOWN FOR GOOD.
DO YOUR WORST...

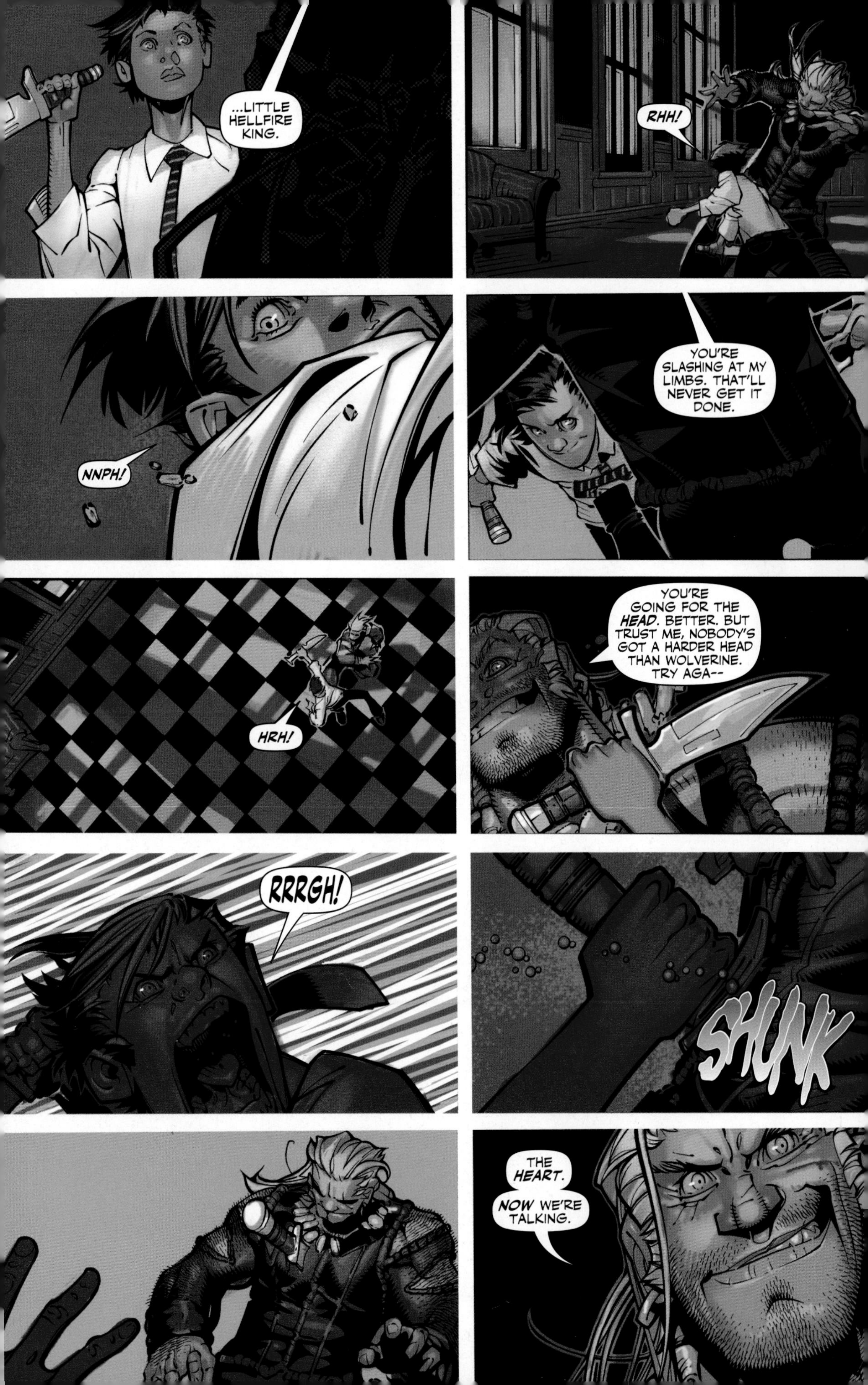

...LITTLE HELLFIRE KING.
RHH!
NNPH!
YOU'RE SLASHING AT MY LIMBS. THAT'LL NEVER GET IT DONE.
HRH!
YOU'RE GOING FOR THE HEAD. BETTER. BUT TRUST ME, NOBODY'S GOT A HARDER HEAD THAN WOLVERINE. TRY AGA--
RRRGH!
SHUNK
THE HEART.
NOW WE'RE TALKING.

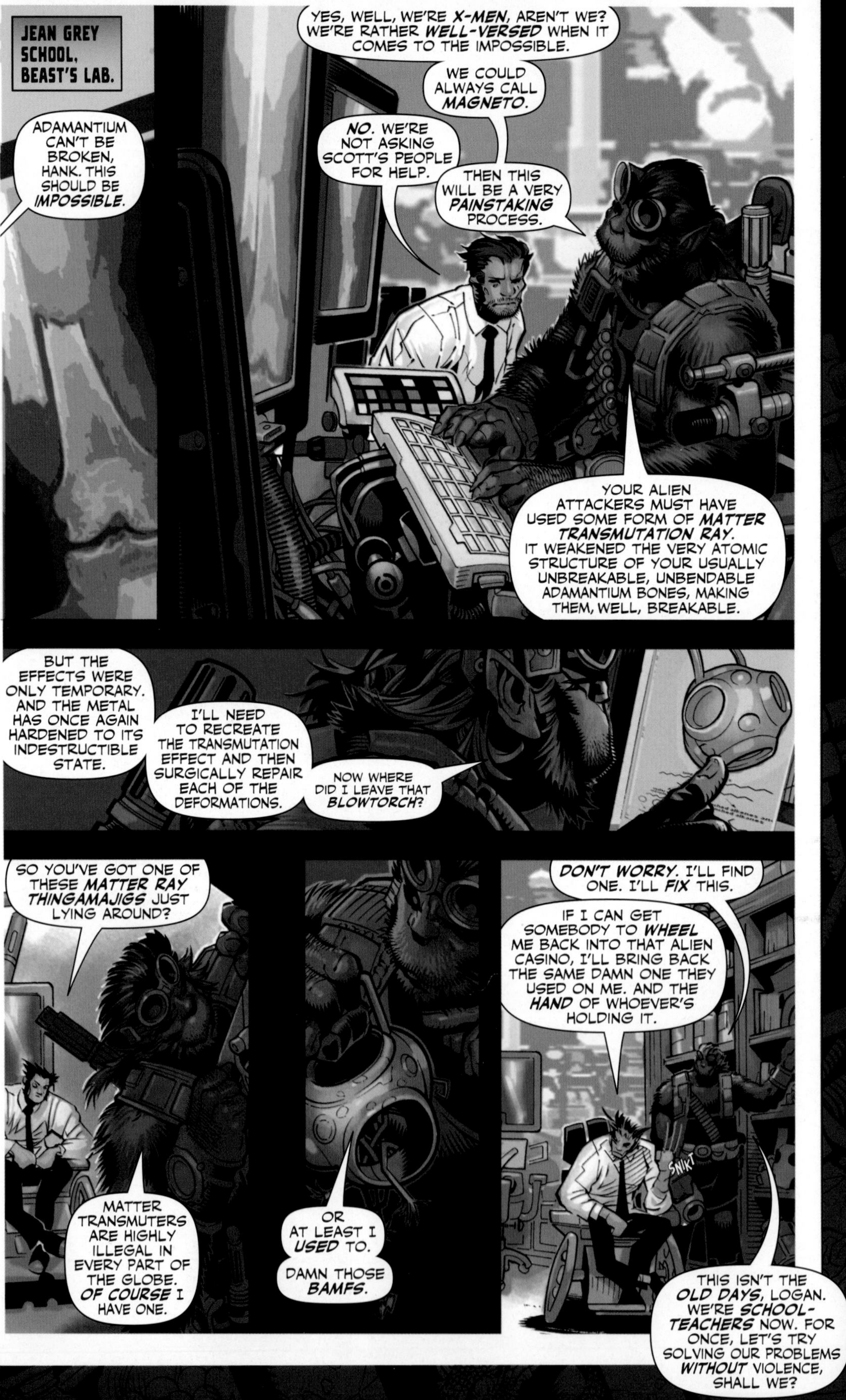

JEAN GREY SCHOOL, BEAST'S LAB.
ADAMANTIUM CAN'T BE BROKEN, HANK. THIS SHOULD BE IMPOSSIBLE.
YES, WELL, WE'RE X-MEN, AREN'T WE? WE'RE RATHER WELL-VERSED WHEN IT COMES TO THE IMPOSSIBLE.
WE COULD ALWAYS CALL MAGNETO.
NO. WE'RE NOT ASKING SCOTT'S PEOPLE FOR HELP.
THEN THIS WILL BE A VERY PAINSTAKING PROCESS.
YOUR ALIEN ATTACKERS MUST HAVE USED SOME FORM OF MATTER TRANSMUTATION RAY. IT WEAKENED THE VERY ATOMIC STRUCTURE OF YOUR USUALLY UNBREAKABLE, UNBENDABLE ADAMANTIUM BONES, MAKING THEM, WELL, BREAKABLE.
BUT THE EFFECTS WERE ONLY TEMPORARY. AND THE METAL HAS ONCE AGAIN HARDENED TO ITS INDESTRUCTIBLE STATE.
I'LL NEED TO RECREATE THE TRANSMUTATION EFFECT AND THEN SURGICALLY REPAIR EACH OF THE DEFORMATIONS.
NOW WHERE DID I LEAVE THAT BLOWTORCH?
SO YOU'VE GOT ONE OF THESE MATTER RAY THINGAMAJIGS JUST LYING AROUND?
MATTER TRANSMUTERS ARE HIGHLY ILLEGAL IN EVERY PART OF THE GLOBE. OF COURSE I HAVE ONE.
OR AT LEAST I USED TO.
DAMN THOSE BAMFS.
DON'T WORRY. I'LL FIND ONE. I'LL FIX THIS.
IF I CAN GET SOMEBODY TO WHEEL ME BACK INTO THAT ALIEN CASINO, I'LL BRING BACK THE SAME DAMN ONE THEY USED ON ME. AND THE HAND OF WHOEVER'S HOLDING IT.
SNIKT
THIS ISN'T THE OLD DAYS, LOGAN. WE'RE SCHOOL-TEACHERS NOW. FOR ONCE, LET'S TRY SOLVING OUR PROBLEMS WITHOUT VIOLENCE, SHALL WE?

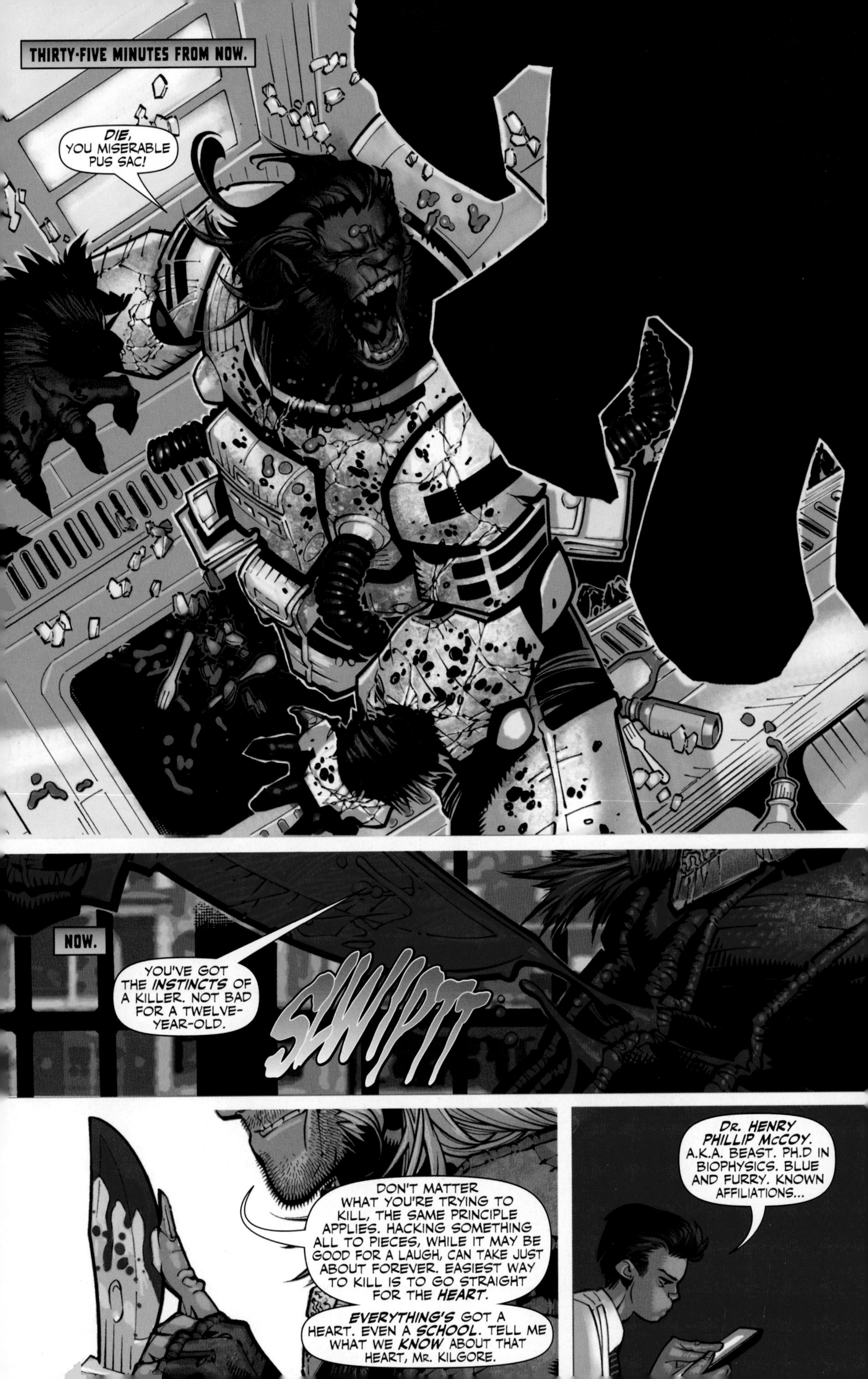
THIRTY-FIVE MINUTES FROM NOW.
DIE, YOU MISERABLE PUS SAC!
NOW.
YOU'VE GOT THE INSTINCTS OF A KILLER. NOT BAD FOR A TWELVE-YEAR-OLD.
SLWIPTT
DON'T MATTER WHAT YOU'RE TRYING TO KILL, THE SAME PRINCIPLE APPLIES. HACKING SOMETHING ALL TO PIECES, WHILE IT MAY BE GOOD FOR A LAUGH, CAN TAKE JUST ABOUT FOREVER. EASIEST WAY TO KILL IS TO GO STRAIGHT FOR THE HEART.
EVERYTHING'S GOT A HEART. EVEN A SCHOOL. TELL ME WHAT WE KNOW ABOUT THAT HEART, MR. KILGORE.
DR. HENRY PHILLIP McCOY. A.K.A. BEAST. PH.D IN BIOPHYSICS. BLUE AND FURRY. KNOWN AFFILIATIONS...

HENRY TO TOWER. BEAST FORCE ONE HAS LIFTOFF.

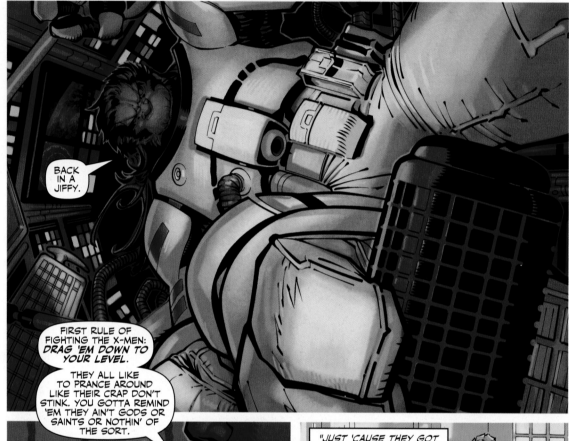

BACK IN A JIFFY.

FIRST RULE OF FIGHTING THE X-MEN: *DRAG 'EM DOWN TO YOUR LEVEL.*

THEY ALL LIKE TO PRANCE AROUND LIKE THEIR CRAP DON'T STINK. YOU GOTTA REMIND 'EM THEY AIN'T GODS OR SAINTS OR NOTHIN' OF THE SORT.

"JUST 'CAUSE THEY GOT WINGS, THAT DON'T MAKE 'EM ANGELS.

"ALL THEY ARE IS BAGS OF MEAT AND BONE JUST LIKE THE *REST* OF US. THEY CAN BLEED. AND YOU BEST BELIEVE THEY CAN BE *BROKEN.*"

EVEN A SMARTY-ART FANCY PANTS LIKE DR. HENRY PHILLIP McCOY, PH.D.

NOW...READ THAT PART AGAIN ABOUT "*KNOWN AFFILIATIONS.*"

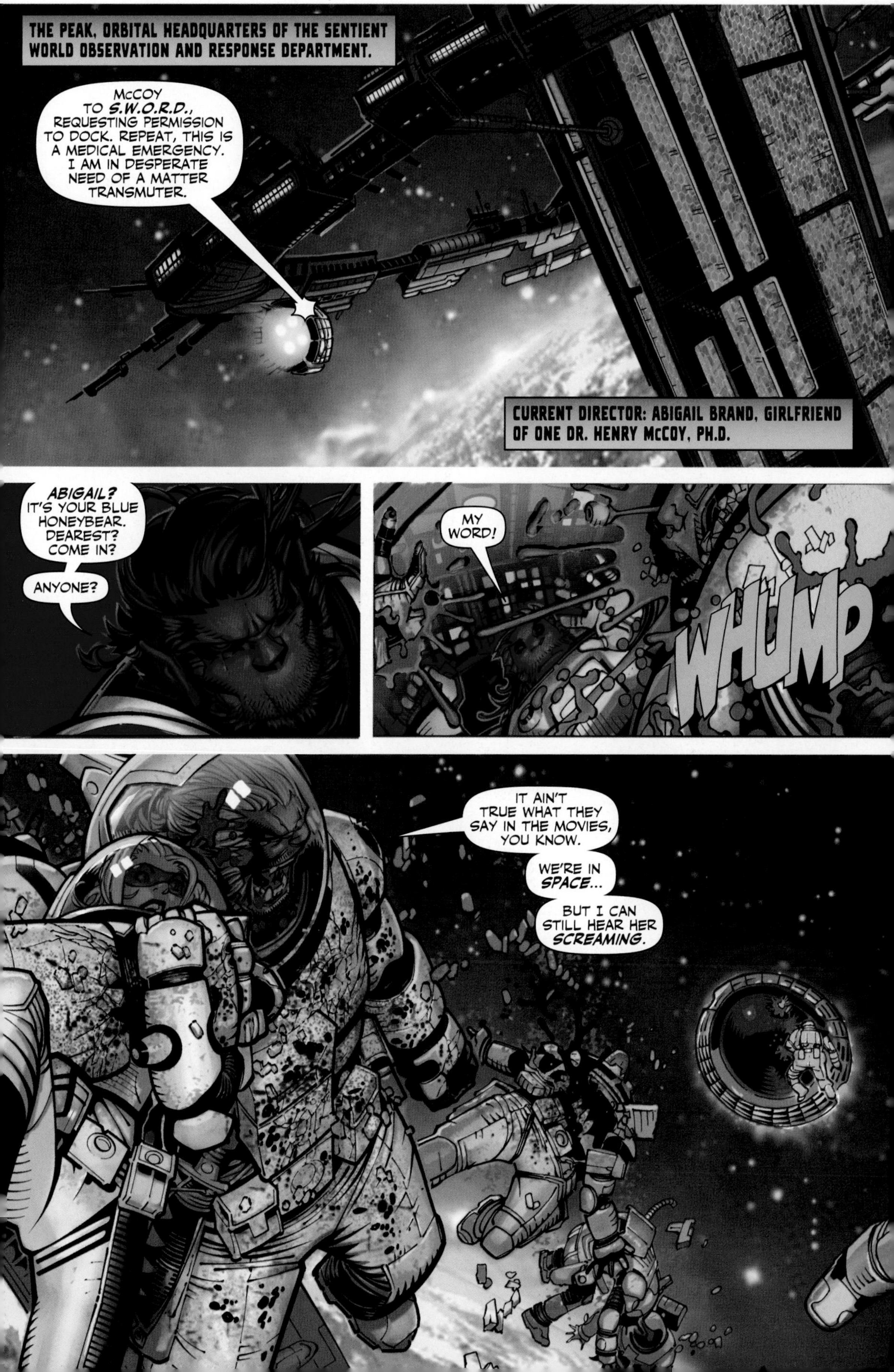

THE PEAK, ORBITAL HEADQUARTERS OF THE SENTIENT WORLD OBSERVATION AND RESPONSE DEPARTMENT.
McCOY TO S.W.O.R.D., REQUESTING PERMISSION TO DOCK. REPEAT, THIS IS A MEDICAL EMERGENCY. I AM IN DESPERATE NEED OF A MATTER TRANSMUTER.
CURRENT DIRECTOR: ABIGAIL BRAND, GIRLFRIEND OF ONE DR. HENRY McCOY, PH.D.
ABIGAIL? IT'S YOUR BLUE HONEYBEAR. DEAREST? COME IN?
ANYONE?
MY WORD!
WHUMP
IT AIN'T TRUE WHAT THEY SAY IN THE MOVIES, YOU KNOW.
WE'RE IN SPACE...
BUT I CAN STILL HEAR HER SCREAMING.

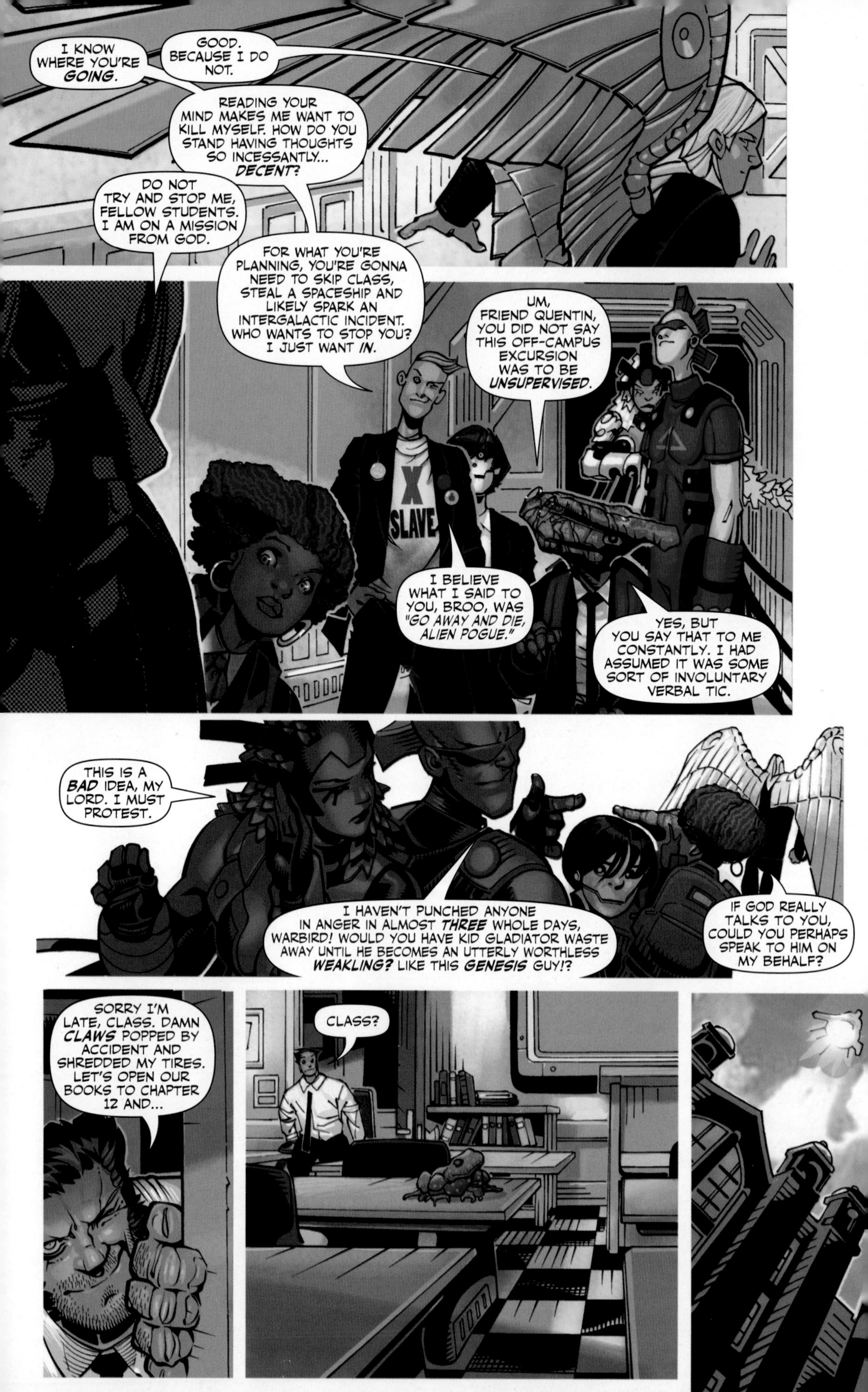
I KNOW WHERE YOU'RE *GOING.*
GOOD. BECAUSE I DO NOT.
READING YOUR MIND MAKES ME WANT TO KILL MYSELF. HOW DO YOU STAND HAVING THOUGHTS SO INCESSANTLY... *DECENT?*
DO NOT TRY AND STOP ME, FELLOW STUDENTS. I AM ON A MISSION FROM GOD.
FOR WHAT YOU'RE PLANNING, YOU'RE GONNA NEED TO SKIP CLASS, STEAL A SPACESHIP AND LIKELY SPARK AN INTERGALACTIC INCIDENT. WHO WANTS TO STOP YOU? I JUST WANT *IN.*
UM, FRIEND QUENTIN, YOU DID NOT SAY THIS OFF-CAMPUS EXCURSION WAS TO BE *UNSUPERVISED.*
X SLAVE
I BELIEVE WHAT I SAID TO YOU, BROO, WAS *"GO AWAY AND DIE, ALIEN POGUE."*
YES, BUT YOU SAY THAT TO ME CONSTANTLY. I HAD ASSUMED IT WAS SOME SORT OF INVOLUNTARY VERBAL TIC.
THIS IS A *BAD* IDEA, MY LORD. I MUST PROTEST.
I HAVEN'T PUNCHED ANYONE IN ANGER IN ALMOST *THREE* WHOLE DAYS, WARBIRD! WOULD YOU HAVE KID GLADIATOR WASTE AWAY UNTIL HE BECOMES AN UTTERLY WORTHLESS *WEAKLING?* LIKE THIS *GENESIS* GUY!?
IF GOD REALLY TALKS TO YOU, COULD YOU PERHAPS SPEAK TO HIM ON MY BEHALF?
SORRY I'M LATE, CLASS. DAMN *CLAWS* POPPED BY ACCIDENT AND SHREDDED MY TIRES. LET'S OPEN OUR BOOKS TO CHAPTER 12 AND...
CLASS?

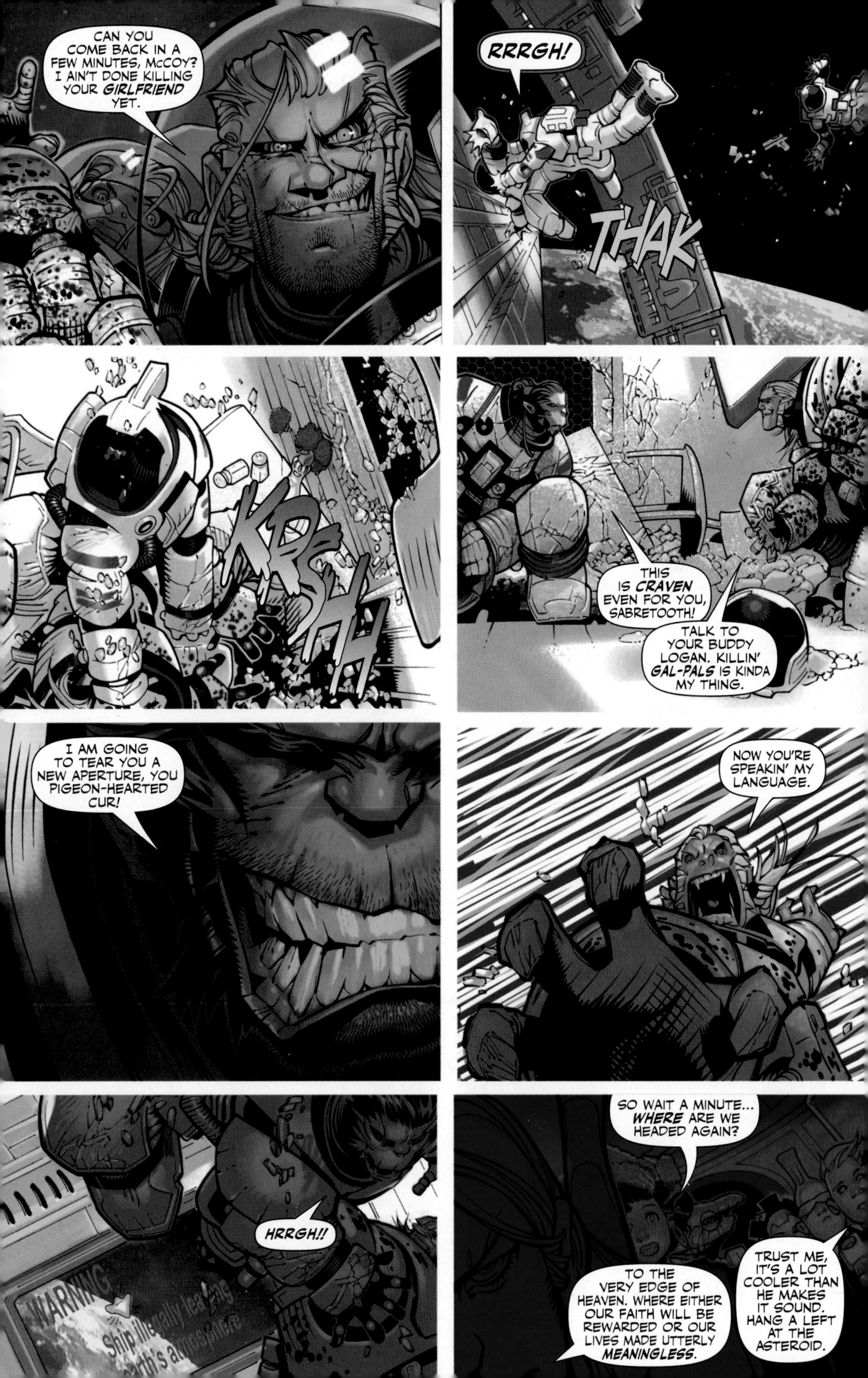
CAN YOU COME BACK IN A FEW MINUTES, McCOY? I AIN'T DONE KILLING YOUR *GIRLFRIEND* YET.
RRRGH!
THAK
KRSHH
THIS IS *CRAVEN* EVEN FOR YOU, SABRETOOTH!
TALK TO YOUR BUDDY LOGAN. KILLIN' *GAL-PALS* IS KINDA MY THING.
I AM GOING TO TEAR YOU A NEW APERTURE, YOU PIGEON-HEARTED CUR!
NOW YOU'RE SPEAKIN' MY LANGUAGE.
HRRGH!!
WARNING
SO WAIT A MINUTE... *WHERE* ARE WE HEADED AGAIN?
TO THE VERY EDGE OF HEAVEN. WHERE EITHER OUR FAITH WILL BE REWARDED OR OUR LIVES MADE UTTERLY *MEANINGLESS*.
TRUST ME, IT'S A LOT COOLER THAN HE MAKES IT SOUND. HANG A LEFT AT THE ASTEROID.

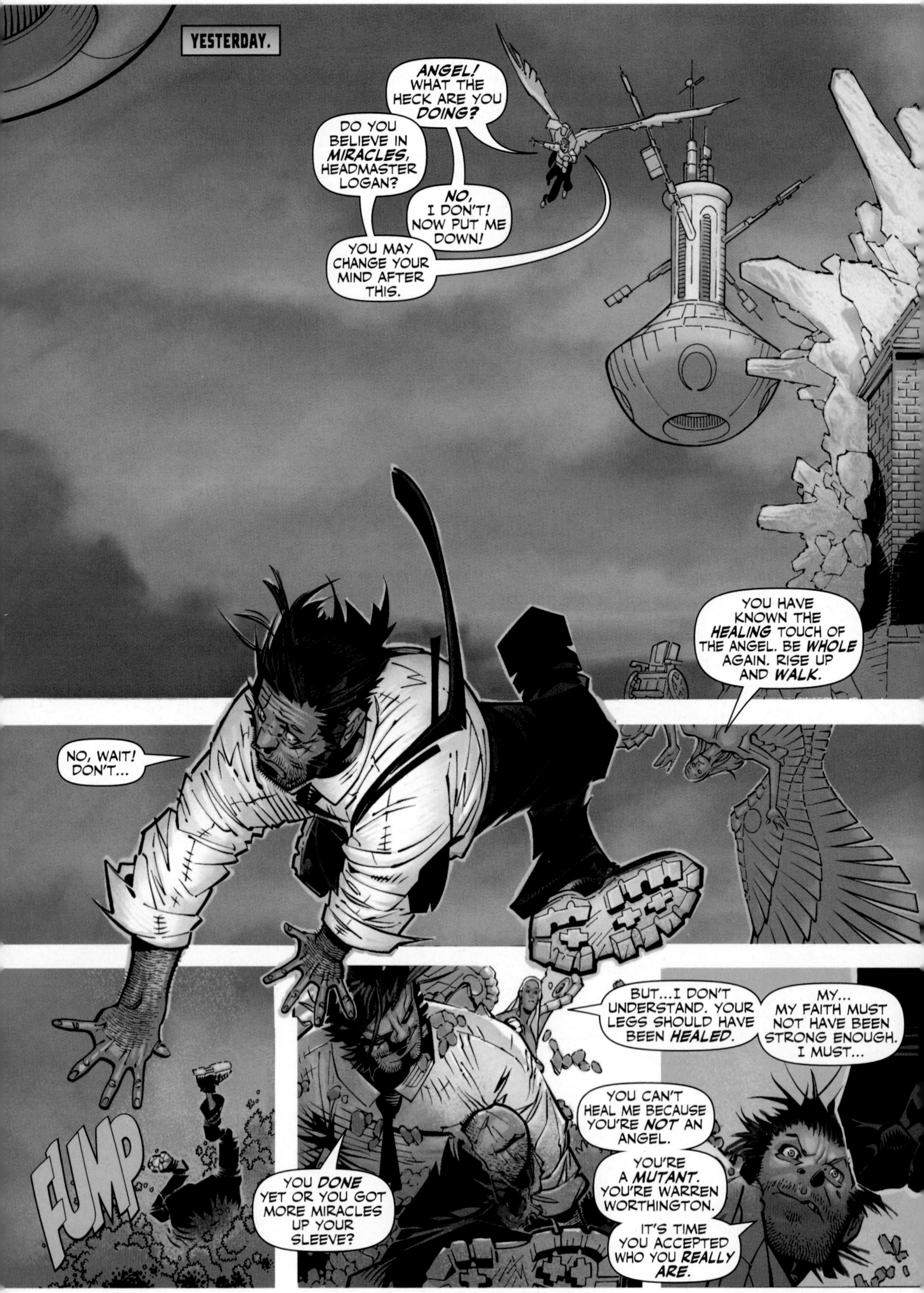
YESTERDAY.
ANGEL! WHAT THE HECK ARE YOU DOING?
DO YOU BELIEVE IN MIRACLES, HEADMASTER LOGAN?
NO, I DON'T! NOW PUT ME DOWN!
YOU MAY CHANGE YOUR MIND AFTER THIS.
YOU HAVE KNOWN THE HEALING TOUCH OF THE ANGEL. BE WHOLE AGAIN. RISE UP AND WALK.
NO, WAIT! DON'T...
FUMP
BUT...I DON'T UNDERSTAND. YOUR LEGS SHOULD HAVE BEEN HEALED.
MY... MY FAITH MUST NOT HAVE BEEN STRONG ENOUGH. I MUST...
YOU DONE YET OR YOU GOT MORE MIRACLES UP YOUR SLEEVE?
YOU CAN'T HEAL ME BECAUSE YOU'RE NOT AN ANGEL.
YOU'RE A MUTANT. YOU'RE WARREN WORTHINGTON.
IT'S TIME YOU ACCEPTED WHO YOU REALLY ARE.

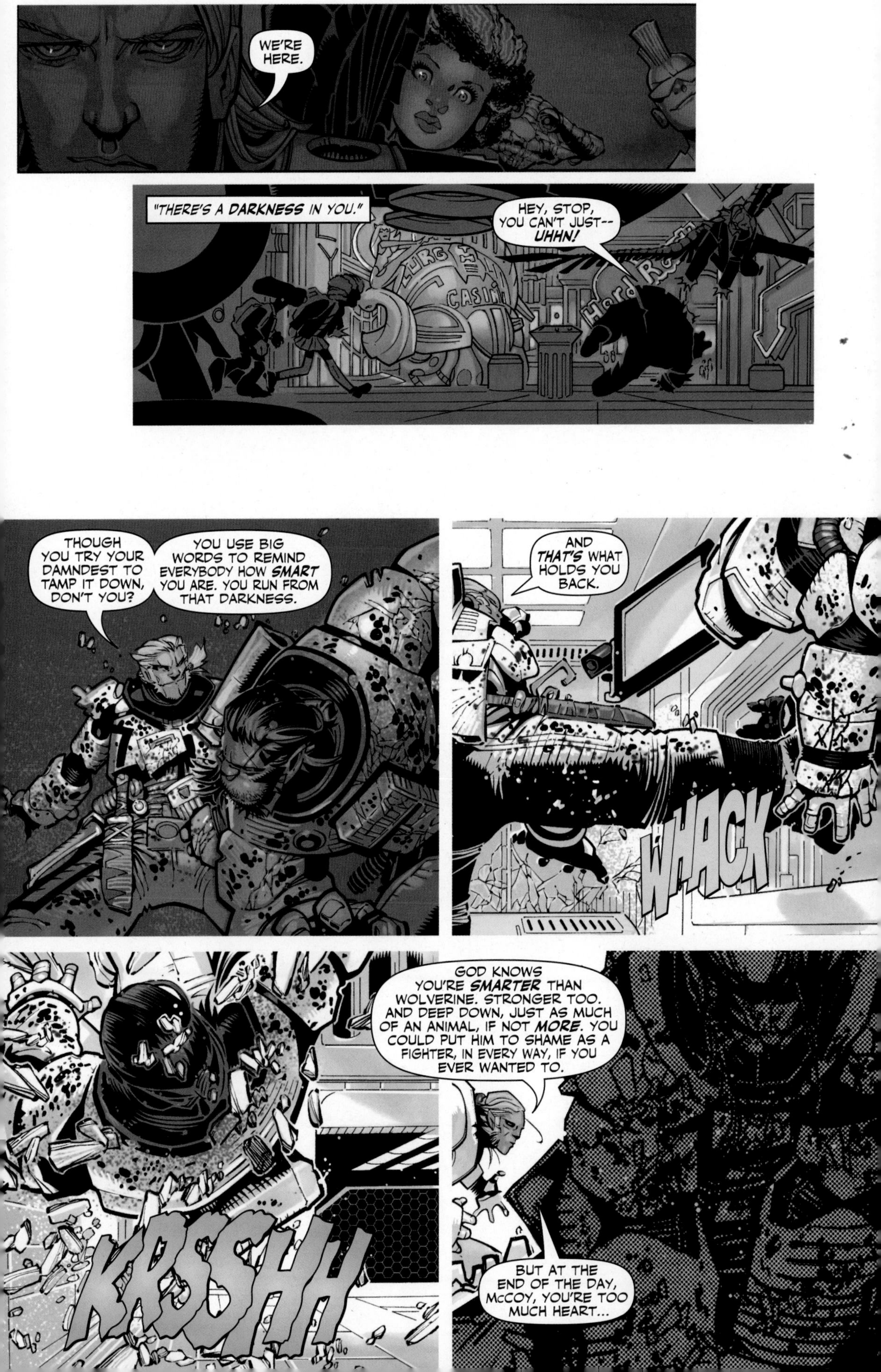
WE'RE HERE.
"THERE'S A DARKNESS IN YOU."
HEY, STOP, YOU CAN'T JUST-- UHHN!
ZURG CASINO
Hard Ro
THOUGH YOU TRY YOUR DAMNDEST TO TAMP IT DOWN, DON'T YOU?
YOU USE BIG WORDS TO REMIND EVERYBODY HOW SMART YOU ARE. YOU RUN FROM THAT DARKNESS.
AND THAT'S WHAT HOLDS YOU BACK.
WHACK
KRSHH
GOD KNOWS YOU'RE SMARTER THAN WOLVERINE. STRONGER TOO. AND DEEP DOWN, JUST AS MUCH OF AN ANIMAL, IF NOT MORE. YOU COULD PUT HIM TO SHAME AS A FIGHTER, IN EVERY WAY, IF YOU EVER WANTED TO.
BUT AT THE END OF THE DAY, McCOY, YOU'RE TOO MUCH HEART...

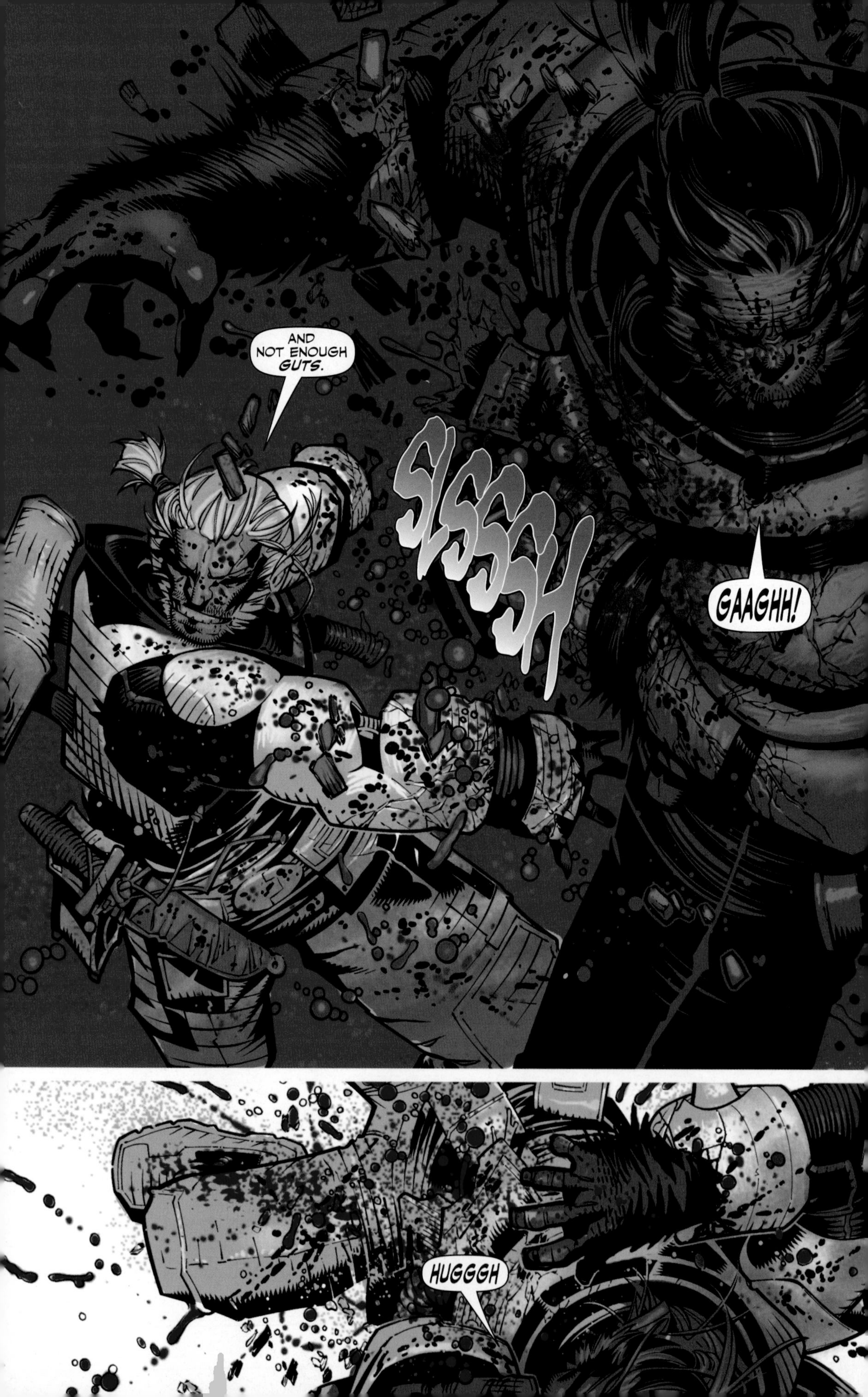
AND NOT ENOUGH GUTS.
SLSSSH
GAAGHH!
HUGGGH

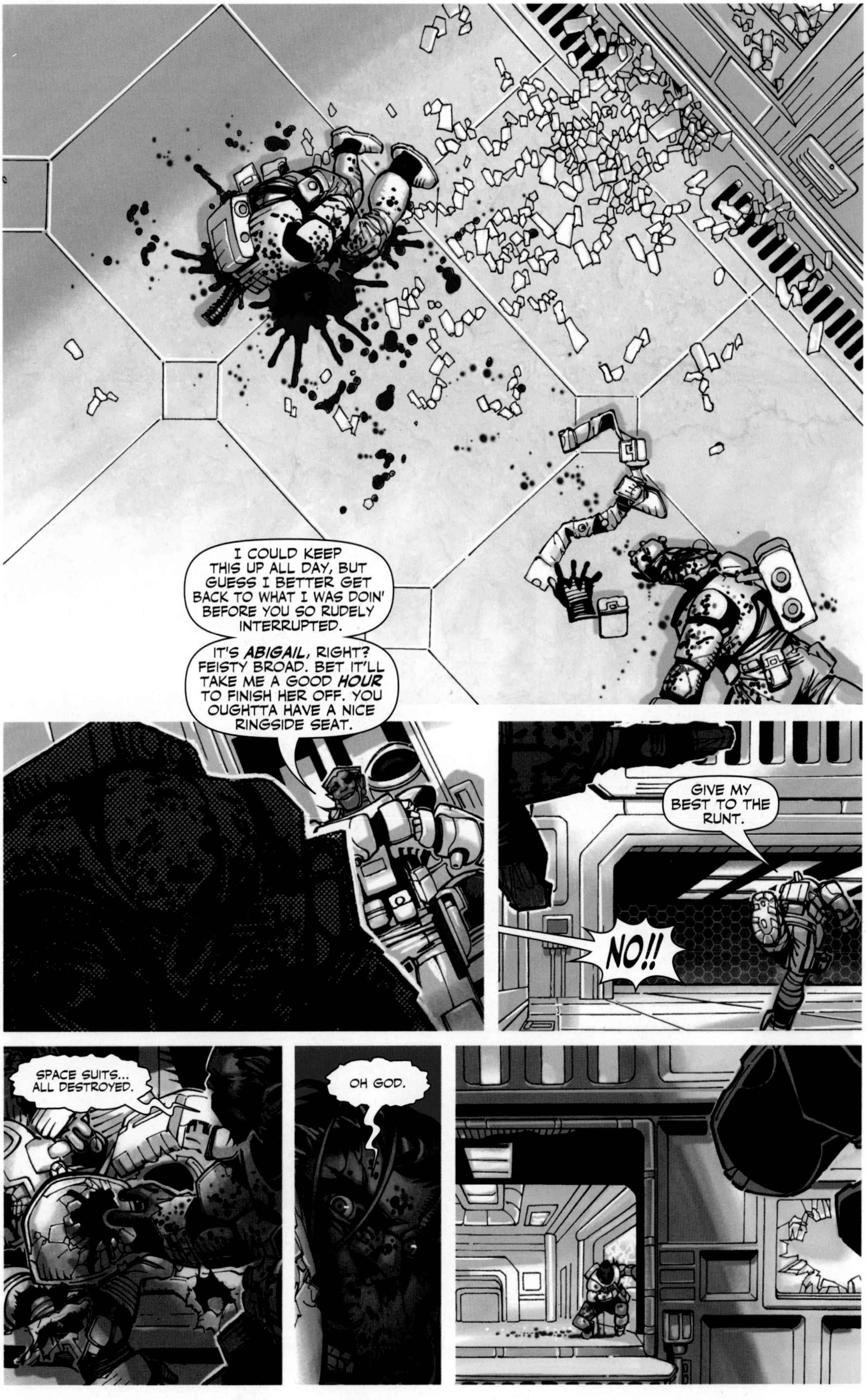
I COULD KEEP THIS UP ALL DAY, BUT GUESS I BETTER GET BACK TO WHAT I WAS DOIN' BEFORE YOU SO RUDELY INTERRUPTED.
IT'S ABIGAIL, RIGHT? FEISTY BROAD. BET IT'LL TAKE ME A GOOD HOUR TO FINISH HER OFF. YOU OUGHTTA HAVE A NICE RINGSIDE SEAT.
GIVE MY BEST TO THE RUNT.
NO!!
SPACE SUITS... ALL DESTROYED.
OH GOD.

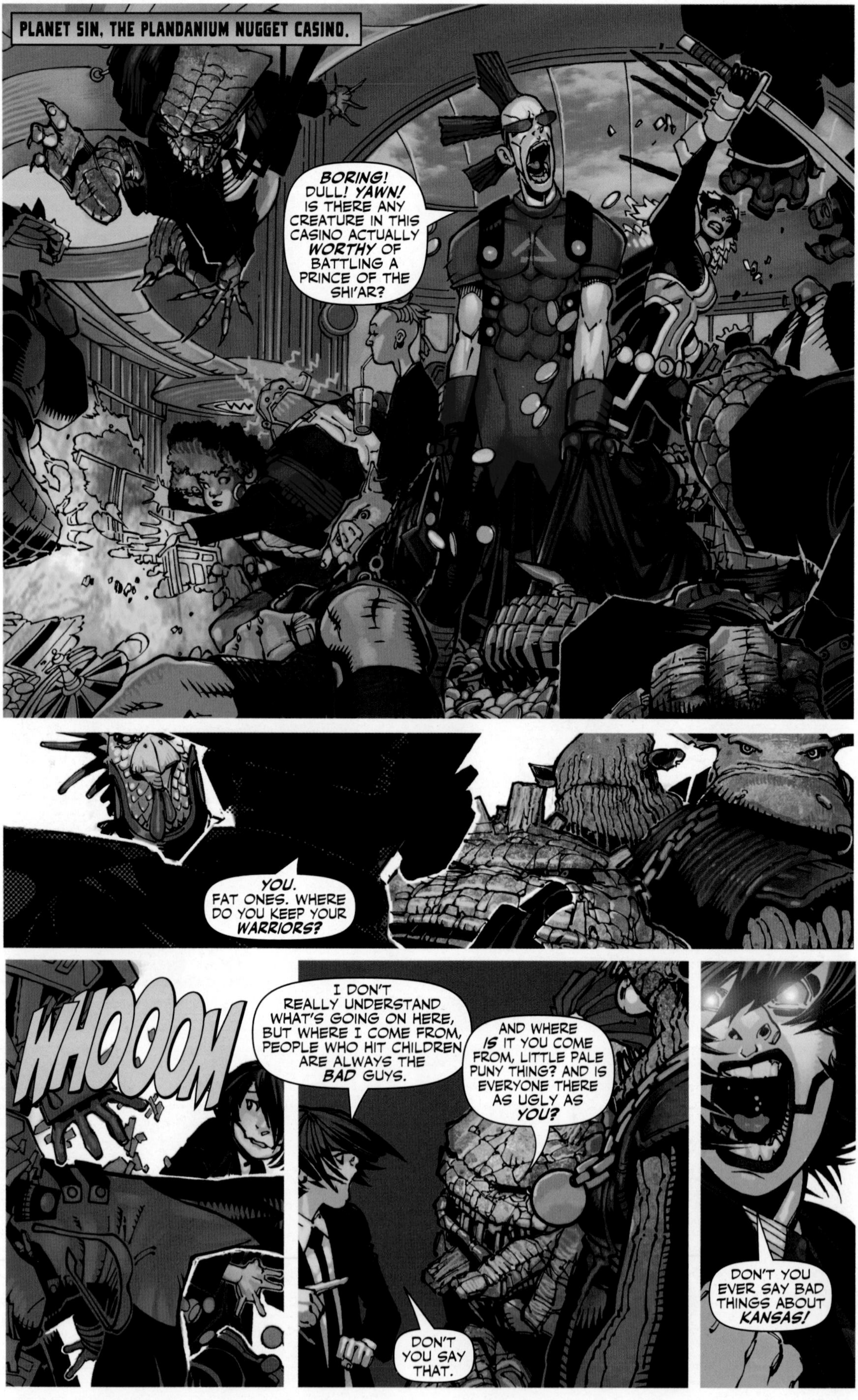
PLANET SIN, THE PLANDANIUM NUGGET CASINO.
BORING! DULL! YAWN! IS THERE ANY CREATURE IN THIS CASINO ACTUALLY WORTHY OF BATTLING A PRINCE OF THE SHI'AR?
YOU. FAT ONES. WHERE DO YOU KEEP YOUR WARRIORS?
WHOOOM
I DON'T REALLY UNDERSTAND WHAT'S GOING ON HERE, BUT WHERE I COME FROM, PEOPLE WHO HIT CHILDREN ARE ALWAYS THE BAD GUYS.
AND WHERE IS IT YOU COME FROM, LITTLE PALE PUNY THING? AND IS EVERYONE THERE AS UGLY AS YOU?
DON'T YOU SAY THAT.
DON'T YOU EVER SAY BAD THINGS ABOUT KANSAS!

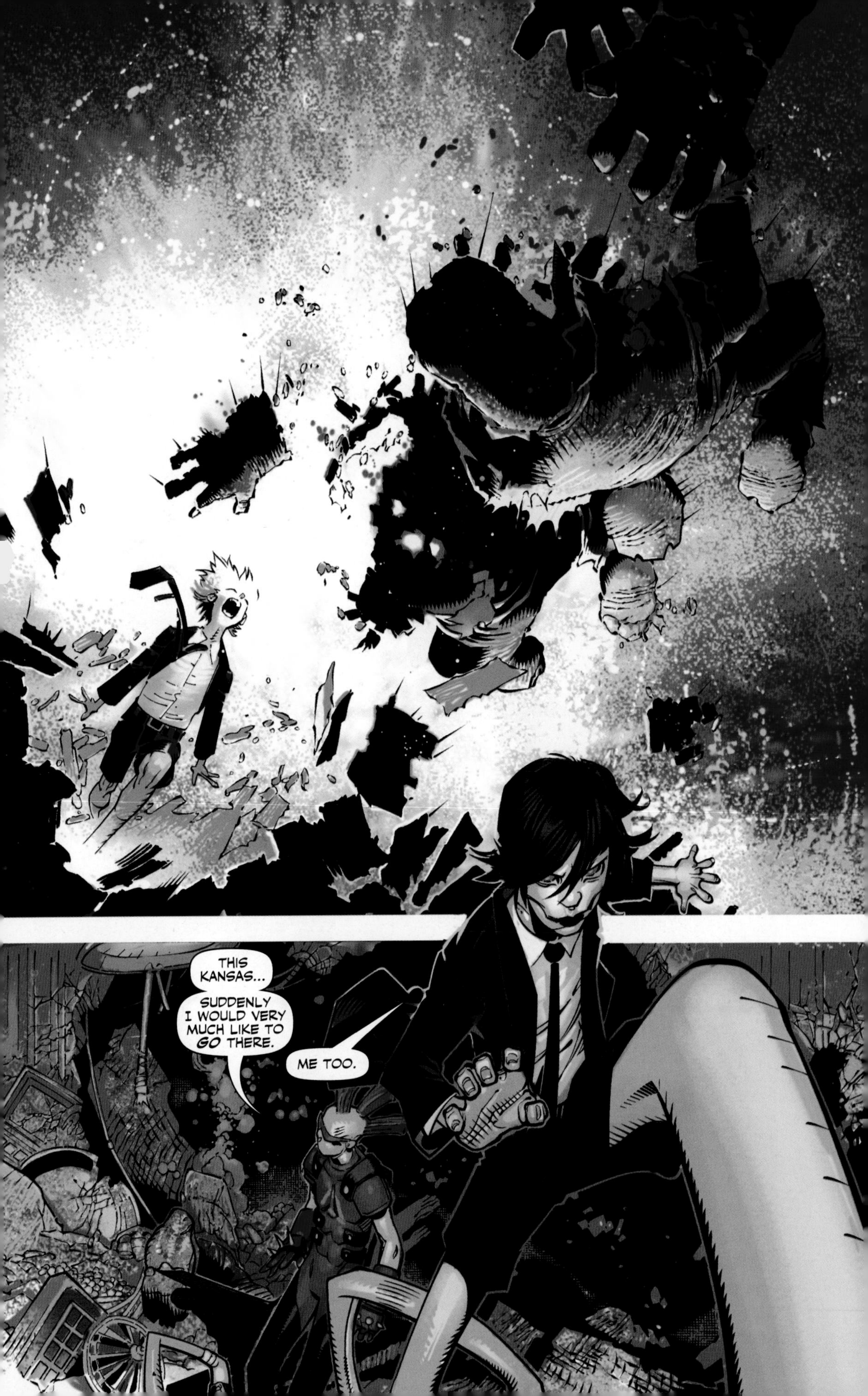
THIS KANSAS... SUDDENLY I WOULD VERY MUCH LIKE TO GO THERE.
ME TOO.

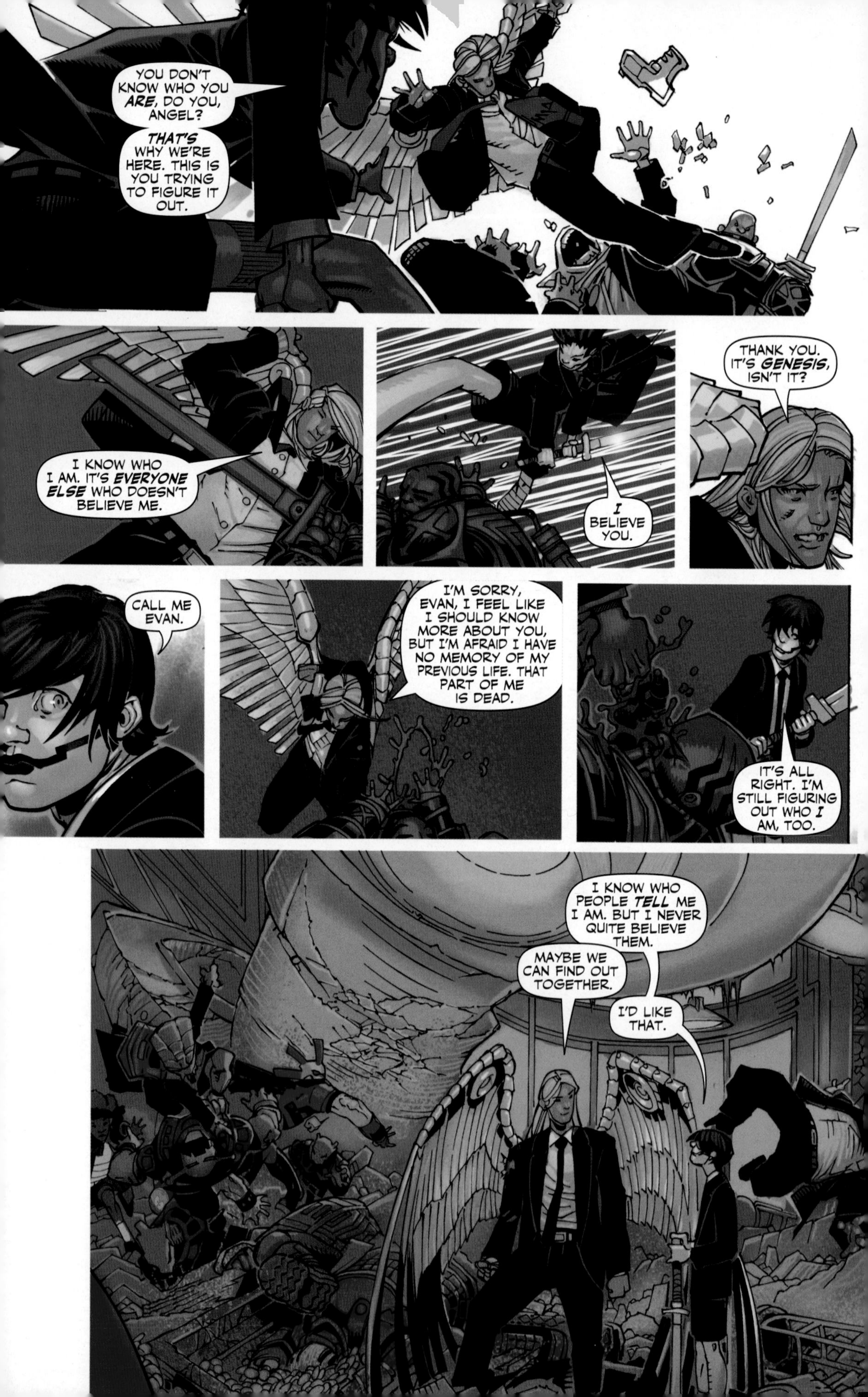
YOU DON'T KNOW WHO YOU ARE, DO YOU, ANGEL?
THAT'S WHY WE'RE HERE. THIS IS YOU TRYING TO FIGURE IT OUT.
I KNOW WHO I AM. IT'S EVERYONE ELSE WHO DOESN'T BELIEVE ME.
I BELIEVE YOU.
THANK YOU. IT'S GENESIS, ISN'T IT?
CALL ME EVAN.
I'M SORRY, EVAN, I FEEL LIKE I SHOULD KNOW MORE ABOUT YOU, BUT I'M AFRAID I HAVE NO MEMORY OF MY PREVIOUS LIFE. THAT PART OF ME IS DEAD.
IT'S ALL RIGHT. I'M STILL FIGURING OUT WHO I AM, TOO.
I KNOW WHO PEOPLE TELL ME I AM. BUT I NEVER QUITE BELIEVE THEM.
MAYBE WE CAN FIND OUT TOGETHER.
I'D LIKE THAT.

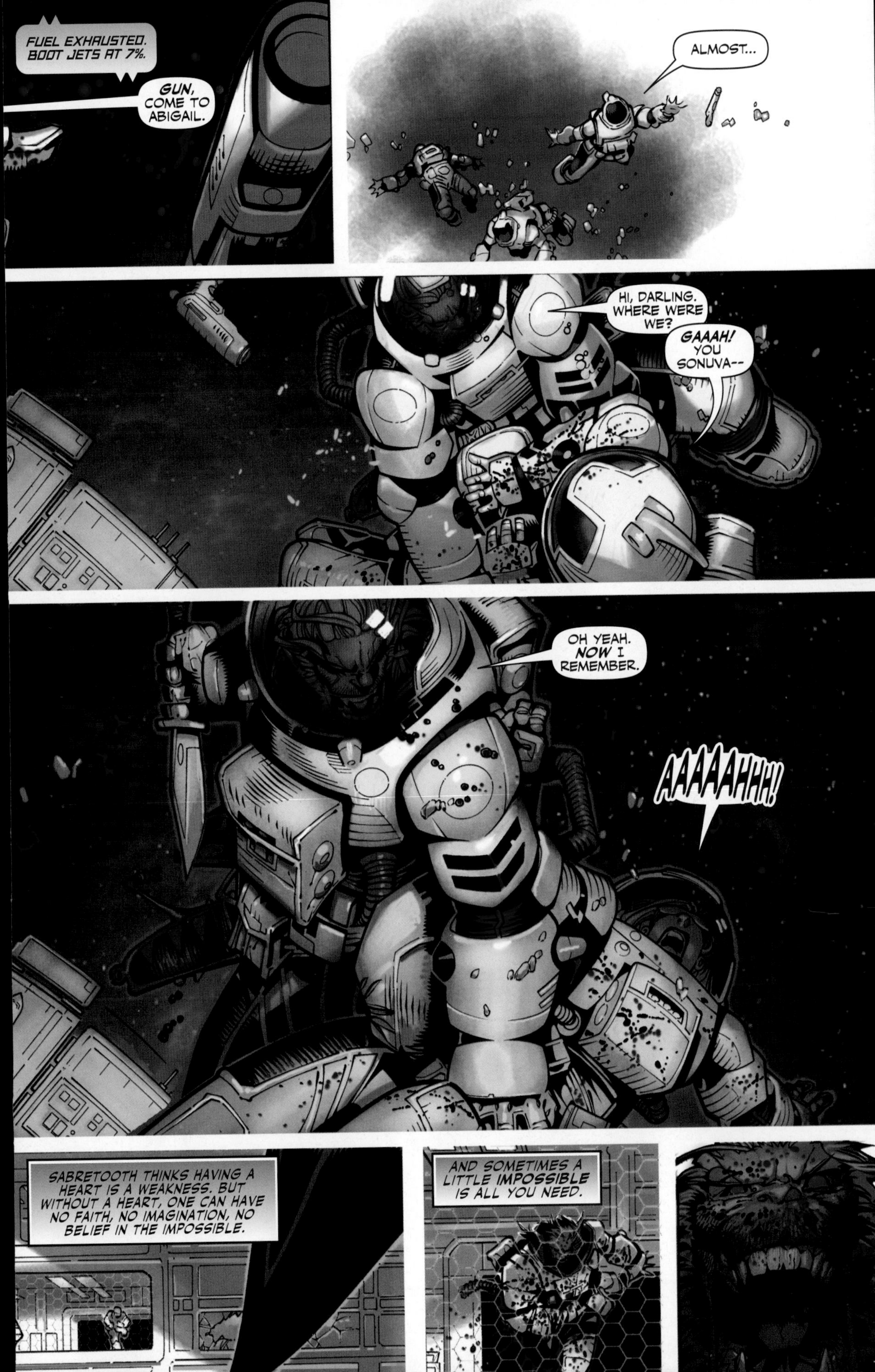
FUEL EXHAUSTED. BOOT JETS AT 7%.
GUN, COME TO ABIGAIL.
ALMOST...
HI, DARLING. WHERE WERE WE?
GAAAH! YOU SONUVA--
OH YEAH. NOW I REMEMBER.
AAAAAHHH!
SABRETOOTH THINKS HAVING A HEART IS A WEAKNESS. BUT WITHOUT A HEART, ONE CAN HAVE NO FAITH, NO IMAGINATION, NO BELIEF IN THE IMPOSSIBLE.
AND SOMETIMES A LITTLE IMPOSSIBLE IS ALL YOU NEED.

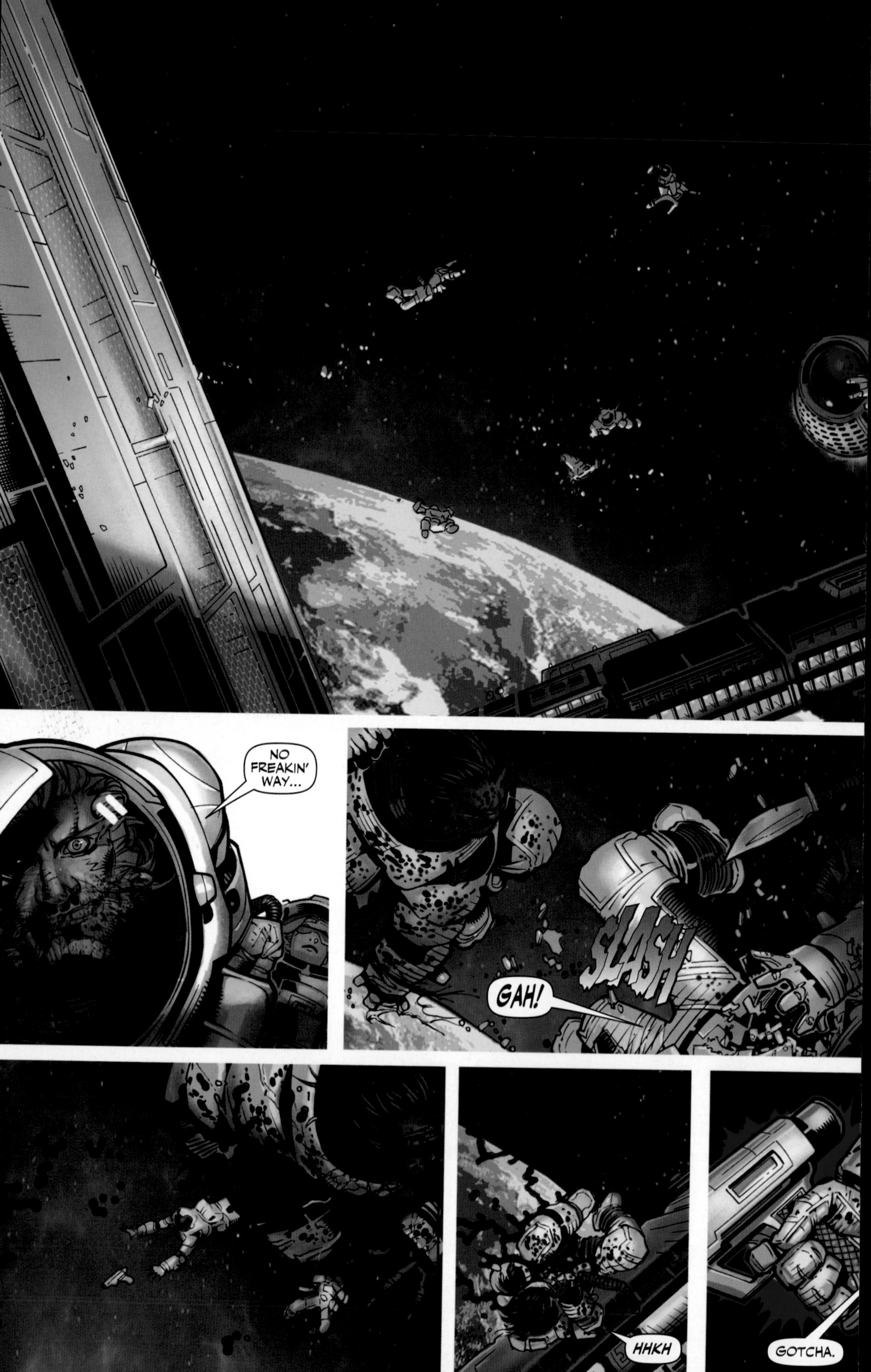
NO FREAKIN' WAY...
SLASH
GAH!
HHKH
GOTCHA.

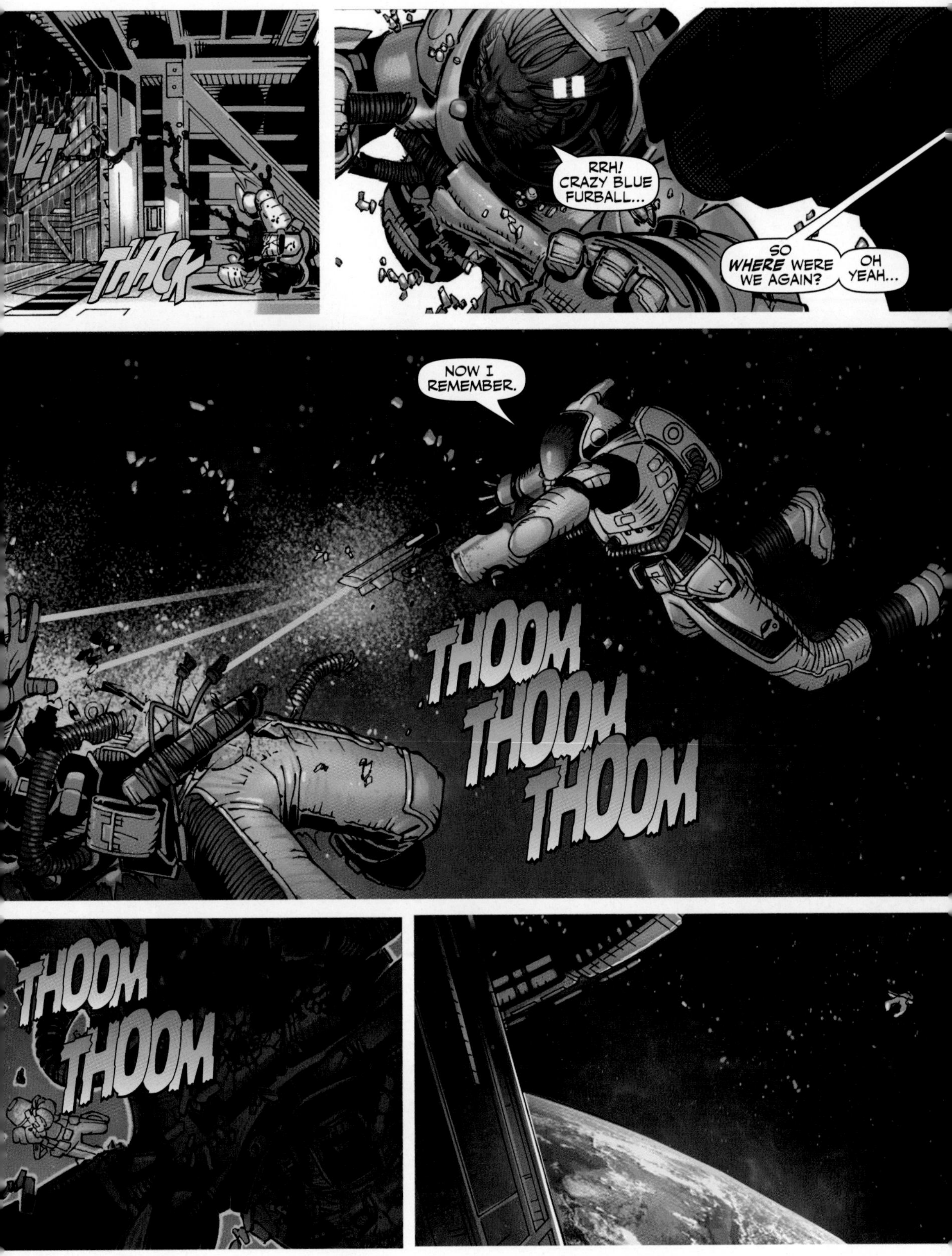
VZT
THACK
RRH! CRAZY BLUE FURBALL...
SO WHERE WERE WE AGAIN?
OH YEAH...
NOW I REMEMBER.
THOOM
THOOM
THOOM
THOOM
THOOM

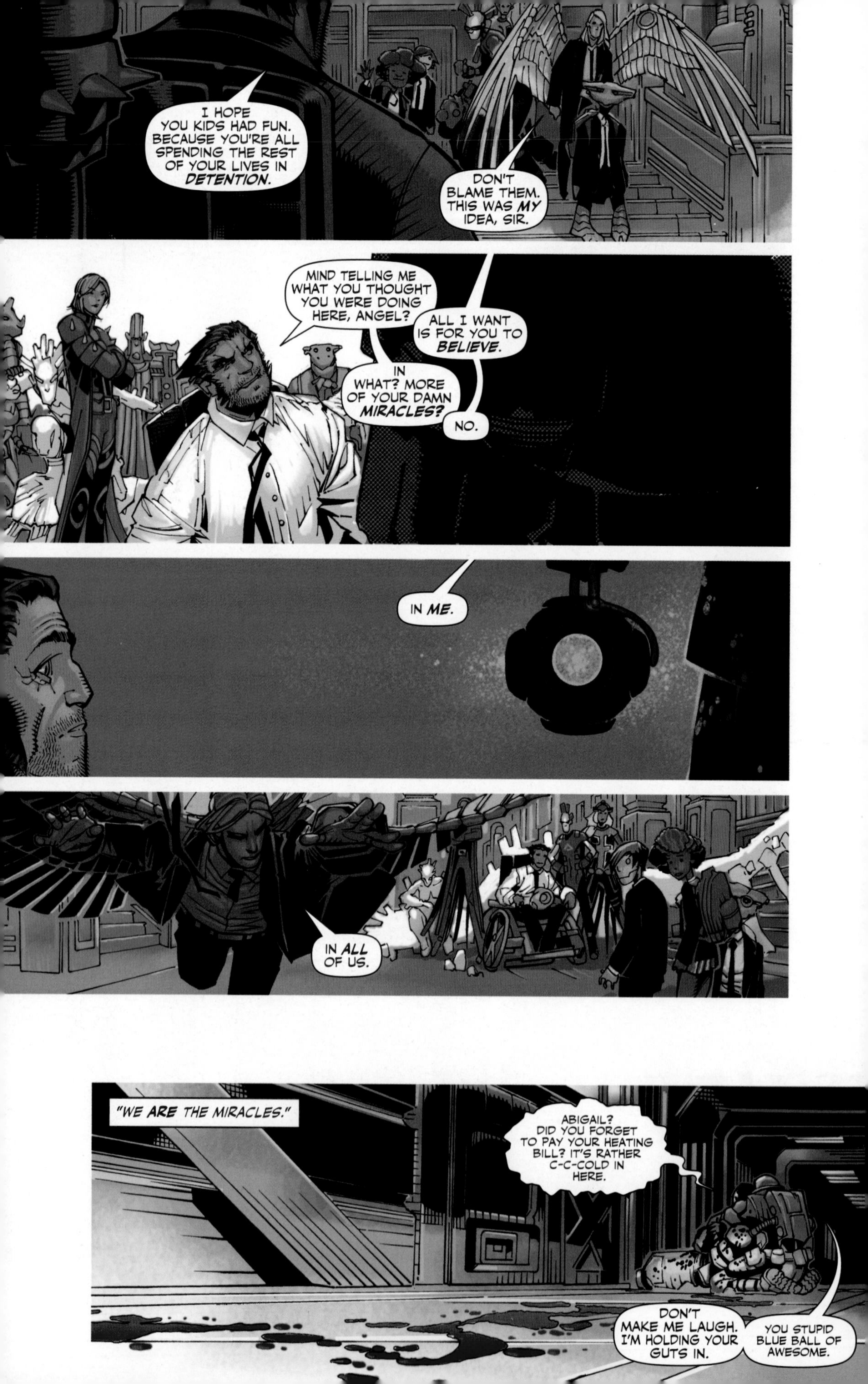
I HOPE YOU KIDS HAD FUN. BECAUSE YOU'RE ALL SPENDING THE REST OF YOUR LIVES IN DETENTION.
DON'T BLAME THEM. THIS WAS MY IDEA, SIR.
MIND TELLING ME WHAT YOU THOUGHT YOU WERE DOING HERE, ANGEL?
ALL I WANT IS FOR YOU TO BELIEVE.
IN WHAT? MORE OF YOUR DAMN MIRACLES?
NO.
IN ME.
IN ALL OF US.
"WE ARE THE MIRACLES."
ABIGAIL? DID YOU FORGET TO PAY YOUR HEATING BILL? IT'S RATHER C-C-COLD IN HERE.
DON'T MAKE ME LAUGH. I'M HOLDING YOUR GUTS IN.
YOU STUPID BLUE BALL OF AWESOME.

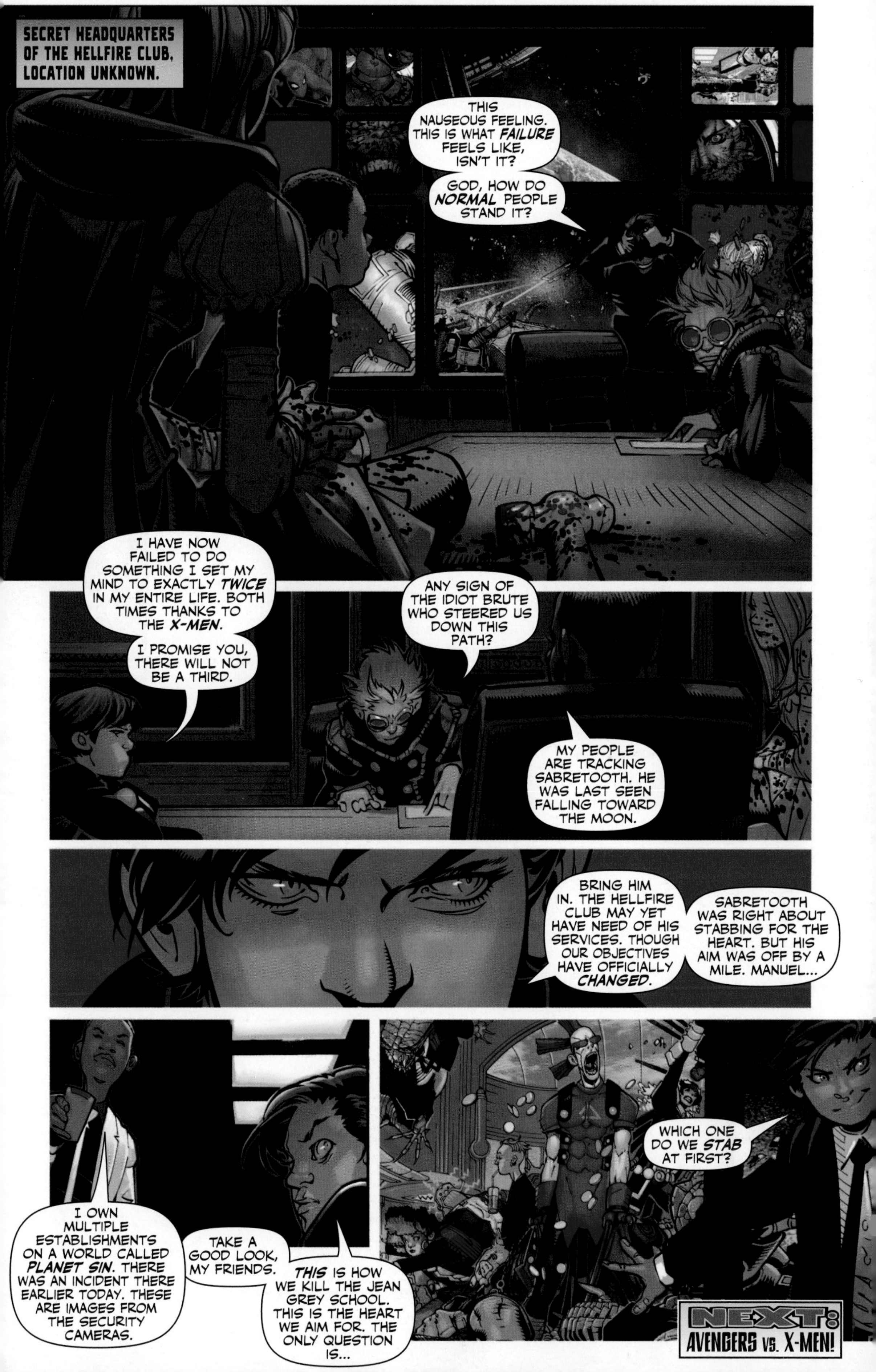
SECRET HEADQUARTERS OF THE HELLFIRE CLUB, LOCATION UNKNOWN.
THIS NAUSEOUS FEELING. THIS IS WHAT FAILURE FEELS LIKE, ISN'T IT?
GOD, HOW DO NORMAL PEOPLE STAND IT?
I HAVE NOW FAILED TO DO SOMETHING I SET MY MIND TO EXACTLY TWICE IN MY ENTIRE LIFE. BOTH TIMES THANKS TO THE X-MEN.
I PROMISE YOU, THERE WILL NOT BE A THIRD.
ANY SIGN OF THE IDIOT BRUTE WHO STEERED US DOWN THIS PATH?
MY PEOPLE ARE TRACKING SABRETOOTH. HE WAS LAST SEEN FALLING TOWARD THE MOON.
BRING HIM IN. THE HELLFIRE CLUB MAY YET HAVE NEED OF HIS SERVICES. THOUGH OUR OBJECTIVES HAVE OFFICIALLY CHANGED.
SABRETOOTH WAS RIGHT ABOUT STABBING FOR THE HEART. BUT HIS AIM WAS OFF BY A MILE. MANUEL...
I OWN MULTIPLE ESTABLISHMENTS ON A WORLD CALLED PLANET SIN. THERE WAS AN INCIDENT THERE EARLIER TODAY. THESE ARE IMAGES FROM THE SECURITY CAMERAS.
TAKE A GOOD LOOK, MY FRIENDS.
THIS IS HOW WE KILL THE JEAN GREY SCHOOL. THIS IS THE HEART WE AIM FOR. THE ONLY QUESTION IS...
WHICH ONE DO WE STAB AT FIRST?
NEXT: AVENGERS VS. X-MEN!

ISSUE #5 LETTERS COLUMN

Hello! This is Professor Rachel Grey handling the mail-call for this month. After being away in space for so long, I'd kind of forgotten that mail existed. Not sure why I told you that, but hey, WHY NOT? If you can't reference your recent space trip, what's the point of doing it? Anyway, let's dive into the mail.

Dear X-Staff,

I'd been away from the world of the X-Men for a while (hell, I'd been away from reading comics, period) up until a little more than a year ago, when I started reading Uncanny X-Force... which led to me reading the Schism mini... which led me to reading Wolverine and the X-Men. And I must say that, with the school in Westchester back in operation, THIS is the X-Men I fell in love with when I was 13 years old.

I just have to ask one question about issue 2: how was one of the inspectors transformed into "a Sauron"? I thought Dr. Lykos (who, I must admit, I would like to see again) was the only one.

And I echo one of the letters in issue 4 - more Lockheed, please! (He's second only to Toothless among my favorite dragons.)

A great many thanks,
Matt Cloutier

Thanks for the letter, Matt. About the Saurons, I don't really know. Hank tried explaining it to me, but I got lost about five words in. Something about a mutagen drug activation or something. There's a reason I don't teach biology. Way more of a physics girl. As for Karl Lykos, I have no interest in seeing him again. He's a pretty big jerk, Matt. And I'll pass on the compliment to Lockheed. How to Train Your Dragon is one of his favorite movies, too, though he finds some of the dragons rather stereotypical.

Dear X Team,

I'm seriously waiting for Broo to go absolutely insane and start attacking people. His face are what my nightmares consist of. I'm pretty sure that Logan is using "Angel" for his money. I'm totally going to investigate this and find out the dirt! Also, what is lunch like at the school?

Daniel Bellay

I have to admit that I didn't love the idea of having a Brood at the school, but I have to say he's a good kid. Really smart, nice. It's kind of crazy knowing where he came from. As for your accusation of our illustrious Headmaster "using" Angel for his money, that's a pretty jerky comment, Daniel. Not only are Logan and Warren friends (sure, they fight and almost kill each other every once in a while, but most of us do with Logan), but Warren has always been very generous with the X-Men. Knowing how much all this costs, we really need it and I'm sure Warren would want us to have it, if he had any memory. And lastly, if you want to know about lunch you should follow the official Jean Grey School Twitter account: @JGSchool. We tweet morning announcements every school day!

Dear X Team,

If Jason Aaron's take on Quentin Quire doesn't seem at least familiar to you, then you didn't go to high school anywhere near me. From the cover that drips with attitude to the machine gun tempo of snarky retorts, the creators of Wolverine and the X-Men #3 get anti-social teenage behavior on every level. I've been enjoying this new direction for Wolverine and Marvel's young mutants so far, but this issue is just way too much fun to be ignored.

I could go on for while about how well Aaron nails his characterizations, but the acid test is looking at the dialogue. Wolverine's lines show him to be a regular "one of the guys"-type dude when interacting with Captain America and a responsible protector when managing his team in combat. However, we don't lose the brusque individualism that he's known for and demonstrates when dealing with Quire. Broo doesn't have much face-time here, but his endearing frames may have made him my second favorite character in the series. Everybody is a little nutty in this book, but they're real to the point that I could see myself hanging out with them.

There's quite a bit of collaboration going on with this issue's artwork. Surprisingly, the collaboration comes together nicely. The images are appropriately muted during Wolverine's conversation with Cap. After resuming action in the present, the art rushes back to full volume, with characters pushing their way into each frame like caffeinated monkeys. The raucous layouts and over-sketched textures once again set a gritty, energetic tone for the book. For readers who may have been overwhelmed by Bachalo's crowded pencilwork in previous issues, the flashback and coda to this story help to air out the more frantic pages. Aaron's script and Bachalo's pencils make the ride an exceedingly enjoyable one. There's energy and attitude to spare, and I'm already excited about the next issue. I had a ton of fun reading this issue.

Carmen Stokes

Okay, this is officially weird, now. Bobby and Kitty told me that people would talk about mysterious figures named Jason Aaron, Chris Bachalo and Nick Bradshaw, so I did some research. Turns out this Jason person is a bearded hillbilly. Chris and Nick are both Canadian, and I think we all know what that says about them. NEXT!

Hi bubs,

I love the new Iceman. Wolverine's faith in him is paying off. Untapped potential no more. Iceman is showing what he is capable of. I can't wait to see what else this comic holds for Iceman in the future.

This may well be the best written and drawn Marvel comic being made now.

Richard Vasseur

Wow, you sure have some deep feelings for Iceman, huh? He's a nice guy and all, but let's not get carried away. I mean, you can't laugh at your own jokes so much and still expect people to take you seriously. After he kissed Kitty, I told her as much.

Dear Ms. Grey/Summers:

You are my favorite X-Man. Have been for awhile. See, not all of the general public is hateful of mutants. Are you going by Summers again? I love your new costume by the way. It seems like it takes a bit from each of your eras. Who designed it? Why did you decide it was time for a new look? I am so happy that you are getting to take such an active role with Wolverine and his X-Men at the new Jean Grey School. I marveled when it seemed that you were only going to be allowed to work with Rogue and her Legacy X-Men.

The reason I am writing is that I am concerned about you as a fan. For one, it seemed you were more powerful when you first appeared and even when you were with Excalibur, but then there were all these training sessions with Professor X and Emma Frost. You seem to be so easily defeated, outsmarted, and outdone of late. There was that alien in space and now Kid Omega. Are you not an Omega Level mutant? Is it because you no longer host the Phoenix Force?

I'm just afraid you're going to be marginalized, placed on the sidelines, and not be well utilized in upcoming battles in the way you deserve to be. Why wouldn't the Phoenix want you? You used its powers the longest (even longer than Jean) and you were never corrupted. I think you were the most proficient with them, too. Even with the recent blue version you no longer wield. You are the original. Okay, second original, but first daughter.

Freddie Rodriguez

Now THIS was unexpected. What a nice surprise. Thank you very much, Freddie. I have no clue what you're talking about as far as whether the Phoenix WANTS me or not. Do you know something? To answer your other questions, I don't think I'm considered an Omega Level mutant since I lost the Phoenix Force, but that doesn't really bother me. First of all, who decides that? Usually arrogant jerks (sound like any pink haired riffraff?). Second of all, it's a LOT of pressure and takes a ton of control. You sneeze and all of the sudden half a city is missing. As for my costume, I designed it myself! Isn't it amazing? I just decided it was time for a change. This is great. More letters like this, people!

That's all for this month. Don't forget to follow @JGSchool on Twitter and we'll see you next month!

Best,

Rachel.

Well, hello there! It's Vice Principal Dr. Henry McCoy opening up the mail-bag this time, and what a delight it is for this blue-haired biologist. Postal correspondence in print has always been a particular interest of mine ever since I pored over the Letters-to-the-Editor column in the Biological Journal of the Linnean Society as a child. In fact, I attempted to dig into my archives in preparation for this but the Bamfs seem to have made off with several of my favorite volumes. But one must persevere!

Dear X-Faculty,

I'm writing in regards of two individuals who should be considered as prospective faculty members. I'm sure, it's overwhelming attempting to teach your student body (Beautiful Cover of WATX #4) which is why I'd like you to consider bringing aboard two experienced teachers whom you may be overlooking. I am talking about Aurora (Jeanne-Marie Beaubier) who is an experienced history teacher at Madame Dupont's School For Girls, and perfectly able to head your History Department, and Rhapsody (Rachel Argosy) of Twin Forks H.S., Maine. A talented and experienced Music teacher and as I see your Music and Arts Department needs rounding out (ahem cough cough). Please consider these former teachers for your school as I think they truly would fit in amongst your special school.

Thanks,
Moises Hernandez

First, Mr. Hernandez, I commend you for putting your thoughts into words and sending them forth! Ah, discourse! We shall take your recommendations into consideration, though I have my doubts about Ms. Argosy's music education credentials. She once tried to argue that Scarlatti and his cohorts of the "Neapolitan school" actually conceived the Neapolitan chord. Everyone knows it had been in use for decades before those composers, talented as they may be, put them into more common practice.

Hello Dr. McCoy,

Just let me start by saying that I have thoroughly enjoyed your first adventures at the Jean Grey School for Higher Learning and really like seeing the school back up and running; it just seems right that you're back in New York.

The new school seems very advanced from what I can tell, and it looks quite impressive. Is there any chance that we may get to see some of your original designs for the school? It would be great to see some sketches, notes, and/or blueprints detailing the layout and features. I mean the danger room is incorporated into the whole school, even the bathroom, how is that not amazing?!?

While we're talking about technical matters, can I make a course suggestion for next semester; Blackbird 101. This would be the class where students learn to design, repair, maintain, and pilot the X-Men's signature aircraft. It could make for some very fun learning experiences. I would suggest that you teach all the technical details and let Icemen cover piloting; he would probably be the most laid back in a stressful environment like that.

Speaking of Bobby, can you tell him and Kitty that they should get together? They would make a great couple, and obviously there is something there between them. It would be nice to see two of my favorite X-Men together as a couple.

Next, what are the Bamfs? I know they look like miniature Nightcrawlers, but where did they come from? I'm just curious if I missed their origin or if it has yet to be explained.

Lastly, is there any chance that some of the members of X-Factor will be guest lecturing in the near future? I figure that with them being on Wolverine's side, they are likely to turn up at the school sooner or later. Thanks for taking the time for all of the fan letters and good luck as the school year continues.

Andy G.

Many thanks for your letter, Andrew, my lad. Firstly, we do have plans to bring a few members of X-Factor Investigations in for lectures. I am particularly looking forward to Alexander Summers' series of lectures on Fluid Dynamics. Secondly, I do my best to stay out of the romantic affairs of my colleagues. I have talked to both Bobby and Kitty and the main advice I gave them was to avoid fishing off the company pier, as it were. My paramour and I worked together for a span and it put a lot of stress on the relationship. Thirdly, I haven't yet been able to pin down the origins of those Bamf pests. There is just so much going on that it's hard to prioritize solving that particular mystery. Point the fourth, we do plan on incorporating Blackbird training in our syllabus. Lastly, I would share my blue-prints for the School, but truthfully, I didn't make very many (there just wasn't time and I knew what I wanted) and the few that I did delineate on vellum got destroyed with Krakoa's lava explosions.

Dear Miss Pryde,

Although I originally had my doubts, your school, under the capable claws of Mr Logan, has already become one of my favourite places in the Marvel Universe. I must say, it is already ten times more enjoyable reading about your antics than that of Prof X's school. I suspect the big difference is probably General Summers not being part of the academic staff. He is truly the perfect definition of a "stick-in-the-mud."

The students are a great collection of strange and fantastic characters! Brilliant stuff adding Krakoa Junior and Kid Gladiator to the class list! I do have a request. Please consider adding Maggott to the academic staff! Since Bobby has seemingly made a strange step towards maturity, you'll need a good joker to keep the team balanced.

Thank you for putting life back into the X-world!

From a long-time X-fan
Johan Botes

You are too kind, Mr. Botes. Though the Xavier Institute will always have a place in my heart, I also find our Jean Grey School far superior in design, functionality and sheer brilliance, if you would permit some tooting of one's own horn. When last I heard about Maggot, he was zombified by Selene. As far as I know he metamorphosed back to dead from undead. But if he turns up alive again, which does tend to happen no matter the odds, we shall have to evaluate his qualifications for professorship.

Dear X-Crew,

I am in love with Wolverine and the X-Men...I've always loved the X-Men, but his new story has just blown me away. I love the entire story line. It's amazing and everything I wanted from restarting the school again. And having my all-time favorite character as the headmistress makes it even better. Kitty Pryde is amazing I love her. I would love to see her powers evolve because that girl can be unstoppable. Also seeing all the BAMFS makes me miss Nightcrawler so much... he's the greatest X-guy ever!!! I would love to see him brought back into the story somehow. I mean doesn't Kitty miss him too when she sees the BAMFS weren't they best friends?! I would just love to see Kurt and Kitty together...just saying that would be awesome!!! So if it's possible please bring Nightcrawler back into the story!!! This story is amazing so far and I can't wait to see what all happens in the future. Thank you so much for creating such an awesome comic series....you all rock!!!!! I love how there are different versions of the same story...I love X-Men Legacy with Rogue and Gambit!! I hope to see them grow closer like before!! But that story line is great, too!!!

Niki Busler

P.S. loving the twitter accounts for the Jean Grey School...those tweets make my day the very best!!!!

You are not alone in your melancholy regarding our dearly departed Kurt Wagner. Not only was it wonderful to have another furry fellow around, but he was a wonderful man who brought so much mirth to the world! As for your requests about the evolution of our Headmistress's powers, your suggestion seems to imply that Miss Pryde isn't unstoppable currently. She has single-handedly saved the X-Men and the Earth as many times as anyone and I would be horrified at the prospect of facing her in hand-to-hand combat as she fights dirty! Regardless, thank you for your kind words, Ms. Busler, and you have my gratitude for mentioning our Twitter accounts. The @JeanGreySchool account has been very helpful for us here at the school and I recently joined in on the fun, so you can follow me on Twitter under my screen name @HenryMcCoyPhD! You can find me there until the next time I have the honor of opening the post parcels!

Sincerely,

Hank

ISSUE #7 LETTERS COLUMN

As if being a student at the Jean Grey School wasn't bad enough, now I'm being forced to answer the letters? Hello, plebs, it's your future overlord Quentin Quire and that filthy Canadian Wolverine is making me respond to your ridiculous letters. I've got things to do (I'm hatching several different ways to get rid of these awful teachers including one method of Nega-Banding them all to various lingerie models), but the hairy dwarf of a Headmaster doesn't seem to care. Better get this nonsense over with.

Dear Educators,

Why hasn't Quentin Quire been expelled yet? He seems like a total bad seed! And speaking of bad seeds...what is going on with Broo? I knew you couldn't trust anyone with more than fifty teeth. Also, keep up with the Twitter updates. They are awesome!

Daniel Bellay
Fairmont, WV

You know, maybe this won't be so bad. You seem like a pretty smart guy, Daniel. I've been asking why they haven't expelled me since Day 1! What I take away from the question is that I just need to work harder to bring this godforsaken place to the ground. And with that Sleazoid Broo, the teeth aren't the worst of it. His cloying brown-nosing makes me want to vomit every time he speaks. The one statement you make that makes me reconsider your place in my new world order is the one about the school Twitter account. I can't read that garbage. You know, I may have to hack it and lay some truth on the world.

Hello JGS Faculty,

I'm quite sure you'll have no idea what I'm talking about, but I want to compliment everyone involved with Wolverine and the X-Men on a fantastic job on their run so far!!! Aaron, Bachalo, Bradshaw, and the rest of the crew are doing an awesome job and the issues have been really enjoyable!!! Sorry to whichever one of the headmasters is reading this and has no idea what I'm talking about, go find Deadpool or She-Hulk, they'll explain it to you!!!

I am rather curious if Rachel is still harboring any ill will towards Headmaster Logan for gutting her so many years ago in Uncanny X-Men #207, or has she buried the hatchet? And I'm a little confused with Angel, has his age regressed as well? He doesn't look like someone in their late 20's, early 30's anymore since his "rebirth". Also what happened to Ariel? I thought she would be a faculty member there since she brought Rogue there from Utopia or was she just

Rogue's ride and now has fallen back into character limbo? Also I know Rogue and the others have their own book in Legacy, but is there any chance we will see characters from that book show up in Wolverine and the X-men? It just seems weird for everyone to be under one roof and hardly see them.

Well I have to run, apparently someone left a portal open and I have Bamf's trying to take away my keyboard! Keep up the great work! "BAMF" D'oh!

Rick Hearn

You sure ask a lot of questions, Rick. Why do you care so much about the old fogies who teach at this poor excuse for an institution of higher learning? Shouldn't you be more worried that Prof Grey hasn't lobotomized that claw-bound clod rather than "harboring ill will"? That just shows a lack of telepathic skill. Angel looks plenty old to me, but he also looks plenty dumb. As for Ariel, I am kind of bummed that she didn't stick around. I thought I might have a chance with her.

Dear JGS Staff,

I have to say that I'm loving the school. Wolverine as a fierce killing machine is amazing, but seeing him as an inspiring father figure, like the Professor was, is sensational.

I am disappointed that Kitty isn't having a speed-evolving baby. It would be fun to have a baby even if it was only a baby for a little while. Everyone would have to take care of him/her.

Could you tell Bobby that he needs to step up his game? He was a big part in the first fight against the New Hellfire Club, but after that he hasn't done much. He is one of the best X-Men. I would like for him to explore the reaches of his powers because isn't he an Omega Level mutant?

I have really loved the kids in the school. Idie, Broo, and Genesis are great! I'm sad that Krakoa isn't put as a character in the opening page that says "Previously..." Krakoa should have more time as a character, possibly getting a physical body composed of Earth. Also, since Krakoa doesn't really have a body, is he a mutant? I think Beast suggested that he might be. I like that the school is open to people that are not mutants, but aliens too.

Oh, and a question for whoever is hosting today's letter page, why did you chose Wolverine?

From a post-M-day deactivated Mutant,
Adam Campbell

PS - I am turning 13 tomorrow, so if this got printed, that would be amazing!

I didn't choose to go with Wolverine and how can you possibly talk about the school and not mention the most interesting student? For shame, Adam. Anyway, I couldn't agree with your disappointment in Headmistress Pryde and Ice-Idiot any more than I already do.

Happy 13th birthday. When I was 13, I telepathically made all the actors in our school production of Oklahoma! berate a jerky jock in a big song-and-dance number. What are you going to do? NEXT!

Dear Faculty,

I'm relatively new to this whole super-powered scene, besides the broad-shouldered cartoons from my youth, and there are a couple things that have been bugging me. First of all, is Quentin Quire's hair naturally pink? Sure, he's got that rebellious streak in him (who didn't at that age?) but when he shares classrooms with a gladiatorial space prince and a gelatinous skeleton, I really have to wonder whether great power comes with pastel hair colors.

My other question is in regards to the Bamfs. Basically...what are they? They look like a cross between mischievous monkeys, swarming mice, and our favorite blue teleporter. Are they some byproduct of mutant and animal gene splicing, or did Kurt have a weekend he wouldn't want to talk about if he could remember it in the first place?

Keep on keepin' on,
Ben Littlejohn

Is my pink hair natural? Is your face? I have no clue what the Bamfs are, other than annoying. They get some credit for creating diversions for me to do whatever I want, but they have also gotten in the way of me getting some action. And that's unforgivable.

That's the last letter, so I'm outta' here. This ship isn't going to fly itself. Later, suckers!

Greetings! What an utter pleasure and honor it is to carry the responsibility of answering the mail to the Jean Grey School for Higher Learning. My name is Broo and I'm a student at this wonderful institution. After I got the highest score on the most recent "World History (1880 – 1950): An Eyewitness Account" test, class professor and school Headmaster Logan informed me that I had won this privilege. I was shocked that he would give up such an honor, but ecstatic to perform this school service. My classmate and very good friend Quentin Quire complimented my brown nose and I was on my way!

Dear X-Men East,

I'm not sure what all that "Schism" business was about, but you guys are definitely the "fun" X-Men. Seriously, if Cyclops had a psychotic clown as a nemesis (not that far-fetched), his catchphrase would be "Why so serious?" I'm not saying you guys don't know when to knuckle down and take care of business, but you permit yourselves to enjoy it when one goes your way for a change. Kurt would have fit right in. Any chance his doppelgänger will spend some time at the school?

In your line of work, I suppose it isn't right to play favorites, but I am particularly partial to Broo. He's so polite and eager to learn! I'm a bit concerned by the treatment he has received from some of his fellow classmates. Surely, bullying is looked down upon at Jean Grey? Yeah, I know that his species is hated and feared and has the potential to end life as we know it on earth, but hasn't the same been said about mutants? He's on the right path, so help him stay on it.

Hoping to hear reports of your exploits for years to come,

Greg H.

What a lovely letter, Greg. Thank you oh so very much for writing in. I'm not sure what bullying you're talking about, but I can assure you that the students here have been utterly welcoming to me. I had expected the fact that most of my species are violent and dangerous enemies of Earth to cause problems, but that hasn't been the case at all! Just the other day, while enjoying the Earth practice of a toilet face-bath, my school chum Glob Herman talked about how I wasn't nearly as terrifying as he thought I'd be. Which is a relief. Though sometimes I do worry that my fellow students' hygiene could improve as few others have taken their face baths as far as I know. Regardless, I am very happy to be at the school and not out West with the other X-Men. Apparently, they don't offer even a single advanced biophysics class!

Dear X-Office,

I love this new school you've started and love that my favorite X-Man, Beast, is teaching there. For a long time I've loved Hank McCoy--he's funny, a great fighter and the kind of person you can aspire to be, and he has a great new uniform.

Anyway, I have a few questions about the school such as why do you have those floating towers and what are they for? What's up with the ice building? Is it for Iceman's classes? Is the spaceship Wolverine used to go into space the new Blackbird? Why did Gladiator really send his son to the school and not the Imperial Guard Academy? Will Krakoa be a student in the school? Anyway, I love your new school and hope to read about your future field trips from Jason Aaron.

Sincerely,
Elmi Hassan

P.S. If you're reading this Beast, I'll keep your secret about your friends in the Lighthouse. Also, good luck fighting Sabretooth.

Isn't Vice Principal McCoy fantastic, Elmi? I dare say that he is my favorite professor here at the school, although Professor Drake is a wonderful Algebra teacher and is only too happy to discuss advanced calculus with me after each class. To answer your questions, the floating towers house both some of the dormitories and classrooms. It is sometimes difficult to get to them, so at one point I had to fashion a jet scooter from parts I found around school. It does have a second seat, in case any of the other students have forgotten my many offers of rides. The Ice Tower houses some classrooms, labs and faculty offices, though most of the professors have moved their offices to the main building complaining of cold temperatures. As for Kubark, or as you know him, Kid Gladiator, I am told that he was kicked out of the Imperial Guard Academy. Krakoa is indeed a student, and quite a good one!

Dear Headmaster Logan,

As my favorite X-Men, you have done quite a lot in your adventures, but teaching is probably your biggest feat. Your time as an animalistic soul was fun, but a loving teacher is what the students need. I support your decision to found the Jean Grey School all the way. Your choice of staff was great, and I am so happy that the X-Men are in New York again. It had to be done.

I loved how Krakoa was handled, but he isn't added as a character in the front page of the book. S/He (Krakoa) has potential as a great character, if he could create a body composed of earth, he could become a real team member.

Have you gotten a chance to talk to Kitty and Bobby about their relationship? They at least have to talk to Human Resources. An X-Men couple is what Team Logan needs. Unless there is another couple, I would like to see Shadowcat and Iceman talk about their status as a couple, or single.

The students are great, Genesis, Idie, Kid Gladiator, and the new take on Angel are all magnificent. Quentin is a great kid, so don't be too tough on him.

Will Professor Xavier make a guest appearance to check on the school?

Sincerely,
A post M-Day deactivated mutant,
Adam Campbell

Many apologies, Adam. I tried to get answers to your questions directly from Headmaster Logan, but he reminded me that he had given me this job and instructed me "not to bother him about it." I'm a little confused as to how this is a bother, but there is a very confusing earth saying about strokes that I hear quite often. I also tried to talk to Headmistress Pryde and Professor Drake about the interpersonal relationship that you seem to think is burgeoning, but they were quite evasive! Professor Xavier has had a few brief visits to the school and it was an honor to meet him. It would be a dream to discuss some of his genetic theories and how he would address some very interesting theories I have on Brood evolution. And I share your hope that Headmaster Logan isn't too tough on friend Quentin. Just the other day Quentin sold me a pool pass, which he assures me is QUITE the privilege here.

I would like to keep answering your mail, but I have to get to class!

Cordially yours,

BROO

ISSUE #5 JEAN GREY SCHOOL LIVE TWEET

@JeanGreySchool Jean Grey School
Welcome to The Jean Grey School of Higher Learning and our live tweet of Biology.

@JeanGreySchool Jean Grey School
Please put on your pressure suits and prepare for your Pym Particle infusion!

@JeanGreySchool Jean Grey School
We will start with a roll call! @idie_okonkwo?

@idie_okonkwo Idie
Here, Professor.

@JeanGreySchool Jean Grey School
. @KidGladiator1 ?

@JeanGreySchool Jean Grey School
. @KidGladiator1 ?! You have to respond out loud! A raised fist doesn't cut it!

@KidGladiator1 Kid Gladiator
Yes, I am here! Unfortunately I am not allowed to be anywhere else!

@QQuire Quentin Quire
BORED.

@JeanGreySchool Jean Grey School
Thanks for that. @GlobHerman?

@_Broodling_ Broo
Oh, oh, do respond quickly. I so want the learning to commence!

@GlobHerman Glob Herman
GLOB IS HERE!

@JeanGreySchool Jean Grey School
. @GenesisHero ?

@GenesisHero Genesis
Present.

@JeanGreySchool Jean Grey School
Thank you, Evan. @_Broodling_ ?

@_Broodling_ Broo
Here and eager to embark upon today's scholarly adventure!

@JeanGreySchool Jean Grey School
I'm sure you are. And I almost hate to ask, but @QQuire ?

@QQuire Quentin Quire
As though I had a choice in the matter. Quite obviously, I'm here.

@JeanGreySchool Jean Grey School
Terrific. With all students here, I'll turn it over to Vice Principal @HenryMcCoyPhD!

@HenryMcCoyPhD Doctor Henry McCoy
Welcome to the @JeanGreySchool Biology 101 class, this is coming to you live from within the circulatory system of an adult male mutant!

@HenryMcCoyPhD Doctor Henry McCoy
That mutant's identity will remain secret in order to protect his medical privacy.

@JanitorToad Toad
This feels weird.

@HenryMcCoyPhD Doctor Henry McCoy
Thanks to the miracle of size-altering Pym Particles, today we will view the wonders of the mutant body up close!

@QQuire Quentin Quire
I got caught doing that same thing on my computer in Psyche class and got detention for a week.

@idie_okonkwo Idie
This all seems very… indecent. I feel like I should cover my eyes.

@GenesisHero Genesis
Where I come from in Kansas, I'm pretty sure this sort of thing is illegal.

@GlobHerman Glob Herman
It smells like feet. Are we inside somebody's feet?

@_Broodling_ Broo
So much learning feel like like I'm going to hyperventilate. Keep it together, Broodling.

@KidGladiator1 Kid Gladiator
This is boring! When do we start the dissection?

@HenryMcCoyPhD Doctor Henry McCoy
Wrong class… alien-boy-whose-name-I-still-cannot-remember. We are not dissecting anything today.

@HenryMcCoyPhD Doctor Henry McCoy
We are merely observing, and experiencing firsthand the intricate beauty of mutant physiology.

@KidGladiator1 Kid Gladiator
You mean… we're just LOOKING at someone's guts?

@KidGladiator1 Kid Gladiator
I've been doing that since I was 12! Usually because I punched someone too hard in the stomach.

@HenryMcCoyPhD Doctor Henry McCoy
There will be NO punching here today! All students are to keep their hands to themselves!

@idie_okonkwo Idie
You hear that, @QQuire? Hands to yourself.

@QQuire Quentin Quire
I read minds, you know, @idie_okonkwo. I can see that you like me. No sense trying to hide it.

@idie_okonkwo Idie
Really? What am I thinking about right now?

@QQuire Quentin Quire
…

@QQuire Quentin Quire
That's a uh… that's a rather viciously clever

use for your ice powers.

@idie_okonkwo Idie
Now imagine it with fire.

@QQuire Quentin Quire
I'll just be over here then.

@JanitorToad Toad
Can't believe I let @HenryMcCoyPhd talk me into this.

@JanitorToad Toad
I've seen the way these kids treat a bathroom. God knows what kind of mess they'll make of my insides.
23 hours ago

@GlobHerman Glob Herman
Check it out! It's like a swimming pool!

@QQuire Quentin Quire
.@idie_okonkwo though really, I could be talked into it. ngl.

@GlobHerman Glob Herman
WE'RE ALL SWIMMING IN BLOOD!

@idie_okonkwo Idie
Oh gross, @GlobHerman is peeing!

@GlobHerman Glob Herman
What? Am not!

@QQuire Quentin Quire
Dude, you're see-through! We can all tell when you're peeing!

@GlobHerman Glob Herman
C'mon, I can't help it. It's like a swimming pool in here. Swimming pools make me pee.

@GlobHerman Glob Herman
Besides, isn't peeing like, one of the natural wonders of the mutant body and all that we're supposed to be here learning about and stuff?

@HenryMcCoyPhD Doctor Henry McCoy
If you need to pee, at least wait until we get to the bladder!

@JanitorToad Toad
Why do I smell pee?

@JanitorToad Toad
I clean toilets for a living. I know what pee smells like.

@GenesisHero Genesis
Boy, wait until I tell mom and dad about all the crazy things I've seen since I came to this school. I bet they won't believe it.

@GenesisHero Genesis
I wonder why they haven't replied to any of my letters?

@QQuire Quentin Quire
Must make you hungry, huh, @_Broodling_? Looking at all these nice juicy innards.

@_Broodling_ Broo
I am quite satiated, friend @QQuire, but I appreciate the concern.

@_Broodling_ Broo
As always my breakfast of scrambled tofu, soy milk and raw granola was most deliciously nourishing.

@QQuire Quentin Quire
First chance I get, I'm pushing you down the intestinal tract.

@_Broodling_ Broo
My, that sounds like a wondrous adventure! Are we headed there next? Good thing I brought along my spelunking gear.

@GlobHerman Glob Herman
Huh. Wonder what happens if I yank on these stringy things.

@JanitorToad Toad
Aah! My arm won't stop flailing!

@HenryMcCoyPhD Doctor Henry McCoy
What did I say about keeping your hands to yourself!

@idie_okonkwo Idie
.@HenryMcCoyPhd Where in here is the soul and when will we be seeing it?

@HenryMcCoyPhD Doctor Henry McCoy
That question would be better asked in @JGS-Headmistress' religion class, @idie_okonkwo.

@HenryMcCoyPhD Doctor Henry McCoy
Do I smell smoke?

@HenryMcCoyPhD Doctor Henry McCoy
PUT OUT THAT FIRE!

@KidGladiator1 Kid Gladiator
I'm just burning some of these old bushes with my eyebeams. Kid Gladiator refuses to be chilly!

@HenryMcCoyPhD Doctor Henry McCoy
Those aren't bushes! Those are nerve clusters!

@JanitorToad Toad
AAAAAAAAAAAAAAAAAAAAAAAAAAAAAAAA AAAAHHHH!!!

@HenryMcCoyPhD Doctor Henry McCoy
That's another demerit for you, young man.

@KidGladiator1 Kid Gladiator
Ha! KID GLADIATOR HAS MORE DEMERITS THAN ANYONE!

@KidGladiator1 Kid Gladiator
What are demerits?

@GlobHerman Glob Herman
.@QQuire just graffitied this dude's skin. From the inside!!! LOL! OMEGA GANG RULES!

@QQuire Quentin Quire
You're not in my gang anymore, @GlobHerman.

@GlobHerman Glob Herman
Fine, then I'm starting my own. GLOB GANG RULES!

@QQuire Quentin Quire
I have no idea what I ever saw in this guy.

@GenesisHero Genesis
This man we are inside is evil. I can smell it in his flesh. I have an excellent nose when it comes to smelling evil.

@QQuire Quentin Quire
Really? Have you ever tried smelling yourself?

@GenesisHero Genesis
What do you mean by that, @QQuire?

@QQuire Quentin Quire
Nothing, Kid A. Nothing at all.

@GenesisHero Genesis
This is not a good man, I'm telling you. I just hope none of us become tainted by this experience.

@GlobHerman Glob Herman
Heh. @GenesisHero said taint. Ahuhahuh.

@QQuire Quentin Quire
Please tell me we're not going there.

@HenryMcCoyPhD Doctor Henry McCoy
Not to alarm anyone, but there appear to be some white blood cells following us. We should move the tour along with a bit more haste.

@JanitorToad Toad
This is driving me nuts! They feel like… like little ants under my skin. Can't… help… but SCRATCH!

@idie_okonkwo Idie
What's happening?

@GlobHerman Glob Herman
Earthquake!

@HenryMcCoyPhD Doctor Henry McCoy
Everyone, hold on!

@_Broodling_ Broo
Weeeeeeee!

@idie_okonkwo Idie
.@GenesisHero Are you all right?

@GenesisHero Genesis
I think so, @idie_okonkwo, but thank you. Sorry, but I should go check on the others.

@idie_okonkwo Idie
Genesis is cute. Too bad he's not the least bit interested in me.

@GenesisHero Genesis
How do you tell someone they have the most beautiful eyes you've ever seen? I wish I knew.

@GlobHerman Glob Herman
Whoa. Where are we now?

@KidGladiator1 Kid Gladiator
I want to go back and fight the white blood cells! KID GLADIATOR FEARS NO ANTI-BODY!

@HenryMcCoyPhD Doctor Henry McCoy
No need for alarm, children, we've simply fallen down into the stomach. Do not panic. This is only hydrochloric acid.

@QQuire Quentin Quire
There are an alarming number of dead flies in here.

@GenesisHero Genesis
See, I told you this guy were evil.

@idie_okonkwo Idie
.@HenryMcCoyPhd Will this be on the test?

@HenryMcCoyPhD Doctor Henry McCoy
Ah, hydrochloric acid. You were always my favorite acid.

@GlobHerman Glob Herman
My face is melting.

@_Broodling_ Broo
Yes, mine too, friend @GlobHerman! Melting from the awesome power of learning!

@GlobHerman Glob Herman
No. Feels more like the acid.

@HenryMcCoyPhD Doctor Henry McCoy
Perhaps this would be a good time to wrap up our live tweeting event. Please go back to your regularly scheduled lives, good people.

@HenryMcCoyPhD Doctor Henry McCoy
Be sure to keep the proverbial eye out for future such twitter events from your friends here at the @ JeanGreySchool for Higher Learning.

@HenryMcCoyPhD Doctor Henry McCoy
And if no one has heard from us within another hour or so, someone please call Ant-Man for help.

@JanitorToad Toad
I think I'm gonna be sick.

@GlobHerman Glob Herman
I'm peeing again.

@QQuire Quentin Quire
.@GlobHerman out. of. the. gang. membership revoked.

@GenesisHero Genesis
We sure didn't have anything like this back on the farm.

@JeanGreySchool Jean Grey School
Thank you all for joining us in this Live Tweet! Now, move on to your next period classes, everyone!

ISSUE #6 JEAN GREY SCHOOL LIVE TWEET

Jean Grey School @JeanGreySchool
Good afternoon! It's time for the Biology 101 Live Tweet. Please take your seats.

Jean Grey School @JeanGreySchool
Make sure you subscribe to the Twitter List at twitter.com/#!/JeanGreySchool/jean-grey-school

Jean Grey School @JeanGreySchool
With that, please pay attention to your teacher @HenryMcCoyPhD!

Doctor Henry McCoy @HenryMcCoyPhD
Ah, good morning students! Apologies for not being in the classroom with resident students. I do have a good reason, though.

Doctor Henry McCoy @HenryMcCoyPhD
Your @JGSHeadmistress is infested with myriad miniature Brood running rampant. Not a normal Vice Principal job, but such is life!

Doctor Henry McCoy @HenryMcCoyPhD
Luckily, technology saves us from missing out on learning the wonders of Biology!

Doctor Henry McCoy @HenryMcCoyPhD
Instead of a normal roll call, I'm going to just ask you to state your name and that you are present, for the sake of visiting students.

Doctor Henry McCoy @HenryMcCoyPhD
Please add the hashtag #JGS_BIO101 to your present call tweet. My name is Hank McCoy and I'm present #JGS_BIO101

Rockslide @SANTORULES
I'M ROCKSLIDE AND TOTALLY HERE #JGS_BIO101

Broo @_Broodling_
Broo here. Present with all relevant body parts seemingly intact for the moment. #JGS_BIO101

Genesis @GenesisHero
I'm here, @HenryMcCoyPhD. #JGS_BIO101

Kid Gladiator @KidGladiator1
Consider me present. Even though I am somewhere inside the digestive system of @JGSHeadmistress. #JGS_BIO101

Idie @idie_okonkwo
I'm here, professor. #JGS_BIO101

Anole @_Anole_
Here, @HenryMcCoyPhD! #JGS_BIO101

Glob Herman @GlobHerman
Wish I wasn't, but totally am. #JGS_BIO101

Quentin Quire @QQuire
The name's Quire. Quentin Quire. At your service. #JGS_BIO101

Broo @_Broodling_
The name's Quire. Quentin Quire. At your service. #JGS_BIO101

Quentin Quire @QQuire
Suck on that, nerd. #JGS_BIO101

Quentin Quire @QQuire
At the school, in space, in Sleazoid's mind controlling his little claws, I'm everywhere. Inset maniacal cackle here, etc.

Broo @_Broodling_
sigh This must be what earthlings call "one of those days".

Doctor Henry McCoy @HenryMcCoyPhD
Is that everyone? I'll give a few more moments.

Kid Gladiator @KidGladiator1
Gah! Stuck! Doesn't @JGSHeadmistress know that you're not supposed to swallow chewing gum! #JGS_BIO101

Rockslide @SANTORULES
SERIOUSLY lame, having a school that makes you attend CLASS in a FALLOUT SHELTER. That turtle didn't have quizzes during "Duck n Cover".

Doctor Henry McCoy @HenryMcCoyPhD
We'll be getting to our lesson today, entitled "Oh, Spleen, You Are Wonderous, Yet Maligned in Pop Culture. Why?" But first, POP QUIZ!

Doctor Henry McCoy @HenryMcCoyPhD
Yes, it's the Pop Quiz I promised last class. But at the Jean Grey School, we do things differently.

Doctor Henry McCoy @HenryMcCoyPhD
Here, to avoid cheating (and, well, just to show off) we do our Pop Quizzes Psychically. Thanks to Rachel Grey for facilitating this.

Anole @_Anole_
Pop Quizzes are THE WORST.

Rockslide @SANTORULES
@_Anole_ you SAID it.

Doctor Henry McCoy @HenryMcCoyPhD
No need to answer audibly. Prof Grey will be putting the questions into your minds and pulling the answers out. Muss and fuss eliminated

Rockslide @SANTORULES
Professor Grey doesn't have anything better to do than pick our brains for how dumb we are?

Idie @idie_okonkwo
@SANTORULES It's going to keep us honest. Cheating is a sin.

Doctor Henry McCoy @HenryMcCoyPhD
Question #1...

Glob Herman @GlobHerman
What is, "This blows?"

Doctor Henry McCoy @HenryMcCoyPhD
Excellent job, @_Broodling_. Hydrogen bonds ARE what hold DNA molecules together. +1

Rockslide @SANTORULES
@_Broodling_ Teacher's pet ravenous space beast.

Broo @_Broodling_
.@SANTORULES Your compliments don't sound like compliments sometimes, Santo. But know that I understand you anyway.

Doctor Henry McCoy @HenryMcCoyPhD
Sorry, @squideye, covalent bonds is incorrect. -1

Kid Gladiator @KidGladiator1
The condition of this digestive tract is deplorable! Strontian intestines are vastly superior! I could digest a whole pineapple if I wanted!

Doctor Henry McCoy @HenryMcCoyPhD
Oh, @SANTORULES, "bail bonds" is not correct. -1

Rockslide @SANTORULES
@HenryMcCoyPhD COME ON. I can't help what my brain thinks!

Anole @_Anole_
That answer sounded familiar. So hopefully that means it was somewhere in my head, right? Hope Professor Grey found it!

Doctor Henry McCoy @HenryMcCoyPhD
Question #2...

Doctor Henry McCoy @HenryMcCoyPhD
So close, @omgitzjojo, but "ribose" is not quite the correct sugar found in DNA. -1

Genesis @GenesisHero
I wonder if my mom and dad are reading this. I hope they don't see me get a wrong answer!

Doctor Henry McCoy @HenryMcCoyPhD
Your answer of "Splenda", while charming, isn't correct, @QuentinQuire.

Quentin Quire @QQuire
.@HenryMcCoyPhD That was just to distract you from what I was actually thinking.

Doctor Henry McCoy @HenryMcCoyPhD
This one seems to be quite difficult. @_Broodling_, you are correct in your answer of deoxyribose. +1 for you.

Glob Herman @GlobHerman
Professor Grey never seems to approve of the things she finds in my head. Like that thing about Spider-Woman that one-- Ahh, brain freeze!

Idie @idie_okonkwo
I like this method of testing. It reminds me of the day of judgment when our lives will be laid bare for all to see.

Doctor Henry McCoy @HenryMcCoyPhD
Question #3…

Doctor Henry McCoy @HenryMcCoyPhD
Anyone? Anyone other than @_Broodling_?

Doctor Henry McCoy @HenryMcCoyPhD
Okay, go ahead @_Broodling_.

Broo @_Broodling_
Nucleotides participate in cellular signaling and are incorporated into cofactors of enzymatic reactions, of course.

Broo @_Broodling_
I'm sure my fellow students had it on the tip of their minds, Professor.

Doctor Henry McCoy @HenryMcCoyPhD
"@_Broodling_ Nucleotides participate in cellular signaling and are incorporated into cofactors of enzymatic reactions, of course" Well done

Anole @_Anole_
I hope Professor Grey wasn't in my head for the two seconds my mind drifted to Josh Hutcherson.

Kid Gladiator @KidGladiator1
I just killed four Brood with a half-digested shard of cauliflower. That has to be worth a high number of points, am I right?

Doctor Henry McCoy @HenryMcCoyPhD
Question #4… We'll go a touch easier here.

Doctor Henry McCoy @HenryMcCoyPhD
Correct, @Miss_Yabs, @JanitorToad's blood pressure diagnosis is hypertension. +1

Rockslide @SANTORULES
If I wore one of those Doctor Head-Mirror things, would it reflect the answer Professor Grey was looking for back at her?

Anole @_Anole_
@SANTORULES You are why our school is always on the brink of losing its accreditation.

Rockslide @SANTORULES
@_Anole_ Aw, come on. It's worth a shot.

Doctor Henry McCoy @HenryMcCoyPhD
Incorrect, @KidGladiator1. We would not diagnose it as "normal weak earthling blood." -1

Kid Gladiator @KidGladiator1
First, this quiz is nonsense as my answer is absolutely true. Secondly, I deserve extra points for breaking 3 Brood jaws mid-answer.

Glob Herman @GlobHerman
Wait, why does @KidGladiator1 get to run around inside Ms. Pryde and all I got was sucked down Toad's intestines? Definitely not fair.

Idie @idie_okonkwo
@GlobHerman Don't be jealous. I am sure he is seeing how sinful she is in there.

Glob Herman @GlobHerman
@idie_okonkwo Yeah, like that doesn't sound totally awesome.

Doctor Henry McCoy @HenryMcCoyPhD
Question #5…

Doctor Henry McCoy @HenryMcCoyPhD
No, @GenesisHero, metalloenzymes are not what carry CO_2 through the bloodstream. -1

Genesis @GenesisHero
I knew I should have thought "metalloprotein"!

Quentin Quire @QQuire
Man, there are a ton of alien hotties in this casino. And all Professor McStab's-a-Lot wants to do is gamble?

Doctor Henry McCoy @HenryMcCoyPhD
Incorrect, @ArmaanBabu, metalloprotein isn't correct either. -1 It was a trick question to make sure you all were paying attention!

Doctor Henry McCoy @HenryMcCoyPhD
Correct, @_Broodling_. Carbaminohemoglobin IS the obvious answer and the vehicle for CO_2 in the bloodstream.

Broo @_Broodling_
I wish I could help you all, but it's explicitly against the rules. I would love to put together a study group, though!

Doctor Henry McCoy @HenryMcCoyPhD
Last question. Question 6…

Rockslide @SANTORULES
OH--what I really need is a MAGNETO HELMET. A quiz-proof Magneto Helmet. And I would look WICKED.

Doctor Henry McCoy @HenryMcCoyPhD
Correct, @_Anole_! The three parts of the small intestine are duodenum, jejunum, ileum +1!

Anole @_Anole_
Yes! And I didn't even know I knew that!

Kid Gladiator @KidGladiator1
I knew that! I'm looking right at them!

Broo @_Broodling_
I've seen on television how much fun those can be!

Doctor Henry McCoy @HenryMcCoyPhD
You misthought "jejunum" as "jejejunum", @FoeApple. -1 Better luck next time!

Genesis @GenesisHero
I miss scantrons.

Doctor Henry McCoy @HenryMcCoyPhD
Hmmm… Didn't quite get the results I was hoping with this Pop Quiz. I may need to adjust future quizzes.

Doctor Henry McCoy @HenryMcCoyPhD
Regardless, I think we're on the road to having many published biologists in days to come!

Kid Gladiator @KidGladiator1
Gah! I just got bit by a Brood! Just a paltry little scratch... but I am now feeling a bit... strange.

Rockslide @SANTORULES
I am not joking. I am going to be rocking a Mags-style, quiz-buster from now on, see if I don't.

Idie @idie_okonkwo
Not my best grade, but at least I passed. On judgment day, the grades will be much harder to attain.

Anole @_Anole_
@idie_okonkwo Girl, you need to cut that out.

Glob Herman @GlobHerman
I least I didn't have to write nothing. I was gonna get a zero either way.

Doctor Henry McCoy @HenryMcCoyPhD
Thanks to all non-residential students who joined us today. This was lovely fun.

Doctor Henry McCoy @HenryMcCoyPhD
Now, there's a Brood biting down on my arm that needs attention. Adieu!

Bobby Drake @IceIceBobby
Just watched @HenryMcCoyPhD and Prof Grey administer a quiz and it sent shivers up my spine.

Doctor Henry McCoy @HenryMcCoyPhD
You know how hard it is to send shivers up Iceman's spine?

ISSUE #7 JEAN GREY SCHOOL LIVE TWEET

Jean Grey School @JeanGreySchool
Welcome to the latest Jean Grey School live tweet. I am Headmistress Katherine Pryde and I'd like to welcome you here.

Jean Grey School @JeanGreySchool
Seeing how we're under attack (both the school and my innards) this Live Tweet is going to be a bit different.

Jean Grey School @JeanGreySchool
The sad truth is that mutants are often targets in this world, but here at the Jean Grey School we don't let it get in the way of education.

Jean Grey School @JeanGreySchool
We're going to prove that today, as the professors host a Master Class entitled "High-Stakes Combat: A First Hand Perspective"

Broo @_Broodling_
I hope fighting for my life doesn't make me miss any valuable learning opportunities!

Quentin Quire @QQuire
Fighting for your life is the ONLY learning opportunity we've had at this school worth anything so far.

Genesis @GenesisHero
Can't wait for this! And can't wait to tell Uncle Cluster about it!

Jean Grey School @JeanGreySchool
So while the professors defend the school, we're going to turn it into a lesson! PROGRESSIVE EDUCATION!

Broo @_Broodling_
"Progressive education" is one of my favorite kinds of education!

Dr. Xanto Starblood @xantostarblood
.@JeanGreySchool You call this "Progressive Education"? My 2nd doctorate from the Magestarial University of Skrullos was more progressive!

Jean Grey School @JeanGreySchool
Professor Drake will start us off.

Bobby Drake @IceIceBobby
HEY THERE! I imagine that I'm kicking this off because I am the most experienced X-Man at the school.

Doctor Henry McCoy @HenryMcCoyPhD
.@IceIceBobby Excuse me, Robert?

Bobby Drake @IceIceBobby
It's true, multitudes. I was, in fact the second X-Man EVER! And even though some of my compatriots are older...

Doctor Henry McCoy @HenryMcCoyPhD
.@IceIceBobby Tread lightly, Robert...

Quentin Quire @QQuire
I love it when Olds call other people old and completely miss their own oldness. #trueadventuresofTheOlds

Rockslide @SANTORULES
.@QQuire Dude, are you still in space?

Quentin Quire @QQuire
.@SANTORULES Not only am I in space, but I just won more money than your pebblebrain could imagine and now I get to fight a bunch of aliens.

Quentin Quire @QQuire
.@SANTORULES Also, did I mention the alien babe factor? It's out of control out here.

Dr. Xanto Starblood @xantostarblood
.@QQuire I agree with you, young man. Planet Sin does have quite attractive ladies.

Rockslide @SANTORULES
. @QQuire WHAT!?!? DUDE, @_anole_, THAT SHOULD BE US! WE SHOULD BE FIGHTING ALIENS!

Anole @_Anole_
.@SANTORULES I dunno about that, but I find it a bit ridiculous that the most demerited student at the school gets taken on a special trip.

Quentin Quire @QQuire
.@_anole_ And so what do we learn? Demerits are meaningless. Add THAT to your progressive education syllab-s.

Anole @_anole_
.@QQuire Hopefully you can pick up the nasty thoughts I'm thinking at you right now. :-P

Bobby Drake @IceIceBobby
...I do have the most X-Men seniority. One of the first bits of wisdom that I learned and want to impart...

Kitty Pryde @JGSHeadmistress
I think I'm going to barf and not just from the thousands of Brood fighting my friends on my intestines.

Dr. Xanto Starblood @xantostarblood
.@JGSHeadmistress It's so wonderful when an experiment does what you want it to do!

Bobby Drake @IceIceBobby
...is to expect the unexpected! Sometimes you shrink down and go chasing a rude alien student inside a coworker.

Bobby Drake @IceIceBobby
You expect the thousands of alien parasites (no offense, @_Broodling_!)...

Broo @_Broodling_
.@IceIceBobby None taken, Professor!

Bobby Drake @IceIceBobby
But you don't expect a student to get Broodified.

Kid Gladiator @KidGladiator1
SCRATCHBITEPUNCHPUNCHPUNCH!

Idie @IDIE_OKONKWO
I don't see how that makes @KidGladiator1 any more of a monster than the rest of us...

Bobby Drake @IceIceBobby
You can't let these surprises catch you off guard. You have to expect the unexpected. You have to be ready for—

Kid Gladiator @KidGladiator1
PUNCHSCRATCHEYEBLASTEYEBLASTEYEBLAST!!!

Doctor Henry McCoy @HenryMcCoyPhD
It appears that my esteemed colleague's experienced face just got burnt off. I assume it's karma for that "old" comment.

Anole @_anole_
If MY face got burnt off, what would it look like when it grew back? (DO NOT REPLY TO THIS TWEET, @SANTORULES!)

Kitty Pryde @JGSHeadmistress
I'll take it from here, @HenryMcCoyPhD. Fights rarely come when you are ready for them.

Kitty Pryde @JGSHeadmistress
Sometimes they come when you're home alone around Christmas and all your teammates are on the town...

Kitty Pryde @JGSHeadmistress
Sometimes they come when you're studying for a big physics exam and tending bar at an esteemed university...

Rockslide @SANTORULES
.@JGSHeadmistress You were a BAR TENDER? Maybe this place is cooler than I thought...

Kitty Pryde @JGSHeadmistress
And sometimes they come when your teammates are fighting an alien army in your seemingly pregnant body...

Kitty Pryde @JGSHeadmistress
Fights come when they come and they rarely give you time to plan or even think. That's why training and learning are SO IMPORTANT!

Dr. Xanto Starblood @xantostarblood
.@JGSHeadmistress I cannot tell you how many of my peers neglect to train themselves in the deadly arts. Essential study, IMHO!

Kitty Pryde @JGSHeadmistress
You have to know how to handle yourself so inherently that you don't NEED to think.

Kitty Pryde @JGSHeadmistress
And even then sometimes you need help from annoying little Gremlins who steal your underwear from time to time.

Idie @IDIE_OKONKWO
Honestly, I don't know how such an immoral woman was put in charge of a school!

Kitty Pryde @JGSHeadmistress
That last bit may not be applicable in all situations.

Doctor Henry McCoy @HenryMcCoyPhD
.@JGSHeadmistress Well said, Katherine.

Bobby Drake @IceIceBobby
.@JGSHeadmistress Yeah, that was GREAT, Kitty.

Doctor Henry McCoy @HenryMcCoyPhD
.@IceIceBobby How's that head feeling, oh experienced one?

Bobby Drake @IceIceBobby
.@HenryMcCoyPhD Yeah, yeah, yeah. Remember when you turned yourself blue and furry?

Doctor Henry McCoy @HenryMcCoyPhD
.@IceIceBobby Of course, Robert, my friend. It was the day I learned yet another way to be more handsome than you.

Doctor Henry McCoy @HenryMcCoyPhD
But that's beside the point. Now let me share some pointers with our students.

Doctor Henry McCoy @HenryMcCoyPhD
When you go into battle it's important to assess your situation carefully.

Doctor Henry McCoy @HenryMcCoyPhD
Analyze your enemy (or enemies). What are their biological attributes, speculate their origins, carefully estimate the size of the force.

Dr. Xanto Starblood @xantostarblood
.@HenryMcCoyPhD For example: do they reveal their strategies on their planet's primitive social media platforms?

Doctor Henry McCoy @HenryMcCoyPhD
Are there any apparent weaknesses you can exploit? If they are a growing force, is there a way to cut off their supply?

Doctor Henry McCoy @HenryMcCoyPhD
Formulate your plan, based on your inferences. What are the consequences, both positive and negative, inherent in each plan?

Doctor Henry McCoy @HenryMcCoyPhD
From the specific to the general… The Brood have no easy weakness. They require extreme force and their numbers are increasing rapidly.

Doctor Henry McCoy @HenryMcCoyPhD
So it is important to find the egg sac. Check. Now all we need are some adequate explosives! What scientist doesn't carry those?

Doctor Henry McCoy @HenryMcCoyPhD
There are certainly negative consequences at play, but the needs of the situation outweigh them…

Doctor Henry McCoy @HenryMcCoyPhD
So you plant your explosives, set the timer and get as far away as possible.

Kitty Pryde @JGSHeadmistress
.@HenryMcCoyPhD That sounds like a heck of a—Wait a minute. Did you just say what I think you—

Doctor Henry McCoy @HenryMcCoyPhD
.@JGSHeadmistress Many apologies, Katherine, but this ensures that both you and the rest of us live to see another day!

Dr. Xanto Starblood @xantostarblood
.@HenryMcCoyPhD Ha! I never would have expected my foes to set off explosives inside one another's body! Successful distraction, indeed!

Dr. Xanto Starblood @xantostarblood
Not to worry, little @_Broodling_, it appears I shall have ample time to kill you before your professors can intrude!

Broo @_Broodling_
I do wish you would reconsider your position on my continued survival, Professor @xantostarblood…

Doctor Henry McCoy @HenryMcCoyPhD
What's that, @_Broodling_? With whom are you conversing that wants you dead?

Quentin Quire @QQuire
.@HenryMcCoyPhD @_Broodling_ Not counting me. #DeathToSleazoids

Broo @_Broodling_
.@HenryMcCoyPhD Prof @xantostarblood? Do you not follow him? Quite an important scientific figure. Also, he is trying to kill me, currently.

Dr. Xanto Starblood @xantostarblood
.@_Broodling_ I am not surprised--@HenryMcCoyPhD is reasonably able for an EARTH scientist, but in galactic terms…

Doctor Henry McCoy @HenryMcCoyPhD
My stars and garters! @xantostarblood has been following our livetweet this whole time?

Kitty Pryde @JGSHeadmistress
Wait…this alien thing has a TWITTER ACCOUNT?

Dr. Xanto Starblood @xantostarblood
.@JGSHeadmistress I take considerable exception to that. I am a scientist, not some THING.

Bobby Drake @IceIceBobby
Anyone else think when our nemesis starts tweeting at us it's time to end the twitter event?

Kitty Pryde @JGSHeadmistress
.@IceIceBobby Seconded!

Dr. Xanto Starblood @xantostarblood
.@IceIceBobby You're no fun at all. Can't multi-task? What's science without a little death-defying risk–taking?

Doctor Henry McCoy @HenryMcCoyPhD
.@xantostarblood I am about to explode my co-worker's innards, and you say we take no risks?

Kitty Pryde @JGSHeadmistress
.@HenryMcCoyPhD DO NOT WANT.

Anole @_Anole_
Geez louise. Who else has a Twitter? Mr. Sinister, you there? Nimrod? Should I be following Sauron?

Doctor Henry McCoy @HenryMcCoyPhD
Well, it seems that we are all about to make an extremely quick exit! Thank you all for joining us for this Master Class.

Bobby Drake @IceIceBobby
It's been… fun? So long as @JGSHeadmistress makes it out alive, we can get back to running a school!

Dr. Xanto Starblood @xantostarblood
.@IceIceBobby No objections here—it will just be less one student.

Bobby Drake @IceIceBobby
We'll see you tomorrow morning at @JeanGreySchool for morning announcements when we get this place back to normal. Well, normal is relative.

ISSUE #8 JEAN GREY SCHOOL LIVE TWEET

Angel @AngelMetalWings
Something is wrong. The miracles I know I have within me will not show themselves.

Angel @AngelMetalWings
This is not right. And I cannot just sit and let this happen.

Broo @_Broodling_
Friend @GenesisHero, waiting for class to start is the most agonizing time of day, isn't it?

Genesis @GenesisHero
.@_Broodling_, I don't think I'd agree with that, but I guess I get where you're coming from.

Kid Gladiator @KidGladiator1
I know exactly where you come from, @_Broodling_, but I do not understand you at all.

Quentin Quire @QQuire
Oh, look at the time, am I really an hour late?

Idie @idie_okonkwo
You are actually five minutes early, @QQuire.

Quentin Quire @QQuire
WHAT?!?!?!?!! I specifically came late. Is there something wrong with my phone?

Broo @_Broodling_
I believe @HenryMcCoyPhD rigged the satellite output to set your clock ahead.

Quentin Quire @QQuire
FASCIST SCHOOL! MESSING WITH MY CELLULAR SIGNALS! I'll show them a thing or two.

Kid Gladiator @KidGladiator1
Bah, this is nothing compared to the fascism my father and I once quelled on the Bagdovan moon of Grodx

Quentin Quire @QQuire
If there was anywhere cool to skip class to I'd suggest—Wait a second—

Broo @_Broodling_
Wait, friend @QQuire, class will start soon. He must be confused. I'll get him.

Quentin Quire @QQuire
.@_Broodling_, go away and die, alien pogue.

Doctor Henry McCoy @HenryMcCoyPhD
"@_Broodling_:I believe @HenryMcCoyPhD rigged the satellite output to set your clock ahead." I amaze even myself! Better get back to flying

Idie @idie_okonkwo
I can't let @QQuire make @_Broodling_ late for class. Come, @GenesisHero, help me.

Kid Gladiator @KidGladiator1
The heir to throne of the Shi'Ar Empire will not be the only student standing here waiting for class to begin!

Kid Gladiator @KidGladiator1
Especially THIS class. I refuse to fight without fighting!!!

Jean Grey School @JeanGreySchool
Hello students! Welcome to our fifth Jean Grey School Classroom Tweet. And it's a GOOD one.

Jean Grey School @JeanGreySchool
Twitterers at home, please take your seats and pay attention.

Jean Grey School @JeanGreySchool
For the first time JGS Class Tweeting history, our illustrious Headmaster/X-Man/Avenger/AlphaFlight-ee/NewFantasticFourian is participating.

Jean Grey School @JeanGreySchool
Yes, Headmaster Logan is going to be tweeting for the first time, teaching the student body (and you students abroad) live on Twitter.

Jean Grey School @JeanGreySchool
Granted, he's refused to have his own Twitter account, but he will be manning the official school account. This one!

Jean Grey School @JeanGreySchool
So, without further ado, ladies and gentlemen, heeeeeeeeeere's WOLVIE!

Jean Grey School @JeanGreySchool
Alright, alright. Enough pomp and circumstance. We opened this school for classes, not to gossip like churchladies.

Jean Grey School @JeanGreySchool
Let's get started.

Kitty Pryde @JGSHeadmistress
HEY! @JEANGREYSCHOOL! You can't just start like that. You have to say what the class is and introduce it.

Jean Grey School @JeanGreySchool
.@JGSHEADMISTRESS, are you kidding me? Fine. This is Fighting Without Fighting. Open to chapter 6 and we'll get started.

Jean Grey School @JeanGreySchool
Class?

Jean Grey School @JeanGreySchool
Aw, you've got to be kiddin me. Where the hell are those little--

Jean Grey School @JeanGreySchool
OKAY! This is Headmistress Pryde commandeering the official school account and avoiding surly Canadian swear words.

Jean Grey School @JeanGreySchool
All students better report to class IMMEDIATELY.

Idie @idie_okonkwo
Are we allowed to be on this ship alone? I thought we needed professor supervision...

Kid Gladiator @KidGladiator1
You call this a ship? Back on Chandilar, I used sturdier vessels than this for target practice! WHEN I WAS 5!

Kid Gladiator @KidGladiator1
Let's hope I do not sneeze and kill us all.

Quentin Quire @QQuire
Looks like our cover's blown. PUNCH IT, DOPEY!

Genesis @GenesisHero
OW!!!

Quentin Quire @QQuire
I was talking to the delusional amnesiac, @KidGladiator1.

Kid Gladiator @KidGladiator1
I APOLOGIZE FOR NOTHING!

Broo @_Broodling_
Wait, fellow students--class is starting. We must get back.

Genesis @GenesisHero
Too late for that, @_Broodling_, we just passed the moon! How about THAT!?

Broo @_Broodling_
I hope the faculty lets me write essays to make up for this rule violation. I have several prepared but would be happy to write more.

Idie @idie_okonkwo
The Earth looks so beautiful from this distance. It almost makes one forget one's monsterdom.

Genesis @GenesisHero
You aren't a monster, @Idie_Okonkwo. @KidGladiator1 might be, but not you.

Kid Gladiator @KidGladiator1
I was an amazing monster when I was half-Brood. By all the gods, THOSE WERE THE DAYS.

Genesis @GenesisHero
.@KidGladiator1, wasn't that just one day?

Kid Gladiator @KidGladiator1
Fine, @GenesisHero, THOSE WERE THE DAY!

Quentin Quire @QQuire
This is too slooooooooow. Hit that red button, blondie.

Angel @AngelMetalWings
Whatever gets us to salvation faster.

Genesis @GenesisHero
WHOOOOOOOOOAAAAAAHHHHH!

Kitty Pryde @JGSHeadmistress
HOW WERE THEY ABLE TO TAKE A SCHOOL SPACE-JET?

Bobby Drake @IceIceBobby
I don't think @HenryMcCoyPhD changed Warren's X-Man security access. Oops?

Kitty Pryde @JGSHeadmistress
And where is that furball when we need him?

Bobby Drake @IceIceBobby
WHOA, WATCH THAT POTTY MOUTH, LOGAN. Alright, we'll take the other jet.

Bobby Drake @IceIceBobby
Jeez.

Quentin Quire @QQuire
Okay, we're here. Slow it down. Everybody be cool.

Broo @_Broodling_
My goodness, what kind of star is THAT? The color of the light emitted it incredible.

Quentin Quire @QQuire
That's not a star, sleazoid, that's the neon of Planet Sin.

Genesis @GenesisHero
So this is basically an intergalactic riverboat Casino? Cool. Uncle Cluster won't believe this!

Angel @AngelMetalWings
If this is the place, @QQuire, let us stop talking and get going.

Quentin Quire @QQuire
Whoa there, All-Business-Angel, let's at least have a little fun while we're breaking every rule.

Idie @idie_okonkwo
Is there anything here that ISN'T sinful?

Broo @_Broodling_
"@_Broodling_: My goodness, what kind of star is THAT? The color of the light emitted it incredible." Cursed fingers. I meant "is" not "it"

Kid Gladiator @KidGladiator1
What does "sin" mean? We do not have this word in the Shi'ar language. Just tell me, is it

something that I can repeatedly punch?

Bobby Drake @IceIceBobby
Where the heck could they have gone?

Kitty Pryde @JGSHeadmistress
Give me a second, @IceIceBobby, and I can track their ship.

Bobby Drake @IceIceBobby
If this leads to more Brood, I quit. And I mean it this time. For actual reals.

Kitty Pryde @JGSHeadmistress
Wait a second, what is Planet Sin?

Broo @_Broodling_
If I may be so bold, @AngelMetalWings, what are we looking for?

Angel @AngelMetalWings
Some magical device that might heal Headmaster Logan's legs. I overheard @HenryMcCoyPhd mention it.

Broo @_Broodling_
A matter transmuter? I have always wanted to use one!

Kid Gladiator @KidGladiator1
Why are you fools busy babbling when there are so many people and things here worth punching?

Anole @_Anole_
Where is everybody?

Rockslide @SANTORULES
.@_anole_ I'm not sure, bro...this place seems DEAD. Wanna TP the girls' dorms?

Rockslide @SANTORULES
Uh...I probably should have direct messaged that.

Kitty Pryde @JGSHeadmistress
Is that smoke coming from that planet casino thing? That's smoke coming from that planet casino thing.

Bobby Drake @IceIceBobby
You know, a lot of this teaching has made me think I need to apologize to Prof X.

Bobby Drake @IceIceBobby
But after this whole thing today? He was lucky he didn't have THESE students.

Idie @idie_okonkwo
Has anyone seen @QQuire? I haven't seen him since I froze that shark alien who was after him.

Genesis @GenesisHero
I think I saw him winning that strange gelatin game over there.

Broo @_Broodling_
LOOK AT THIS! A MATTER TRANSMUTER!

Bobby Drake @IceIceBobby
Hold your horses, Logan. We need to get your ramp down.

Kitty Pryde @JGSHeadmistress
There you all are. Thank God you're alive. YOU ARE IN SUCH TROUBLE!

Kitty Pryde @JGSHeadmistress
I think it's pretty clear that you all get an F for today for Fighting Without Fighting.

Kitty Pryde @JGSHeadmistress
Except for you students joining us...

Kitty Pryde @JGSHeadmistress
Holy cow, we're still in the middle of a Live Tweet!

Jean Grey School @JeanGreySchool
Hello again, JGSFHL twitter followers! @JGSHeadmistress here still, thanking you for bearing with us through all this!

Jean Grey School @JeanGreySchool
Oh, and this was supposed to be Headmaster Logan's debut! Of course, it would be the one time everything goes wrong…

Jean Grey School @JeanGreySchool
I will turn the reins back over to Logan who… I'm sorry, what?

Jean Grey School @JeanGreySchool
…

Jean Grey School @JeanGreySchool
No, Logan, I am NOT going to type that, we're an educational facility, we shouldn't be saying that sort of thing.

Jean Grey School @JeanGreySchool
OK! It looks like this will be the END of our Headmaster's time on Twitter…

Jean Grey School @JeanGreySchool
Thanks for joining us for this Live Tweet, everyone. Sorry that it wasn't more educational.

Jean Grey School @JeanGreySchool
Detentions for all resident students!

Kid Gladiator @KidGladiator1
For something that I assume must be a reward, these detentions are rather incredibly boring.

COVER PROCESS BY NICK BRADHAW

#5

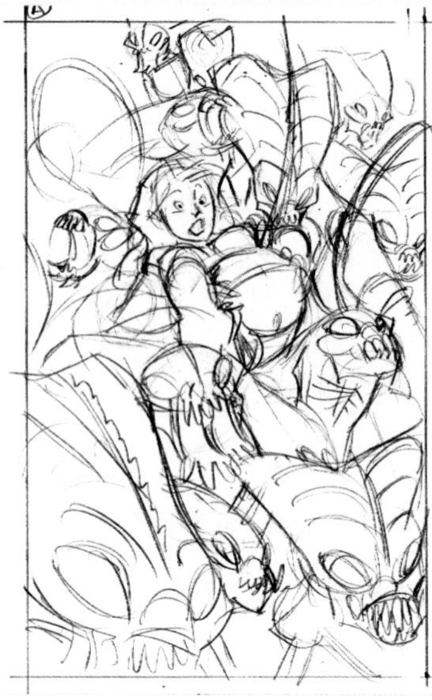

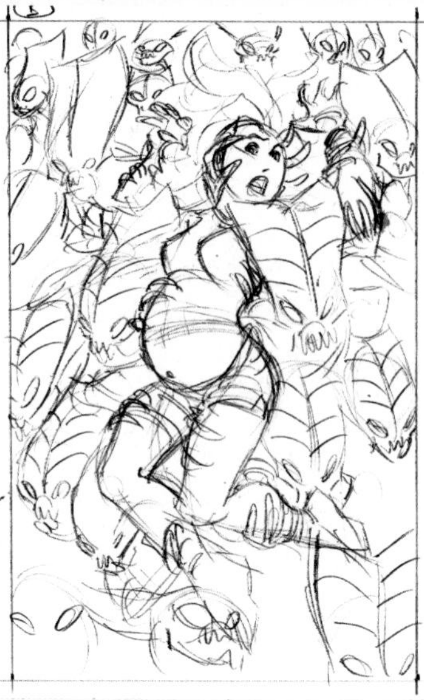

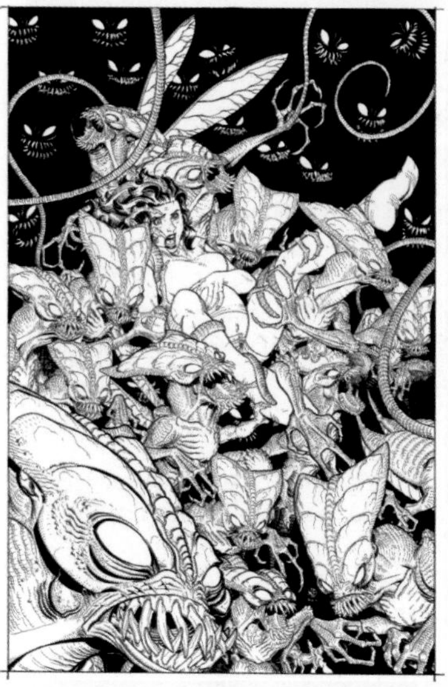

#6

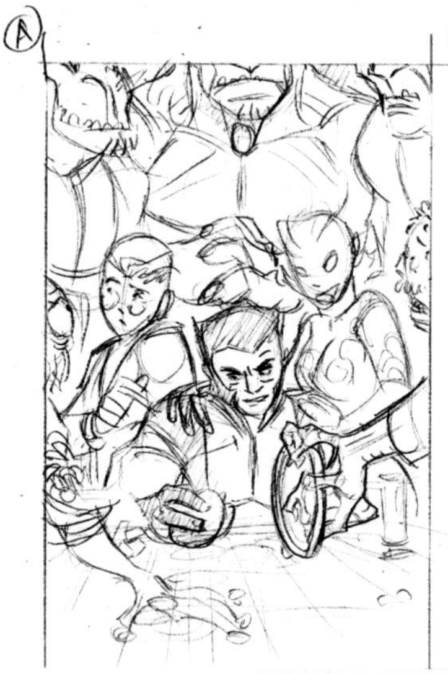

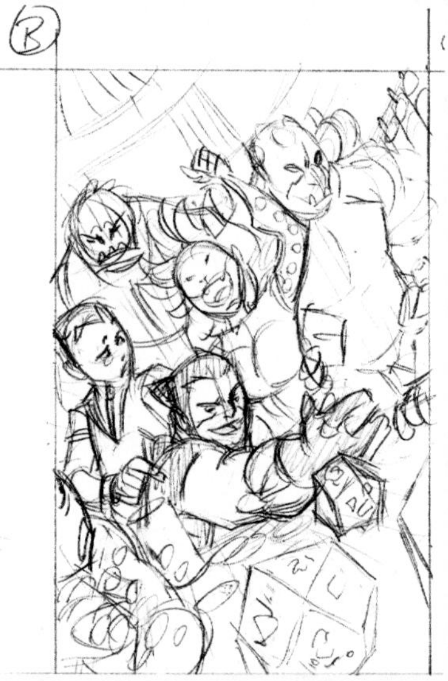

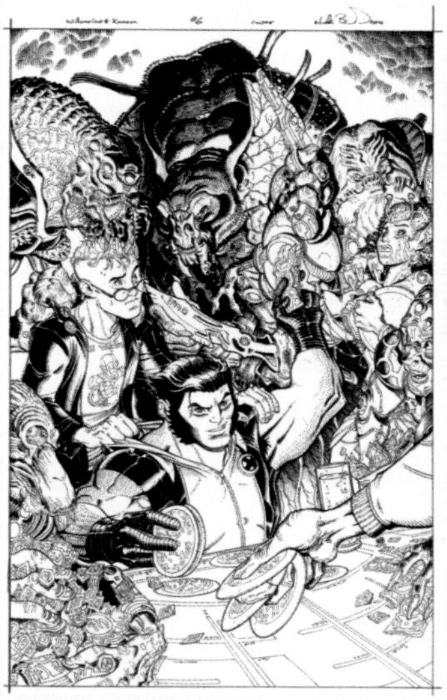

#7

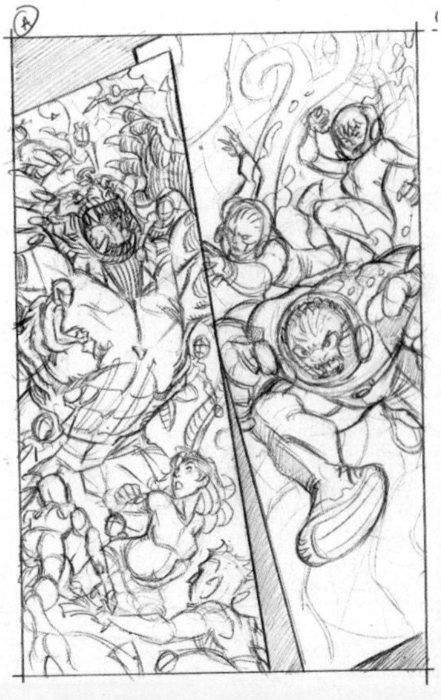

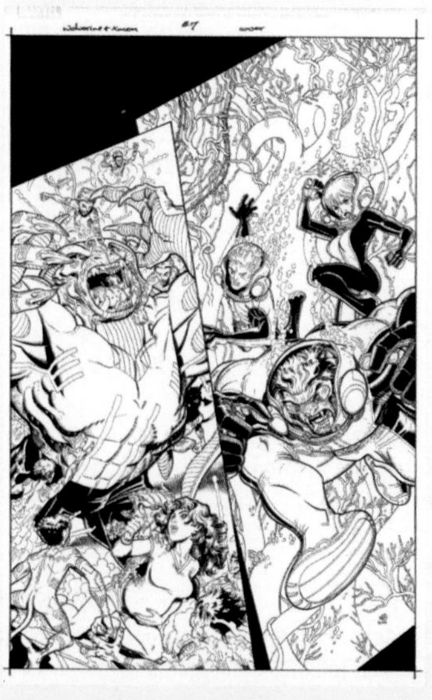

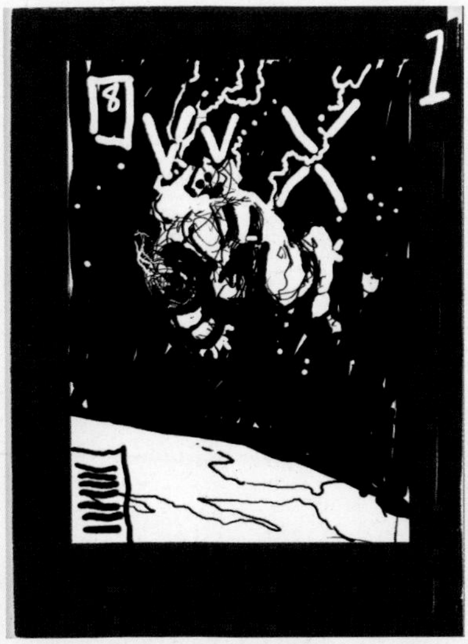
1

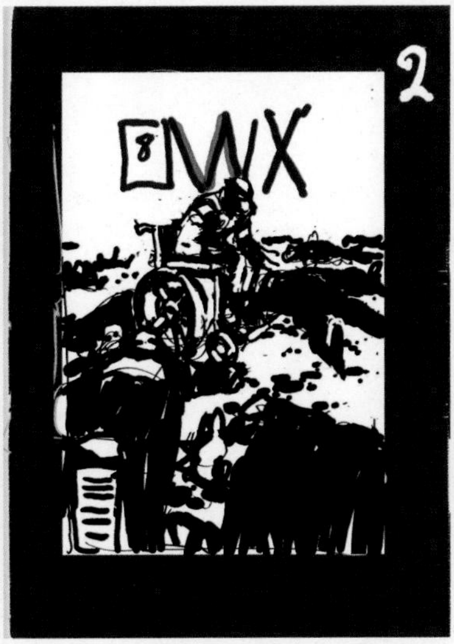
2

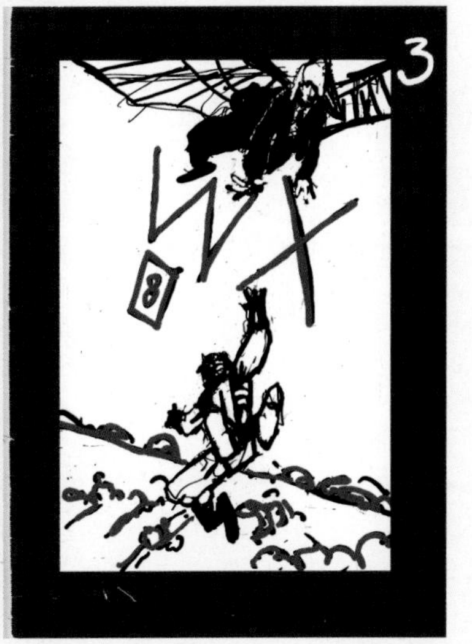
3

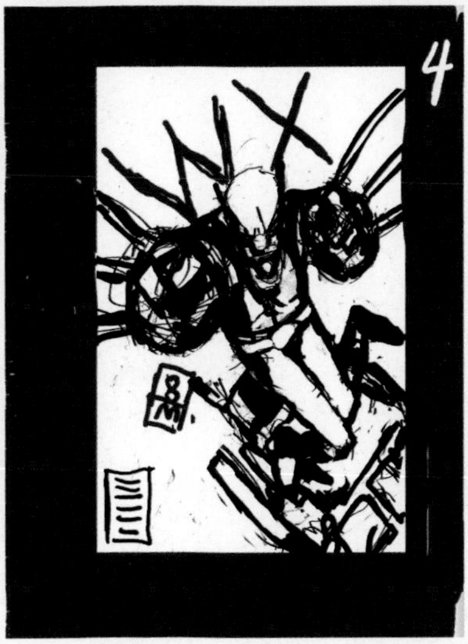
4

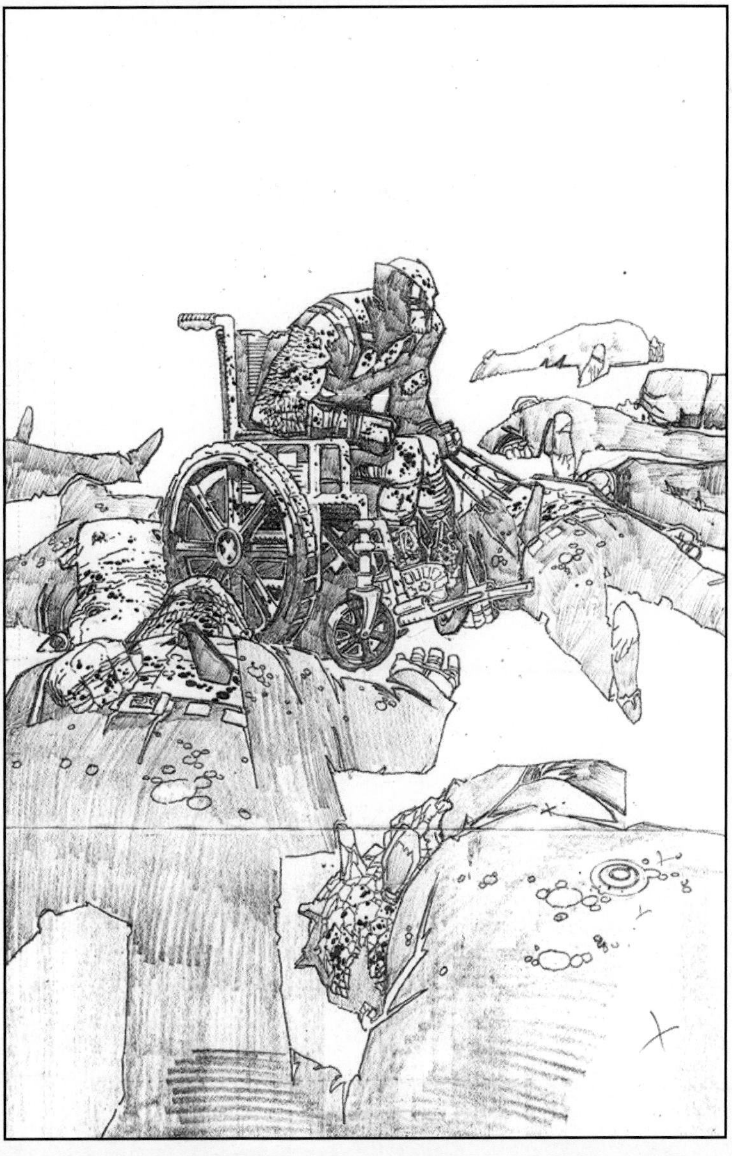

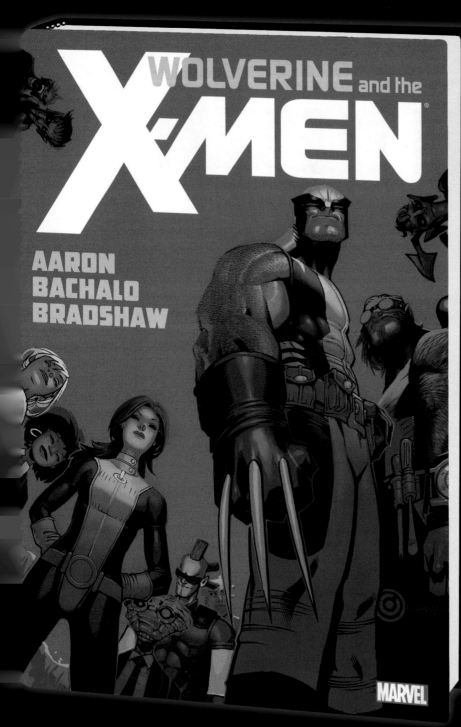